Massacre over the Marne

Patrick Stephens Limited, an imprint of Haynes Publishing, has published authoritative, quality books for enthusiasts for more than 25 years. During that time the company has established a reputation as one of the world's leading publishers of books on aviation, maritime, military, model-making, motor cycling, motoring, motor racing, railway and railway modelling subjects. Readers or authors with suggestions for books they would like to see published are invited to write to: The Editorial Director, Patrick Stephens Limited, Sparkford, Nr Yeovil, Somerset, BA22 7JJ.

Massacre over the Marne

THE RAF BOMBING RAIDS
ON REVIGNY, JULY 1944

by Oliver Clutton-Brock

PSL
Patrick Stephens Limited

First published in 1994

British Library Cataloguing in Publication Data:
A catalogue record for this book is
available from the British Library

ISBN 1 85260 452 2

Library of Congress catalog card no 93 81190

Patrick Stephens Limited is an imprint of Haynes Publishing, Sparkford, Nr Yeovil, Somerset, BA22 7JJ.

Typeset by G&M, Raunds, Northamptonshire
Printed in Great Britain by Butler & Tanner Ltd of London and Frome

Contents

This book is dedicated to the memory of all those who never came back, and to those who waited in vain for them to return.

'I cannot but turn my mind for a moment to those who no longer fill your ranks, those who have given their lives in the service of their country, victims of those accidents which must always be part of any human effort, however well organised that effort may be.'

Sir Stafford Cripps,
Minister of Aircraft Production 1942–45

'Mr Clutton-Brock's vivid story of the bombing of the railway yards at Revigny-sur-Ornain brought back for me, as though they had just passed, those early months of 1944, fifty years ago, when at meeting after meeting the merits of the plan with which my name became associated were being debated by the Commanders of the air forces that were going to be involved.'

Professor Solly (later Lord) Zuckerman,
Scientific Advisor to Air Chief Marshal
Sir Trafford Leigh-Mallory

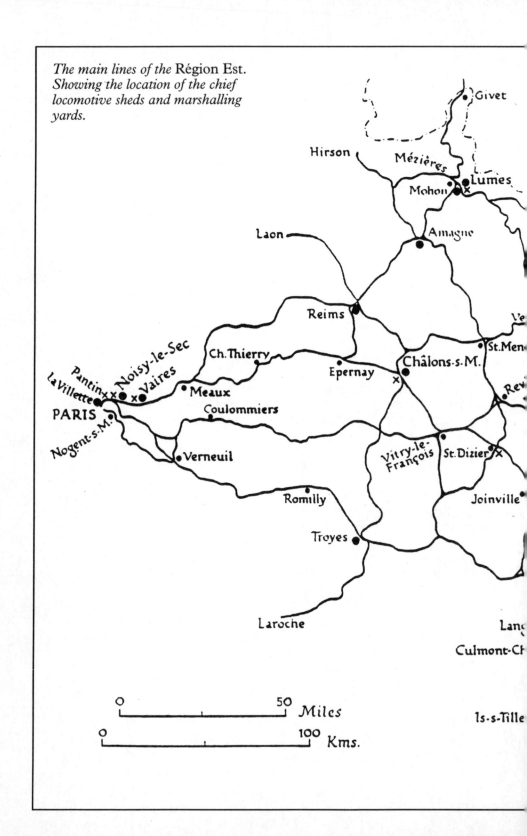

The main lines of the Région Est. *Showing the location of the chief locomotive sheds and marshalling yards.*

Givet

Hirson

Mézières

Lumes

Mohon

Amagne

Laon

Reims

Ve

Ch. Thierry

Châlons-s.M.

St.Men

Noisy-le-Sec

Epernay

Pantin

Vaires

Rev

La Villette

Meaux

PARIS

Coulommiers

Nogent-s.M.

Vitry-le-François

St.Dizier

Verneuil

Romilly

Joinville

Troyes

Laroche

Lang

Culmont-Ch

| 0 | | 50 | Miles |

| 0 | | 100 | Kms. |

Is-s-Tille

EASTERN REGION

- • Locomotive Sheds.
- × Chief Marshalling & Shunting Yards.

Luxembourg   To Trier

Bettembourg

Longwy   Apach

Longuyon
Audun-le-R.   Thionville

Baroncourt   Saarbrücken   To Ludwigshafen

Hargarten   Forbach

rdun   Conflans-   Metz
Jarny

ehould   Sarreguemines   Wissembourg

gny   Pagny   Benestroff   Haguenau

Bar-le-Duc   Lérouville   Champigneulles   Saverne

Commercy   Sarrebourg

Toul   Nancy   Strasbourg

Sorcy   Jarville   Lunéville   Molsheim

Blainville

Neufchâteau   Mirecourt   St. Dié   Sélestat

Epinal   Colmar

Chaumont

Vitrey-Vernois

gres   Mulhouse

nalindrey   Port d'Atelier   Lure   Belfort

Vaivre   Vesoul   Basle
(St.Louis)

To Besançon

Gray

To Dijon

Acknowledgements

This book could not have been written without the generous contributions made by so many people from so many continents. But I must single out Bernard Bertin of Soulaines Dhuys, France, who so readily shared his considerable local knowledge and gave me so many clues and suggestions. The many twisted strands involving the many evaders could not have been unravelled without him. He also 'found' many photographs of evaders and was kind enough to pass them on to me. Thanks, too, go to his very knowledgeable friend and aviation author Jean-Marie Lenours of Romilly-sur-Seine — 'have photocopier will travel'!

The next list is of personnel who flew with the Royal Air Force at the time (not all on the Revigny raids). I have given their squadron numbers in brackets after their names, but not their rank. I have listed awards where known, but no insult is intended if I have accidentally omitted a medal given for bravery in the air:

J. T. Ackroyd (192); E. Annon (298); D. E. Bell (103); L. N. Bignell (166); D. R. Breeze (156); S. P. Broad (166); H. L. Brooks (44); J. T. Brown (467); J. Comley (166); E. W. Cropper (103); G. G. Davies DSO (156); A. E. De Bruin (630); J. A. Diley (49), deceased; F. A. M. Eade (166); W. Fortune (49); D. C. Gibbons (166); J. Griffiths (576); R. A. Hammersley DFM (57); J. K. Harris (166); R. J. Harris (9); J. D. Harvison (49); S. A. Hawken (630); B. J. Hayes DFM (83); G. Hexter DFM (619); R. A. Hilborne (630); W. G. Johnson (467), deceased; D. A. Kelsall (166); C. H. Kroschel (166); L. A. Lewis (166); L. E. S. Manning (57); C. A. McKernan (550); T. F. Millett (166); C. R. Murray (166); J. H. Nicholson (166); N. F. Oates (9); S. Parker DFC (61); C. T. Rose (166); R. G. Royle (44); E. H. Ruston (57); R. Savage (166); C. W. Smithurst (166); G. Tabner (576); T. D. G. Teare (103); R. Trotter DFC (156); J. A. Waugh (102); L. Wharton (44); F. Whitfield DFM (9); F. K. White (467); R. C. Wiseman (156).

The following Luftwaffe night-fighter pilots flew with III/NJG 5 against the Revigny raids:

Major Paul Zorner, commander of the unit, and Fahnenjunker Herbert Altner.

By no means least, my thanks to those persons who, for one reason or another, did not fly with the RAF during the war, but have been most kind and helpful:

The Editor, *Air Mail*; Mrs M. Aitken; Roger Anthoine; Gérard Arcelin; Mrs D. Banville; The Editor, *Belper News*; Pierre Bezins; Mrs G. Booth (Personal Assistant to the late Lord Zuckerman); Mrs L. Breakspear; *Bomber Command Association*; *Bundesarchiv*, Freiburg; Mrs B. H. Carroll; *Commonwealth War Graves Commission*; R. Crompton (re Stalag Luft 7); Pierre Demarson; René Demongeot; Denis Esmard; Henri Février; J. George; Jean Hercot; H. Horscroft (*44 Squadron Association*); Roland Jeanvoine; D. Jones; E. Jones (*Alconbury/Warboys/Upwood 1942–45 Association*); W. E. Jones; Mrs J. King; A. J. Little; F. McMillan (*Air Crew Association*); The Director of National Archives, Canada; Mrs E. O'Collard; G. G. Ogden; Dr J. Ogden; Lady Ogilvie-Forbes; Bernard Parisse (Revigny); Bernard Poitel (Revigny); R. Powers (*Air Gunners Association*); *Public Records Office*, Kew and Chancery Lane; Helmut Peter Rix; J. Sherwin (*102 Squadron Association*); Madame Sinclair (Revigny); Mrs S. G. Westrup (*Elsham Wolds Association*); Lord Zuckerman OM, deceased.

Finally, to Amy Myers who made many helpful suggestions (and without whom this book would probably never have seen the light of day) and to Patrick Stephens Ltd of Haynes Publishing I am sincerely grateful.

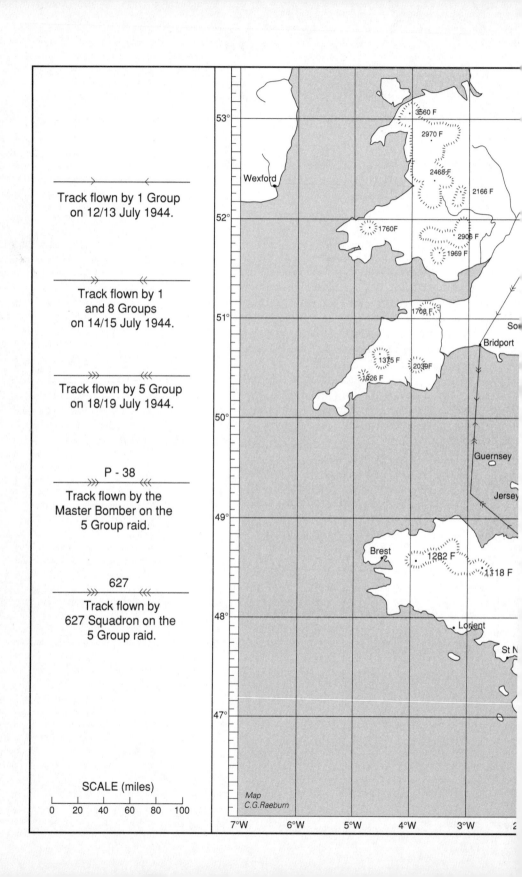

Track flown by 1 Group
on 12/13 July 1944.

Track flown by 1
and 8 Groups
on 14/15 July 1944.

Track flown by 5 Group
on 18/19 July 1944.

P - 38

Track flown by the
Master Bomber on the
5 Group raid.

627

Track flown by
627 Squadron on the
5 Group raid.

SCALE (miles)

0   20   40   60   80   100

Map
C.G.Raeburn

Wexford

53°

52°

51°

50°

49°

48°

47°

7°W   6°W   5°W   4°W   3°W

3560 F
2970 F
2468 F
2166 F
1760F
2906 F
1969 F
1708 F
1375 F
2039F
1626 F
So
Bridport
Guernsey
Jersey
Brest
1282 F
1318 F
Lorient
St N

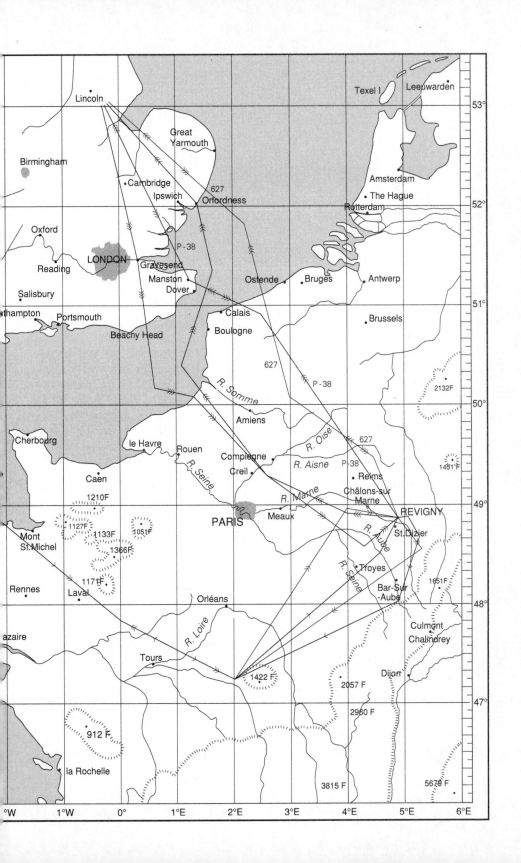

Preface

A long with nearly everyone else, I suppose, I know of the incredibly brave bombing of the Ruhr dams by 617 Squadron in May 1943. I know, too, of the awful Hamburg raids of late July and early August of the same year; of Peenemünde a few weeks later; of the bitter struggle throughout the long winter of 1943–44 against Berlin; of the Nuremberg fiasco of March 1944; and of Dresden in February 1945. These are names famous throughout the annals of RAF Bomber Command. But there were many other Bomber Command raids during the six long years of the Second World War on almost unheard-of targets on which aircrew would make the supreme sacrifice.

One such was Revigny. My curiosity was originally aroused when I noted that, on three separate raids to Revigny in July 1944, a total of forty-one Lancasters were lost. But where was Revigny? And why was the target so important that three raids had to be mounted against it?

★ ★ ★

The first question was easy to answer. Revigny-sur-Ornain (to give it its full name) is a small French town in the Meuse *département* situated on the Ornain river some 240 kilometres due east of Paris. It has a population today of 4,000 compared with 2,500 during the war. Built on the edge of the town was the *camp des permissionaires*, a transit camp for French forced workers going to and from Germany. It boasted no industry in the Second World War other than a tile factory and a nut and bolt factory, and had a railway locomotive depot. Revigny's only claim to fame is that André Maginot, sometime French Minister for War, was born there and that, in 1916, a French gunner succeeded in shooting down a German airship nearby. The town had been badly damaged during the First World War and was to suffer again when the German *panzers* overran the country in 1940. There was also a large cemetery for the dead of the First World War.

Running past the southern edge of the town is a main railway line. In August 1937 the French government passed a decree that merged all existing railway companies into the *Société Nationale des Chemins de Fer*

Français (better known as the 'SNCF'). The SNCF was divided into five regions — North, East, South-East, South-West and West — and Revigny was in the East. In that region were 7,078 kilometres of line, 5,435 of which were double track. Up to the Second World War these lines carried considerable freight, mostly from the Lorraine iron field and the coal and coke traffic emanating from the Ruhr in Germany (and from northern France itself) to feed the Lorraine smelting industry. The East region was the most important freight-carrying section of the national railway and was, in fact, second only to the West region in numbers of passengers carried.

There were two main radial lines in the East region, which diverged a few kilometres east of Paris (the hub of the railway system) at Noisy-le-Sec.* One of the radial lines ran to Châlons-sur-Marne and on, via Nancy and Saverne, to Strasbourg; the other went to Troyes and on, via Chaumont and Belfort, to Basel in Switzerland. Revigny was situated on the more northerly, Strasbourg, line between Vitry-le-François and Bar-le-Duc (205 and 250 kilometres respectively east of Paris). Also at Revigny a major north-south line crossed the Paris-Strasbourg track.

The line from Paris to Bar-le-Duc is the most perfectly graded in the whole of France, with scarcely a noticeable gradient, though there are a few insignificant stretches of 1 in 200 near Meaux (50 kilometres east of Paris) where the line cuts across rambling sections of the River Marne. Otherwise the gradient is no more than 1 in 2500. Between Vitry-le-François and Bar-le-Duc, however, in what is known as the *Champagne humide* region, the line begins to steepen as it reaches and follows the Ornain valley, one gradient being at 1 in 285.

To the east of Bar-le-Duc the line crosses the Portland limestone escarpment that forms the watershed of the Ornain and Meuse rivers. Here there is a 10-kilometre ascent of 1 in 125 with a similar descent to Lérouville, beyond which is the only difficult section of the whole 500-kilometre route. The line then climbs the Meuse valley for 16 kilometres and, at a gradient of 1 in 285, passes through the Corallian limestone escarpment (known as the *Côtes de Meuse*) in the remarkable Toul gap (cut by the Moselle). For most of the remaining distance to Strasbourg the line climbs and descends at gradients of between 1 in 200 and 1 in 300, with the steepest, 1 in 141, being encountered on the drop down to the Rhine Rift valley, whence there is a gentle run to Strasbourg.

To the Germans in 1944, however, these facts and figures would have been of little interest. All they were worried about was keeping these vital tracks open for their own warlike freight.

★　★　★

The second question ('Why three raids?') was not so easy to answer. Clearly something had gone wrong, as it was a fair bet that such losses had not been expected.

The first of the two parts of this book gives a detailed account of the three RAF Bomber Command raids on the railway junction at Revigny,

---

* *Attacked to great effect by RAF Bomber Command on the night of 18/19 April 1944.*

and explains what went wrong. The second part deals with the 59 survivors from the 290 aircrew (of the 41 Lancasters lost) who found themselves alive on French soil after they had either baled out of, or had been involuntarily blown out of, their doomed Lancasters.

It would be easy to blame the planners of the raids for the heavy losses. They knew, for instance, that St Dizier airfield, barely 15 miles from the target, was home to an experienced night-fighter unit. But in war something always goes wrong.

The target should have been destroyed at the first attempt, but, as Sir Arthur Harris had promised Supreme Headquarters that it *would* be destroyed, RAF Bomber Command had to keep at it. Poor weather and the Luftwaffe saw to it that a heavy price was extorted.

The Revigny raids certainly played a small part in the successful removal from France of the German Army, and hence in its ultimate defeat, but it is impossible to say by how much the war was shortened as a result. In reality, they can have made little difference.

Revigny was just another name, another place, another time for dying.

★ ★ ★

One thing that I hope emerges from this book, quite apart from the day-to-day heroism of the average bomber crew, is the wonderful assistance given by the average French family to the airmen whose misfortune it was to be shot down. We might have our national differences today but, when the chips were down . . . well, let's just say that for the French it was all or nothing. It was their life not yours on the line, and that should never be forgotten.

Introduction

By the summer of 1943 the plans for the invasion of the continent ('OVERLORD') were taking shape, and a provisional date was set for May 1944. At the same time it was agreed that ACM Sir Trafford Leigh Mallory be appointed commander-in-chief of all the RAF and USAAF fighter and light and medium bomber forces. But on 6 November 1943 ACM Sir Charles Portal, Chief of the Air Staff, minuted the Prime Minister that a 'detailed plan for the use of heavy bombers in OVERLORD has not yet been worked out'.

He added, however, that the Chiefs of Staff were agreed that by D-Day 'the effort of the Strategic bomber force, or part of it, would be placed at the disposal of the Supreme Commander as the situation might demand'. How much effort would be available was a matter for debate, but Portal thought that it was 'probable that the diversion of the strategic bombing effort from the bombing of Germany would amount to at least 50 per cent'.

Portal also suggested that prior to D-Day 'a considerable effort from the home based heavy bomber force would be required to attack such targets as the enemy fighter control organisation, the transportation system, ammunition and fuel dumps and so on'.

On 23 December 1943 he wrote to Harris suggesting that as the Allies were 'now committed for good or ill to OVERLORD' it was time to examine Bomber Command's role in the operation. On 13 January 1944 Harris, as blunt and forthright as ever, produced a paper (*The Employment of the Night Bomber Force in Connection with the invasion of the Continent from the UK*) in which he said that it was 'clear that the best and indeed the only efficient support which Bomber Command can give to OVERLORD is the intensification of the attacks on suitable industrial centres in Germany'.

Up to the end of February 1944 RAF Bomber Command had, in the three and a half months since it began the so-called Battle of Berlin on the night of 18/19 November 1943, already lost around 600 Lancaster and 300 Halifax crews on raids to German targets, either failed to return or crashed in the UK. By the end of March 1944 the total for both types exceeded 1,100.

Nor was he confident, Harris continued, that his bomber crews could fulfil their new role, pointing out that

> 'the bomber force is trained to fly at night and at night only. It would require at least six weeks of fair weather training to convert crews to day work. Even then, the aircraft are completely unsuited for anything but night operations since armament has largely been sacrificed in the interests of range and bomb carrying capacity . . . Day operations are therefore absolutely out of the question and could in no circumstances be undertaken.'

The day following publication of his paper, Harris was mildly rebuked by the Deputy Chief of the Air Staff, AM Sir Norman Bottomley, who reminded him that 'the closest co-ordination is essential to the successful prosecution of the Combined Bomber Offensive.'

Harris took the hint:

> 'Naturally I did not quarrel with the decision to put the bomber force at the disposal of the invading armies once the die had been cast; I knew that the armies could not succeed without them.'

On 17 February he was again reminded that his overall mission remained

> 'the progressive destruction and dislocation of German military industrial and economic system, the disruption of vital elements of communications and material reduction of German air combat strength by successful prosecution of the Combined Bomber Offensive from any convenient bases.'

Harris believed that his bombers could best support the landings by continuing the 'area' attack on German industry. His American counterpart, however, Lieutenant-General Carl A. 'Tooey' Spaatz, USStAF commander in Europe, disagreed, believing that the enemy's oil facilities should be destroyed. There was, however, yet a third line of thought, namely that the enemy would be unable to prosecute a successful ground defence on the continent were all his lines of communications to be destroyed or so damaged as to make any movement in the critical area extremely hazardous.

This plan originated with Professor Solly Zuckerman (who died in April 1993 as Lord Zuckerman OM KCB FRS), who had had first-hand experience of the effect of Allied bombing when he was attached to ACM Sir Arthur Tedder's staff in the Middle East and the Mediterranean in 1943. Known as 'The Transportation Plan', it was eventually to prevail over the Harris and Spaatz ideas for the crucial period up to D-Day.

The Transportation Plan began in earnest on the night of 6/7 March 1944 with a successful RAF attack on Trappes, after Bomber Command had been given permission to begin its raids on selected rail yards. Thereafter the pace picked up so that in March 1,511 four-engined sorties were flown against nine 'rail' targets; 3,482 in April against 21; and 3,709 in May against 30 such targets. A further 178 sorties against two more in the five June days before the invasion brought the total to 8,880 sorties. By the end of June that total had risen to '13,349 sorties against the railways of North-West Europe, dropping 52,347 tons of bombs, with a casualty rate of 2.6 per cent'.

As the Luftwaffe slowly but surely appreciated the shift of target from Germany to France, so they moved their night-fighters. Heavy bomber losses mounted accordingly — seven in March 1944; 66 in April; 108 in May; 173 in June. Overall RAF Bomber Command dropped 67,974 tons of bombs (over twice as much as all the other air commands put together) in over 17,000 sorties, at a cost of over 400 aircraft for a loss rate of around 2.5 per cent.

The Transportation Plan, however, required that other targets apart from railways be attacked — roads, bridges, canals, ammunition dumps, radar installations, and heavy coastal guns. When the time came, despite the massive aerial bombardment, Allied progress on land was slow. Attacks by the heavy bombers on the 'transportation' targets continued after D-Day, but had to be reduced after 13 June to deal with the menace of the V-1 flying bomb.

By July 1944, with the Allies still bogged down in Normandy by fierce German resistance, the need to attack the enemy's lines of communication was as great as ever. As a continuation of the Transportation Plan, therefore, in the first week of that month Harris was asked by SHAEF to destroy a number of railway junctions in north-eastern France. The last raid on a railway target was made on Connantre on 18/19 August 1944, by which time the German Armies in France had been well and truly routed.

Despite the heavy losses sustained in its prosecution, the Transportation Plan was a success. This is borne out by General Heinrich Hans Eberbach, CO of Panzer Group West, who reported to the Allied Air Commanders' Meeting at Versailles on 26 September 1944 'that the skilful and scientific use of our bombers was the cause of the defeat in France, and he singled out for praise the planning and execution of the attack on the Seine bridges, which made reinforcement in Normandy at the critical time almost impossible. His own words, summing up the effect of Air power on the Germans' ability to defend or counter-attack, are: "France, in which all means of transportation were interrupted, was the cause of our defeat".'

By September 1944 most of France had been liberated. The Germans continued to retreat north of Switzerland, but it took weeks of dour fighting in appallingly wet weather before France was empty of Germans. A number of irregular forces, including the French 'maquis', helped them on their way.

It had been earlier agreed that within Occupied France the French should form a properly structured army ('l'Armée Secrète'). Known also as the FFI (*Forces Françaises de l'Intérieur*), it would be commanded from outside France by General Koenig and would have officers and NCOs with usual army ranks. Some FFI units (usually those with Regular Army officers) were reasonably effective, but others were no more than bands of brigands seeking to profit from friend and foe alike. Maquis was thus the collective word for all guerilla units whether good or bad.

Also operating behind enemy lines after D-Day were a number of three-man uniformed units known as 'Jedburghs', dropped into France by Special Operations Executive ('SOE') and the US Office of Strategic Services ('OSS') to support and direct the French underground activities in a useful direction (see Chapter 11). As well as the 'Jeds', members of the Special Air Service ('SAS') were sent in. They did their fighting as openly as circumstances would permit. Mobility was their key, and they zoomed around in Willis jeeps bristling with machine guns, hitting the Germans wherever they could, leaving a trail of confusion and chaos in their wake. They operated best where conditions were fluid, as they were in eastern France once the Germans were on the retreat; and it was into that area of France from June to September 1944 that squadrons of 1 SAS and 2 SAS Regiments were dropped to hinder and hasten their withdrawal.

This, then, was the situation in France that summer of 1944, when many thought that the war would be over by Christmas. For some, on the Revigny raids, it was over already. For others, in captivity, the war seemed endless, though they were not to know that the Christmas of 1944 would be their last behind the wire.

PART ONE

1

The First Raid – Outward, 12/13 July 1944

It was the practice after the Normandy landings for the Allied Air Chiefs to hold a daily meeting at ACM Leigh-Mallory's HQ at Stanmore. There the great men discussed, amongst other matters, the current ground situation in France. Supplied with the latest intelligence, they could assess the priorities for the air forces. At Stanmore Meeting No 35 on 5 July 1944, for example, further evidence

'was available to show that the Germans despaired of attempting to use Railway communications anywhere West of Paris leading to the battle area. Their activities were now moving further and further East, and the main centre appeared to be as far back as Dijon and Belfort.'

On 8 July, at Meeting No 38, 'Bomber Command agreed to attack Revigny'. Revigny lay on the line from the Ruhr to north-eastern France, and the Germans were making full use of it to supply the battle zone. It therefore had to be destroyed.

Just after midday on 8 July 1944 a raid to Nantes was 'scrubbed', and the target changed to the marshalling yards at Revigny-sur-Ornain. At 1500 hours this raid was also cancelled; it was to have been made in daylight. Revigny was 'on' again on 10 July, and 105 Lancasters of 1 Group were posted, but bad weather forced yet another cancellation at 2105 hours, after crews had been briefed. The next day, 11 July, 1 Group were to try once more, but again it was cancelled, at 1752 hours. For the fourth time, on Wednesday 12 July 1944, the attack on Revigny was authorised.

At around 1000 hours the details of the raid were sent to all 1 Group stations in the usual Form B. The route was interesting, if only for the distance to be covered — nearly 1,550 track miles there and back. It crossed the English coast at Bridport, Dorset, went round the Channel Islands, crossed in over France by le Mont St Michel, kept south of Paris and then swung north-east to the target, 150 miles due east of the French capital. The return journey followed the same route.

Lancasters were to be loaded with six or seven 1,000 lb and four or five 500 lb medium capacity ('MC') general purpose ('GP') bombs according to their type. All the 1,000 lb bombs and 75 per cent of the 500 lb bombs were fused to explode 0.025 seconds after hitting the ground, with the remaining 25 per cent of the 500 lb bombs long-delay fused to explode at any time between 6 and 144 hours after impact.

The fuel load was a minimum of 1,990 gallons. It was reckoned that a Lancaster consumed one gallon every 0.95 miles, and the formula for calculating the required load was simply to divide the total track miles by 0.95. An additional 200 gallons were then added for safety.

Marking for the raid would be carried out by 1 Group's own Special Duties Flight (SDF) which shared RAF Binbrook, Lincolnshire, with 12 Squadron.

1 Group were to provide the aircraft for the Revigny raid. 13 Base were required to supply 86 aircraft (19 from 103 Squadron; 29 from 166 Squadron; 19 each from 550 and 576 Squadrons) and 14 Base would supply 14 (eight from 101 Squadron and six from 300 Squadron). The SDF were putting up seven. One hundred and seven Lancasters in all.

1 Group were also providing a further 100 Lancasters for a raid on the marshalling yards at Tours.* They would be accompanied by 14 Lancasters and three Mosquitoes of 8 (PFF) Group, which would carry out the marking for the raid.

Bomber Command planned to take advantage of the 1 Group raids by combining them with a 5 Group attack on the railway at Culmont and Chalindrey, two neighbouring villages some 60 miles south-east of Revigny. 5 Group would follow 1 Group for as far as possible into France (the Revigny Lancs leading the way) with 5 Group's 157 Lancasters (and four Mosquitoes) bringing up the rear.

The planners hoped to keep the Luftwaffe busy in the Low Countries by mounting four 'Crossbow' (V-1 site) attacks: 105 Halifaxes of 4 Group (accompanied by ten Mosquitoes and four Lancasters of 8 Group) were to attack the V-1 flying bomb sites at Ferme-du-Forestal and les Hauts Buissons (near the northern coast of France), and 99 Halifaxes of 6 Group (with ten Mosquitoes and four Lancasters of 8 Group) were to do the same to the V-1 sites at Bremont and Acquet (also in northern France).

Seventy-eight Wellingtons, 63 Halifaxes and 15 Stirlings of 1, 3, 4, 6, 92 and 93 Groups were to fly diversionary sweeps across the North Sea, either dropping leaflets on eight northern French towns or sowing mines in the 'Rosemary' area (Heligoland Bight). 8 Group would also send eight Mosquitoes on a nuisance raid to the oil plant at Homberg in Germany.

100 (BS) Group would be putting up 96 aircraft whose job, amongst others, was to lay a 'Mandrel' screen across the night sky in front of the German radar. The diversionary sweep would suddenly appear through the screen as if heading for Holland, but would turn back before reaching the enemy coast. Twelve Stirlings of 199 Squadron, RAF, and five B-17s of 803rd Squadron, VIII Bomber Command, USAAF, were used

---

* *12 Base — 16 Lancasters from 12 Squadron, 21 from 100 Squadron, and 19 each from 460 and 625 Squadrons; 14 Base — seven from 300 Squadron and 18 from 626 Squadron.*

for the screen which was, in simple terms, a 'wall' of jamming emitted from powerful transmitters in the aircraft. The Mandrel aircraft were required to fly up and down a precise course until such time as the jamming was no longer required.

★ ★ ★

SDF was formed on 18 April 1944 to provide 1 Group with its own 'pathfinder' force. Its first and only Commanding Officer was S/L Harold Frederick 'Bill' Breakspear, who was taken off operations from 100 Squadron. He chose five other crews from 1 Group — F/L D. F. Gillam (100 Squadron), F/L W. E. Hull (101 Squadron), F/L G. M. Russell-Fry (103 Squadron), F/O J. W. Stewart (626 Squadron), and P/O J. H. Marks (625 Squadron). Eighty airmen were posted from various stations in the Group to support the new unit.

SDF began training on 22 April 1944 and flew its first operation on the night of 30 April/1 May when 116 Lancasters of 1 Group successfully attacked an ammunition dump at Maintenon in northern France. Bill Breakspear was the 'Master of Ceremonies'.

SDF had but a short existence, flying its last sorties early in August 1944. On 10 August the small unit was disbanded, as the 1 Group Operational Report noted:

'The S.D.F. has served its purpose very well and, as the speed of the Allied advance made it very difficult to find suitable targets, it was decided to release the crews for normal duties rather than keep them standing by any longer. The magnificent marking carried out on some of the marshalling yards of France has been amply rewarded by the news of the chaotic state of the enemy's lines of communications.'

Bill Breakspear was some character. Prior to the raid to the German *panzer* training depôt at Mailly-le-Camp, he was summoned by 'Butch' Harris. Harris wanted to know what Bill thought should be done about bombing the tank crews and their tanks before it was too late, given the likelihood of there being bright moonlight. Bill told Harris that in effect it would be madness to try in such conditions. But Harris was adamant. They would go, and that was that. When it was over Harris asked Bill to give his account of what had gone wrong. Bill was not in a good mood (possibly because F/L Hull and crew failed to return and were all killed) and did not bother to salute as he left.

'Breakspear!' bellowed Harris. 'Don't you salute Air Chief Marshals?'

'Not stupid ones, Sir,' replied our hero and stormed out of the room! He lived to tell the tale, and was tour expired after his 31st operation (to Dijon, 5 July 1944).

★ ★ ★

The following account by a Canadian pilot of 166 Squadron, F/O Redmond Banville, written soon after the war, gives a vivid insight into how he spent the day of the first Revigny raid:

'At 10.30 am word came that we were "on" for the night. Ops dinner was on for 5.30 pm so take-off was estimated at 9 pm. The crew and I biked out to our kite R-Robert at 10.45 am bringing out our chutes, Mae Wests and one-man dinghies, to save carting them out after briefing. We ran up the kite checking everything, as is done before every flight . . .

'It was now time for lunch, and after lunch I had a snooze until tea-time — 3.30 pm. I went back to my quarters after tea to do my own pre-operational check . . . I also left the key to my trunk in the table drawer — the crew always used to kid me about that. I told them that if I got the chop, I didn't want some "erk" breaking my trunk open and stealing my cigs . . .

'It was now time for supper, and the speculation was rife as to where we were going. Some of the boys knew the load, nine 1,000 pounders, and the fuel load, 1,800 gallons, and so many bundles of "window" [thin metal strips dropped from Allied aircraft to confuse German radar]. . . So we knew it was a long trip. Guesses ranged from Berlin to Italy and back again . . . but no one is sure until we get to the Briefing Room. We had steak that evening with fried potatoes — a real good meal.'

The navigators and bomb aimers had a separate briefing three-quarters of an hour before the main one at 1830 hours:

'All the specialists had their say, and the CO wished us "God speed" and Briefing was over.

'Amidst lots of kidding among ourselves and other crews, we made our way over to the locker rooms to don our flying clothing and pick up our issue of chocolate bars and flasks of coffee.

'There were crew buses waiting outside after we had dressed and we piled in and were driven out to good old R-Robert.

'Ran the engines up again and checked over all the instruments and equipment — with the exception of the radio. Strict radio silence must be maintained until we arrive back over base and request permission to land. . . Nothing to do now but sit around and wait until 9.10 pm. "A" Flight were to take off first followed by ourselves. As our dispersal was only about 100 yards from the runway in use for the night, we wouldn't start our engines until three or four minutes before take-off.

'The Padré, our Flight CO [S/L Rippon] and the Group Captain drove around to wish us "God speed" — as they did to all crews on ops nights — and promptly at 8.45 pm the quiet of the English countryside was broken by the roar of Merlin engines starting up. In the distance we could make out the sound of engines at Elsham, our main Base. Elsham would be about six miles away.

'At five to nine all of "A" Flight were lined up on the perimeter track, with engines ticking over, with the leading a/c lined up on the runway, waiting for a green light from the Control Van. We watched half a dozen take off and then, with a last pull at a fag, climbed into R-Robert at 9.10 pm.

'As I crawled through the kite I made a last check. Made sure all the escape hatches in the roof were secure. Pressure in the hydraulic jacks sufficient. Crossfeed valve turned off etc. My Mae West was on my seat and as I picked it up I found out it wasn't mine at all — the name inside was W/C Garner, only our CO! Oh well, I'd sneak it into his locker when I got back. He wasn't on ops that night anyway. Little did I know he would never see that particular Mae West again.

'Checked the inter-comm and made sure all crew members were in their places. Asked the R/G if he had secured the entrance hatch and started engines at 9.15 . . . All four power plants started up easily, and I waved the ground crew clear, released the brakes and started to roll out of dispersal.

'The rest of "C" Flight was on the move, but we wanted to be away first — partly just to be first off in the Flight and partly because R-Robert's mark of engine had a bad habit of overheating while idling. Nicky was watching his temp gauges anxiously, both oil and radiator, but everything was under control.

'All "A" Flight were airborne and sure enough we got the green light to taxi out. As we swung on the runway Singleton's V-Victor* was facing us, having taxied up the perimeter track on the other side of the runway. I had my side window open and gave him the old "finger" sign as we swung on.

'I let her roll until my tail wheel was straight, and held her on the brakes, opening engines to 800 rpm to prevent spark-plugs from oiling up. My hands always sweated at this time — this is when you think "My God. Suppose an engine cuts out at 90 to 100 mph and we do a ground loop with 9,000 lbs of explosives and 1,800 gallons of 100 octane fuel and 43,000 lbs of aircraft". Makes you think!

'Another green from control. I waved to the usual collection of spectators (my bat-girl among them — she never missed a take-off) and closed my window.

'With Nicky beside me — the brakes are still on — I opened the inner throttles wide open and released the air, and we started to roll. Until the tail comes up at about 60 mph, a pilot steers these big fellows by manipulating the two outer engines. The tail came up and I called to Nicky "Full power", and released my grip on the throttles. "Full power," he repeated, shoving the throttles through the gate and locking them.

'Now we were belting down the runway — 90, 100, 110, 115 — I held her down until at 120 I heaved her off the ground. We came down and bounced once, and then we were away.

'"Undercarriage up," I called, Nicky repeated and selected the undercarriage up.

'The airspeed climbed slowly to 145 and I eased her into a steady climb, holding the speed at 165. At 1,000 feet, I took off the 25° of flap and turned 90° to port. We could relax now.

'Even at 9.25 it was still broad daylight and I set course for our favourite pub, about three miles from base. As we passed overhead I rocked my wings and, sure enough, there were the proprietor and his

* *P/O Singleton and crew were killed in V-Victor, LM386, on the Stuttgart raid of 25/26 July 1944. Records indicate that on this night, 12/13 July, Singleton was flying T-Tommy, ME835.*

wife way down below waving to us. We did this every ops night, and they were always on hand to wave us on our way.

'We circled for altitude and at 8,000 feet and at 9.45 pm we set course over the centre of our drome — at 165 indicated. I called to Harry Kidd to go back and call out a reading from the Master Unit of the D/R Compass, and Ted, Charley and I all checked our Repeater Compasses against the reading he called out. Then we all settled back — nothing much to watch for until we picked up our own coast in an hour or so.'

* * *

Between 2100 and 2200 hours all the Lancasters of 1 Group took off without mishap, gained height over their airfields and, followed by the 5 Group crews, set course for the first point on the route — RAF Upper Heyford. The four Mosquitoes, because of their extra speed, could afford to leave later and went on a more direct route. The bomber stream, 378 Lancasters, made its way from Upper Heyford to Bridport on the south coast, then set course for a point to the south-west of Guernsey in the Channel Islands.

Red Banville again:

'By the time we crossed our coast it was quite dark, but the shoreline was easily discernible. It was a beautiful night — stars very bright, but no moon, thank heaven.

'All was quiet until we were opposite the Channel Islands when Jerry's defences opened up on some guy who was evidently off course and had strayed over the Islands. However, after a few minutes the firing ceased and all the searchlights (S/Ls) were switched off, and all was peaceful again.

'We were running on time and should pick up the coast of Brittany around 11.40 pm. Sure enough, at 2340 the Ack Ack opened up again, but not very seriously as Jerry was more or less firing blindly. We passed over it and headed for our final turning point before our final leg to the target.'

As the Lancasters came into German radar range, it was the job of one of the crew (usually the bomb aimer or the flight engineer) to throw out packets of 'window'. It was not simply a matter of shovelling the bundles out of the aircraft as fast as possible. The rate at which they were dropped had to be carefully controlled. Windowing did have one potential drawback — experienced German night-fighter pilots made use of the metal cloud by flying to where it was thickest, and then searching visually, their AI having been rendered useless by window.

The Revigny Lancasters were carrying 325 window bundles, and crews were ordered to window at rate 'C' (one bundle per minute) once across the line of 2° East (just to the east of Orléans), increasing to Rate 'G' (five bundles per minute) once 4° East was reached, as they would be nearing the target area. Rate C would be resumed on the homeward route at 4° East and windowing would stop at 2° East. (Revigny lies at 48°49'N/4°57'E).

Assisting with the night's proceedings were four window-dropping and six 'jamming' B-17s of 214 (BS) Squadron. The window B-17s flew only as far as a point off the Dutch coast, but the rest mingled with the bomber stream and flew all the way to their target. It was the job of the six 'jammers' to interfere as much as they could with radio transmissions to and from the enemy night-fighters.

With Guernsey passing to port at around 2330 hours/12 July, the gunners were on the alert for any signs of the Luftwaffe, whose night-fighters were already active. Off Jersey two Ju88s had a nibble at a passing 5 Group Lancaster, which claimed one of them destroyed.

It was 2353 hours. As the bomber stream crossed the French coast over Brittany, the attacks on Bremont and les Hauts Buissons in northern France were due to start, at 0005 hours and 0025 hours/13 July respectively; and the 'Bullseye' diversionary sweep across the North Sea was also timed to suddenly appear on the German radar screens, heading for Holland, once the 'Crossbow' raids had ended. Here was the 100 (BS) Group radar 'wall' in operation.

The plan was working. The attacks on Bremont and les Hauts Buissons had ended by 0030 hours/13 July, and at the same time as the enemy fighters were being drawn to the 'Bullseye' feint at the Dutch coast, the training aircraft of the various groups turned back for the safety of England. The raids to the three French railway targets proceeded south-eastwards with little interference.

But the 'Bullseye' diversion had ended too soon.

The German fighter-controllers saw that the plot was receding, the aircraft were returning to base. All that remained to worry about, therefore, was the raid moving in across France, and likely to pass south of Paris. With only 172 serviceable night-fighters available in northern France and Belgium, directing them to the right part of the sky was always a problem. Those that had gone to the 'Bullseye' raid were landed back and refuelled, having had no success. They took off later to deal with the raids on Acquet and Ferme-du-Forestal and located the Halifaxes but, again, none of the bombers was shot down. The northern night-fighters landed back between 0307 and 0415 hours.

At 4750°N/0000° the Lancasters (call-sign 'Press On') detailed to bomb Tours broke away from the middle of the bomber stream and headed for their target.*

The remainder of the stream, now 264 Lancasters strong, roared on along its south-easterly course, deeper into France and clearly visible on German radar. Contact was made with the bomber-stream at 0040 hours/13 July when an Me110 attacked JB555 (P/O V. P. Tomlin, 576 Squadron), with neither combatant inflicting any serious damage on the other. Between 0049 and 0057 hours six Me110s and one Ju88 were sent to the Paris area to wait for further orders. At 0103 hours, at 6,500 feet and at position 4810°N/0340°E, LL804 (F/S Z. Stepien, 300

---

* *Tours was on the transverse line from Brittany via Vierzon and Bourges to Saincaize, a large marshalling yard on the north-south Paris-Marseilles line. It was bypassed to the north-west and to the south by main lines, but was served by a short line from the junction of St Pierre-des-Corps. Apart from the junctions and cross-lines, Tours also boasted considerable locomotive works and a carriage and wagon repair depot.*

Squadron) was attacked by an Me110. The two gunners scored hits on the night-fighter's cockpit and claimed it as damaged, possibly destroyed.*

Eighteen minutes later, at 0121 hours, several aircraft of I/NJG 5 from St Dizier (only 20 miles south of Revigny) were sent to orbit a beacon (*Schimpanse*) west of their base, while the rest of their *gruppe* were ordered south-west (to orbit the *Bernd/Bella* W/T and visual beacon) to intercept the raid heading for Culmont/Chalindrey. The net was closing.

At 4715°N/0200°E both Groups began shovelling out 'window' at Rate C. The 5 Group Lancasters followed 1 Group's north-east turn to port before easing slightly to port of track and, at 4800°N/0330°E, swinging to starboard with a sudden change of direction to take them to their target.

The overture had ended, now the show was about to begin. Watching the aerial activities carefully, the German night-fighter controller, being fed information from the radar tracking system, had not been deceived by the spurious window traces appearing on the radar screens. The diversionary 'Bullseye' spoof which was due to appear from behind the Mandrel screen apparently heading for the Dutch coast had turned back nearly an hour earlier at 0030 hours, some two minutes after the raid on les Hauts Buissons had finished and 20 minutes after the Bremont attack was over.

The spoof was to have drawn the night-fighters northwards, away from the thrusts to Revigny and Culmont/Chalindrey. As we have seen, it certainly gained the attention of the Germans who, for a time, carefully plotted it at the expense of the 'railway' raids to the south. But once the motley collection of training aircraft had turned back over the North Sea and the 'Crossbow' raids had ended, the enemy had a fairly clear picture of the situation. The controller ordered the fighters to turn round and head south; and the hitherto unused *gruppe*, I/NJG 5, was itself at 0121 hours flung into the fray.

It is at this moment, with the 1 Group Lancasters closing in on Revigny, and 5 Group doing likewise at their target, and with the enemy's fighters closing in on the Lancasters, that the unpredictable weather began to play its part in the proceedings. It was to have dire consequences for the Revigny raid.

There had been a sufficient promise of good conditions to enable the two eastern French raids to go ahead. England was covered by 5-6/10ths cloud which thickened towards the coast (Bridport) and persisted out into the Atlantic. Nearing the French coast at St Malo (Brittany) the cloud lessened and on the way to the target it was virtually clear, save for occasional patches of broken cloud (some crews reckoned it to have been 4/10ths). But as the 1 Group Lancasters neared Revigny, some 50 miles to the north-east, thin layer cloud appeared between 4,000 and 6,000 feet.

This was no immediate problem for the crews, now heading for the briefed assembly point at 4841.30°N/0450.30°E. The use of an assembly

---

* *On 18 July 1944 Stepien's flight engineer, Sgt Jozef Pialucha, was involved in a life-or-death struggle to save the rear gunner who had almost been blown out of his turret by flak. He was awarded the CGM for his bravery.*

point was a precaution to ensure that crews waited for the order to attack should the SDF Master Bomber have to postpone H-Hour (the time the bombing was due to start). In that event they were instructed 'to carry out a wide right-hand orbit' of the assembly point, which happened to be no more than five miles west of the very airfield from which the Me110 night-fighters of I/NJG 5 had recently taken off, and only 15 or so south-west of Revigny. Travelling at about three miles a minute, it would have taken only five minutes for the Lancasters to cover the short distance to the target.

As Main Force began arriving in the area, one of the SDF crews dropped the first of ten 250 lb impact-fused 'Target Indicators Green' over the assembly point. It was 0145 hours. Each 'TI Green' burned for a few minutes only and it was up to the SDF crew to keep the green fire stoked up for the duration of the raid. It was a useful navigation aid, but obviously it could be seen by friend and foe alike. The other six SDF crews, the 'markers', flew on to illuminate the target.

The Lancasters had been flying at the low altitude of 6,000 to 8,000 feet all the way to the target and had been instructed 'to pass over the Assembly Point at the height and airspeed at which they intend to bomb, with bomb doors open'. They were to bomb from a low height to ensure accuracy and at the same time ensure, so far as possible, that no French civilians were killed. It was made absolutely clear at briefing that they were to bomb below whatever cloud there might happen to be. In the event, there was a thin layer of cloud over the target, reported by the crews to be 5 to 8/10ths thick between 3,000 and 6,000 feet. Below this cloud there was considerable haze, which made it difficult for the markers to locate the aiming point.

The Master Bomber had a highly responsible job, and on his skill and experience depended the success of a raid. But on this night the Master Bomber was bedevilled not only by the low haze but also by his H2S set going unserviceable at the critical moment. He was forced to make a D/R run from the assembly point to the target.

Already flying low by the time he had reached the target, he was unable to see clearly and was forced to delay calling in Main Force to bomb. For 15 minutes he searched to find the aiming point. SDF crews were dropping illuminating flares as hard as they could over where they believed the railway junction to be and, with Sod's Law working overtime, the Master Bomber, his H2S already u/s, then lost the use of his VHF radio due to a power failure.

Now all the ingredients for a colossal 'balls-up' were present and the raid was doomed to failure. The patient Main Force crews (collective call-sign 'Ghurka 1 or 2', depending on which wave each was in) had been flying around in ever-decreasing circles for upwards of 15 minutes waiting for the word from 'Chugboat 1' (the Master Bomber) to come on in and bomb the briefed Red Spot Fire ('RSF'). But all they heard was 'Chugboat 2' (the Deputy Master Bomber) plaintively asking 'What's going on?'. They strained to hear any message transmitted (on 5020 kilocycles) and, just as chaos was setting in, some heard 'Lysol', the codeword to 'stop bombing and go home', broadcast not by the Master Bomber but by his Deputy.

It was rare to find on a raid that all crews had blindly followed orders at all times, and the crews of 1 Group were no exception on this night. Many of them, tired of waiting, saw the 60 white flares dropping and that was enough for them. They had not flown all that way just to stooge around in the enemy sky for 15 or 20 minutes, then shoot off home. Under those flares lay their target, and if they could see railway tracks, then that was good enough for them. Bombs away!

They were well aware of the need to avoid bombing civilians and came in low, at heights varying from 3,000 to 8,000 feet — one of the Polish crews of 300 Squadron came in at only 2,300 feet, and one of 166 Squadron at 2,500. Some made timed runs on D/R from the assembly point, others bombed from whatever position was convenient.

All semblance of control had disappeared as Lancasters arrived from all points of the compass, ending their left or right-hand orbits (crews had been briefed to make a left-hand orbit of the target if they had to make more than one bombing run). One 166 Squadron crew (F/O W. C. Hutchinson, ME746) had made three orbits and was then fired on by another Lancaster, sustaining slight damage; the guilty Lancaster was not identified. After all that, Hutchinson did not bomb, one of over 50 to obey orders.

P/O A. A. Moore, RCAF (LM116, 103 Squadron) decided to head for Culmont/Chalindrey and try his luck there. It was 0204 hours, and they were down to 3,000 feet; turning away from Revigny and gaining height, they came to 5 Group's raid where, at 0217½ and now at 7,500 feet, the navigator, P/O Eric Cropper, noted 'Bombs gone on reds and greens'.

The raid was breaking up with no help from the enemy. There were no searchlights and no heavy flak, just four light flak guns operating in the immediate vicinity of Revigny. But just as the raid was collapsing and the aircraft were being turned for home, the Luftwaffe arrived. The Me110 night-fighters of I/NJG 5 that had been sent to orbit in the St Dizier and Chaumont areas now closed in. It would have been difficult for the night-fighters not to have seen the flares (despite the hazy cloud) and it was only a matter of time before they homed on to the milling bombers. At 0153 hours LM133 (P/O E. J. Mann, 576 Squadron) was still some three or four miles short of the target when, with no warning from 'Fishpond', it was attacked and badly damaged by an unseen night-fighter which, luckily, did not continue its attack.

★ ★ ★

Old night-fighter hands aimed for the fuel tanks between the engines on either wing. To aim at the belly of a Lancaster was asking for trouble. Firing at the wings gave them a good chance of avoiding any explosion, and gave the bomber crew a sporting chance of escaping. If the rear gunner was awake, then they aimed for him first; but once fire took hold in the wing, the crew had only a few seconds in which to bale out. The Germans added to their advantage by mounting a pair of upward-firing 20 millimetre cannons (usually the obsolete Oerlikon MG FF), known as *schräge musik*, on their Me110s and Ju88s. This allowed them to manoeuvre into the blind spot beneath the bomber. The first many bomber crews knew about an attack was when cannon shells ripped into their aircraft. Experienced as well as 'green' crews were slaughtered in this way. Major Schnaufer, famous night-fighter pilot, when interviewed on 21 May 1945 by two RAF Bomber Command gunners, claimed that he had attacked 20 to 30 bombers with his upward-firing guns at about 80 yards range, and of these only one in ten ever saw him!

★ ★ ★

The first Lancaster was caught at around 0150 hours. PA999 (P/O J. A. Harrison, 103 Squadron, on his ninth op) was shot down on its way to the target, and crashed near Véel, six or seven miles south-east of Revigny. There was one survivor (see Chapter 11). The blaze from PA999 attracted other impatient Lancasters like moths to a candle, and several bombed the red glow beneath them in the mistaken impression that it was the Red Marker dropped by one of the SDF aircraft.

The crew of LL798 (P/O G. R. Davies, 300 Squadron) admitted after the raid that they had released their bombs on an RSF that afterwards proved to be a burning aircraft. F/S Stepien and crew stated that they had been able to see ground detail when they bombed, but that it 'did not appear to be like railway tracks or roads'.

This illustrates only too well the difficulties that an average bomber crew had in finding, let alone hitting, a target under adverse conditions, even when at an unusually low height. The bombing, such as it was, was scattered and, despite the odd claim to have hit railway tracks, there was no damage to the target.

550 Squadron, for example, despatched 19 aircraft of which only eight of its 17 survivors claimed to have bombed in the target area; and only two of the eight brought back printable photographs — LL748 (W/O T. A. Lloyd) which showed well-illuminated clouds, and LM134 (P/O H. Jones) which showed a bomb flash covering some fire tracks and nothing else. Neither photograph was capable of being plotted. Some crews bombed on clusters of white illuminating flares, but these were widely spaced and gave no assistance to the searching crews who, in reality, were lost. There is no reason to suppose that the experience of 550 Squadron was any different from that of the other squadrons.

Leaderless and unable to see much because of the low haze, the bombers wandered about in the area over Revigny and dropped their bombs believing that they were carrying out their duty. Once done, they could go home. Those that had heard 'Lysol' in time returned, not happy but having done their duty. Some crews failed to hear the broadcasts and bombed as best they could rather than take their 'eggs' back with them. As already mentioned, one enterprising crew joined the attack at Culmont/Chalindrey.

The bombing had been scheduled to last for eight minutes, from 0150 to 0158 hours, with an equal number of aircraft bombing in two waves, each wave to take just four minutes. The first crew bombed at 0152 hours and most of the other crews that managed to bomb had done so by 0205 hours. 'Lysol' was broadcast for a second time at 0202 hours.

F/L Harry Guilfoyle, deputy 'A' Flight Commander, 576 Squadron, circled Revigny in LM227 as his Canadian navigator, George Tabner, gave him directions:

'I kept us positioned on H2S. When we were down to 2,400 feet indicated height (ground elevation 1,500) I called Harry on the intercom to suggest he lower the undercarriage, since we would be in the circuit of the Night-fighter Station which was adjacent if we did another orbit and descended any more. With that we f/o'd back to base!'

With the plan falling apart at the seams and aircraft coming and going on many different headings, the almost inevitable occurred. At 0155 hours two Lancasters orbiting in opposite directions were seen to collide; there were no survivors from LL796 (P/O W. Boocock, 550 Squadron, on his 24th op) or ME674 (F/O C. R. Phillips, 103 Squadron, sixth op), the second and third losses of the night.

F/O Les Graham and crew (NE113, 166 Squadron) were dutifully orbiting the target area when the night-fighters dropped their flares. The wireless operator, Fred Eade, heard a call 'to bomb the reds' followed by 'I'm going down'. The unknown aircraft (perhaps PA999) hit the ground and exploded in a blaze of red, which, as already mentioned, other Lancasters proceeded to bomb. Then the Graham crew had their own problems. Fred Eade was keeping a lookout when he spotted an aircraft coming for them from '2 o'clock'. He told his skipper to pull up quickly and the fighter, for such it proved to be, shot by under their port wing. But it did not get far. Close by, very close in fact, was a second Lancaster and the fighter slammed straight into it. The explosion blew NE113 upside down and flung Les Graham out of his seat. His right leg caught in the throttles — two became fully opened and the other two fully closed. Their guardian angel was certainly with them that night, for the mess was sorted out only when the ground was uncomfortably approximate.

Les flew around for a while to give the compass a chance to settle down, and Fred sorted out the API master unit and put the ammunition belts back into their boxes. They touched down safely at Wittering after being airborne for 9 hours 20 minutes.*

---

* *Les turned to motor-cycling after the war. He was winner of the first World 500cc Championship in 1949, also winning the 1950 and 1951 Swiss and the 1952 Italian and Spanish Grands Prix. He also won the odd TT race on the Isle of Man before the notorious Mountain course claimed his life.*

2

The First Raid – Homeward, 13 July 1944

The German night-fighters had no difficulty following the bombers as they headed away from Revigny, and the Lancaster crews knew that they were around; spotting them, however, was another matter. At his interview with the two RAF Bomber Command gunners, Major Schnaufer said that 'he could usually recognise each bomber he attacked as he invariably came in close enough to see the guns . . . With the Lancaster, the exhausts can only be seen when the fighter is flying directly astern and in line with it; on a dark night these would sometimes be visible at a range of 800 metres but usually less.'

So, even for the great Luftwaffe night-fighter pilots, identification was no easy matter. At 0210 hours, two Lancasters, on their way home, were seen flying close to each other. At some fateful moment the rear gunner of the leading Lancaster must have suddenly seen the blur of an aircraft in the dark sky immediately behind. Although a half-moon had risen half an hour or so earlier, there would have been little light and he would have been unable to have quickly identified the threatening aircraft.

In such circumstances he would have taken no chances. His aim was true and tracer ripped into the starboard inner engine of the following Lancaster, which burst into flames. Horrified observers could clearly see the distinctive bulge underneath the stricken Lancaster identifying it as a 'Y' type. Even as they watched, they saw that the 'fight' was not yet over. As the rear Lancaster went down, its mid-upper gunner returned fire and, with the aircraft so close to each other, he too could not miss. Now the leading Lancaster caught fire. Both were seen to crash to the ground in flames, the first one exploding in a shower of red and green.

The two Lancasters were probably ND993 (F/O P. J. Abbott, 103 Squadron, seventh op), which crashed near the farm 'de la Haie', and PD202 (F/O E. J. Welchman, 166 Squadron, tenth op), which crashed near Prez-sur-Marne, half a dozen miles to the west. There were no survivors.

Five Lancasters had now been lost and 34 men were dead.

Also at 0210 hours, an unidentified night-fighter had the temerity to attack EE193 (Sgt G. H. Town, 550 Squadron) whose gunners (P/O Ball, mid-upper, and F/S Teasdale, rear), in the words of the Squadron diarist, 'accepted the challenge from an enemy fighter and claim to have shot it down in flames and to have seen it hit the deck', the enemy 'having achieved nothing but his own downfall'. The brief battle began with the single-engined attacker firing two rocket projectiles, and ended with six .303-inch Browning machine guns returning fire with interest. This claim was no boast by the 'sprog' 550 Squadron crew, for their victory was witnessed by other crews, including that of P/O R. A. Jones (ED327, 300 Squadron): 'S/E E/A seen shot down in flames by Lancaster over the target. Seen to hit the ground.'

Three more Lancasters were shot down south of the target, all homeward bound on the south-east leg. These were JB644 (P/O J. McLaren, 166 Squadron, 20th op) with two survivors (see Chapter 11); LL896 (F/O R. T. Banville, 166 Squadron, 14th op) four survivors (see Chapter 13) and LM647 (P/O J. E. H. Davies, 550 Squadron, second op) with no survivors. A fourth, LM388 (P/O D. C. Gibbons, 166 Squadron, 19⅓ ops) with five survivors (see Chapters 8 and 9), was caught some 50 miles from Revigny on the long south-westerly track.

The total for the night was now nine Lancasters lost, 51 dead.

The tenth and final loss of the night was ND859 (P/O C. Hart, 576 Squadron, 14th op) which had strayed south of track. It is likely that the navigational error was enough to have placed the Lancaster in the path of the end of the 5 Group raid on its way to Culmont/Chalindrey. If so, then it was ND859 that struck Lancaster LM638 (F/O R. S. Arnold, 44 Squadron) under its port wing. The two aircraft crashed about seven miles apart. All seven crew of LM638 baled out successfully (see Chapter 9).

Giey-sur-Aujon, tucked away in a fold of the Aujon valley, is surrounded by steep hills, and it was on top of one of these that ND859 came down, a mile or so from the village. It smashed into a cornfield and ploughed on into a wood, killing the five men in the forward section. The two gunners, Sergeants C. J. Glenny and P. H. Keeler, survived, but both were captured and sent to Germany, Keeler to Stalag 357 and Glenny to Stalag 13D, Nürnberg, and from there to Stalag Luft III, Sagan, where he remained until the camp was overrun at the end of the war. He was back in England on 8 May 1945 and in Canada soon after, the first time he had seen his native soil in over two years.

According to Henri Février, then a maquisard, one of the gunners was sheltering with a charcoal burner when he was denounced to the Germans. Word of the crash of ND859 had soon reached German ears and a patrol was despatched to locate it. Of course everyone in the village knew about it and one of them, primary school teacher Max Duville, told the Germans where they could find it. The Germans thanked him and set off for the spot but found nothing, which was not surprising as Max had given them false information. This greatly displeased the Germans, who returned to the village and murdered the teacher. On the site of the crash the French have erected a simple memorial to all who died:

Homage aux aviateurs
de la RAF
tombés ici
le 13-7-1944

A là mémoire de Max Duville, Instituteur,
tué par les Allemands le 14-7-1944

At the front of the memorial stand the bent and broken remains of one of ND859's propellers.

★ ★ ★

1 Group's losses were, then, ten Lancasters and 56 men dead. One other 5 Group Lancaster was lost that night, shot down a few miles to the north of the ND859/LM638 collision. This was LM221 (F/O W. A. M. Hallett, 9 Squadron), which probably blew up at 0148 hours/13 July with all its bombs still aboard.

1 and 5 Groups were to suffer no more at the hands of the enemy that night, although Ju88s and Me110s did make contact with the bomber stream from time to time on the long haul out of France. At around 0240-0250 hours various unidentified aircraft put in an attack. The gunners of one of the returning Lancasters, LM122 (F/S J. J. B. Ryder, 576 Squadron, incidentally one of only seven NCO pilots on this Revigny raid), were awake. At 0240 hours LM122 was twice attacked but neither the aircraft nor the crew suffered any damage. A further five attacks were recorded, the last three being over the Brittany coast between 0347 and 0406 hours, no damage being inflicted on any of the Lancasters.

One enemy had been left behind, but for the tired bomber crews a very different but just as deadly enemy lay ahead of them. Before they could climb out of their noisy Lancasters and stand, however shakily, on terra firma, they had to avoid a blanket of dense fog. So far that night the weather had proved unkind to the Revigny crews, and it was not to relent as they looked forward to a landing at base, followed by the usual de-briefing, then breakfast and bed.

At 1740 hours on 12 July the Air Staff had been informed:

'Bases in operational Groups are expected to be generally fit all night. In Yorkshire, however, there is a risk that after 0400 hrs considerable visibility troubles may be experienced . . .'

There was nothing else to indicate that Lincolnshire would be subject to the same problems.

As it turned out, the weather over England that morning of Thursday 13 July, though bad enough, was, according to the prolific 550 Squadron scribe, made worse by the unwelcome attention of certain creatures known as 'gremlins', who were in an unusually evil and playful mood. Not everyone who flew on ops saw these mini-monsters, but those who did had good cause to curse the little creatures with their wicked grins. They were often seen by the dancing light of St Elmo's fire dismantling aircraft engines or radio equipment, drilling holes in fuel tanks, jamming doors and windows and ailerons and generally being destructive and bloody irritating.

As the Lancasters of 1 and 5 Groups approached the English coast and began to claw their way up the centre of England on the reverse of the outward track, they received the unwelcome information that Lincolnshire was disappearing under a sea of mist. The crews of 101

Squadron might not have been unduly worried, however, for Ludford Magna was 'FIDO'-equipped.[*]

On the morning of 13 July, though, the tired 1 Group crews were, in the main, diverted to the airfields of East Anglia. 550 Squadron in particular was unusually widely dispersed, its 17 surviving aircraft landing, with varying degrees of success, at no fewer than ten airfields.

It was now, with touch-down so close, that the wicked little gremlins began to play their naughty games. They poked their ears into the Watch Offices of the 1 Group bases, heard the diversion gen and made for the 550 Squadron Lancasters, which seem to have been singled out for attention. P/O J. Lord (ED562) estimated that there was only some 15 minutes fuel left when, having been diverted to Suffolk, the chosen airfield suddenly disappeared in the mist.

He ordered the crew to jump, trimmed the aircraft to fly straight and level, and followed them earthwards. ED562 plunged to the ground some two miles east of Needham Market at 0720 hours. The crew were all safely gathered up and taken to Wattisham, home of the P-38s of the 479th Fighter Group, VIII Fighter Command, where the Yanks treated them with all their famed hospitality, 'high, wide and handsome' as the 550 Squadron diarist put it.

F/O F. S. Steele (PA995) of the same squadron was *en route* to RAF Mildenhall when he decided to jettison the six 1,000 lb bombs that he had dutifully brought home. From a height of only 400 feet he put them into a field on the starboard side of the railway running between Exning and Burwell. They were dropped 'safe' but, to add to the salvage party's worries, the crew had no idea what the fusing times were! Steele landed safely at 0655 hours and he and his crew remained at Mildenhall until 1643 hours/13 July when they received permission to return to Base.

Other 550 Squadron aircraft had their share of excitement at Hethel airfield in Norfolk, home of the B-24s of the 389th Bomb Group, VIII Bomber Command, Eighth USAAF. LL837 Q-Queenie (sadly to be lost on the second raid with another crew) was one of those to call in there. F/O Les Wareham and crew had been stooging home when they received the diversion message before crossing the Channel. Sgt Tony McKernan, wireless operator:

'Eventually we circled Hethel, flying from one Drem light to the next round the perimeter until, eventually, the Americans fired flares from their caravan to show us the beginning of the runway. Another aircraft of 550, R-Robert, was also in the circuit, also with a full load of bombs — it was quite a dicey night. My skipper put Queenie down as gently as a baby, and we reported to flying control at Hethel, who weren't particularly impressed!

'We arrived back at North Killingholme about 3.00 pm on the 13th,

---

[*] *FIDO (Fog Intensive Dispersal Operation) consisted, in simple terms, of several long lines of hollow pipes with many tiny holes drilled into their upper surfaces and laid alongside the runways. Fuel was then forced along the pipes and ignited as it sprayed out of the holes. The flames created so much heat round the edge of the runway that the fog was 'burned off' and pilots were able to slip in underneath it and land on a now visible runway. Some likened the experience to landing in the jaws of hell.*

to be met by the Wingco who calmly informed us that the same target was on for that night. We were stood down so that the Wingco could take our aircraft, and a crew made up of the various leaders . . .'

Four of 550's Lancasters landed at Hethel without incident, but LM460 R-Robert (F/O H. A. T. Clark) had a few problems. By the time the pilot finally put 'R' down on the ground, he had been in the air for over ten hours and was undoubtedly very tired. On his first attempt to land he was beaten by the poor visibility and, going round again, the fuel gauges were showing empty. Landing as quickly as possible, somewhat worryingly he found that he had touched down at an angle of 30 degrees to the runway and, as it sped across the grass, LM460 headed uncontrollably towards a row of dispersed aircraft. He had no option but to raise the undercarriage in an attempt to bring the aircraft to an abrupt halt. He was successful. Time: 0717 hours.[*]

The 550 Squadron diarist again: 'Shaved, shining and unhurt thanks to lease-lend comforts . . .(and conviviality) they were in the best of spirits according to recent arrivals from Hethel whom they are expected to follow in due course — the last of Mother Carey's chickens.'

550 Squadron, though, did not have a monopoly of bad luck. ND990 (103 Squadron) ran short of fuel as P/O F. G. Durrant tried to land at Elsham Wolds. The weather closed in before he could land and he was diverted to Carnaby landing-strip, two miles from Bridlington.[†] Unable to get there in time, the crew were ordered to bale out, which they did at 0715 hours, and all landed safely bar the flight engineer, who fractured an ankle. ND990 crashed near Lissett, some five miles short of Carnaby.

The last Lancasters to land that morning were those of 101 Squadron, LM462 (F/O G. H. G. Harris) not touching down until 0725 hours, having been airborne for 20 minutes short of ten hours, and having covered the best part of 1,600 track miles (the planned route was measured at 1,571 track miles). As each Merlin engine consumed on average 48 gallons of fuel per hour, the Lancaster would have had little of its 2,000 or so gallons to spare by the time it landed.

Most of the contingent bound for the East Anglian airfields had managed to land back between 0600 and 0700 hours, after a flight of nine hours or more, a considerable part of which could be spent waiting to land if, as usual, there were a stack of aircraft over their particular airfield.

Even though most of the 1 Group crews had not landed at their 'home' base, each had to be de-briefed and fed before they could be sent on their way as soon as possible; but not before the Lancasters had been topped up with fuel and checked for damage. On this morning, though,

[*] *Clark was killed a week later returning from Scholven/Buer in Lancaster DV279. The Norfolk coast was crossed with only one good engine. Clark ordered the crew to bale out while he kept the Lancaster straight and level. Too low to jump, he attempted a landing, but the aircraft hit a power cable and crashed to the ground. Clark was dead. No medals. No glory. Just another statistic.*

[†] *This emergency runway was opened on 26 March 1944. Its extra width of 750 feet and length of 9,000 feet was to prove a great boon to the crews of many crippled aircraft before the war was over. It was also FIDO-equipped.*

cloud covered a greater part of the eastern counties, and the crews' return to base was delayed.*

LL748 (W/O T. A. Lloyd, 550 Squadron) was delayed at Waterbeach until 1715 hours when it was finally airborne for North Killingholme, nearly 11 hours late. Kirmington was a quiet place for most of the day with most of its aircraft stranded at RAF Wittering and not returning until after 1800 hours. The Kirmington Station CO, G/C Gerald Carter, must have been considerably agitated for at 1010 hours/13 July, 166 Squadron were ordered to stand-by for ops again that night. They were not cancelled until 1345 hours!

But, once the dust had settled, staff at Bomber Command HQ were able to assess the result of the Revigny raid, and to count the cost. From the very fact that the raid had had to be called off, they already knew that it had been unsuccessful. As reports trickled in from Intelligence Officers scattered around East Anglia, their worst fears were confirmed; but the fact that some crews claimed to have bombed the target may have given rise to the hope that the railway junction had been 'plastered'.

Despite Group's exhortation before the operation that 'every effort is to be made by crews to obtain the greatest possible accuracy on this important rail junction' and that 'every bomb should fall in the target area', the plain truth was that the target was unscathed. And F/S Dick Greenwood could testify, despite being some way south of the target, that several bomb loads were dropped on him and on the remains of his burning Lancaster.

Of the 100 Main Force Lancasters, 42 claimed to have bombed Revigny; two bombed elsewhere (one a railway line near Blois, the other at Culmont/Chalindrey); 46 did not bomb (complying with orders); two were still outstanding; and ten were missing. Added to the debit side were the three Lancasters that crashed in England — ED562, LM460[†] (both 550 Squadron) and ND990 (103 Squadron). LM133 (576 Squadron) had also been severely damaged by night-fighter attack near the target, and ME746 (166 Squadron) by machine gun fire from another Lancaster. This was a topic that was beginning to cause Bomber Command some concern, as the number of incidents of friendly aircraft firing at each other was increasing for some unknown reason.

Of the 14 casualties, at least six did not bomb. The 42 that bombed dropped 286 x 1,000 lb and 180 x 500 lb bombs. When the French woke up on the morning of 13 July they must have found many holes in many strange places. They were put there at a cost to the RAF of 56 airmen killed. But that is war. Mistakes are made, accidents occur. And tomorrow, or the next day, someone has to go back and finish the job.

---

* *The gremlins, however, were unable to distinguish friend from foe. In the darkness of the morning of 13 July, at around 0430 hours, a Ju88G-1 of 7/NJG 2, equipped with the latest anti-bomber night-fighting apparatus, landed at Woodbridge, Suffolk. The pilot had been chasing a Halifax mining raid to Heligoland when the aircraft's compass toppled. The inexperienced crew then took bearings on a radio beacon that they believed to be to the east. It was in fact in England and to the west. The rest, as they say, is history.*

† *LM460 was in fact repairable and saw out the war before being scrapped in 1947.*

3

The Second Raid – Outward, 14/15 July 1944

As the returning crews had already discovered, the weather over England on the morning of Thursday 13 July was misty; and it was bad enough over the Continent to prevent Bomber Command from laying on any major daylight raids, although 13 Lancasters of 8 (PFF) Group did manage to visit a flying-bomb site in northern France. The following night, 13/14 July, there were no bomber operations, but four Mosquitoes went on a nuisance raid to the oil plants of Homberg and Scholven/Buer.

On 14 July, apart from 19 Lancasters of 8 Group which visited the flying-bomb site at St Philibert-Fermé (albeit bombing through thick cloud), Bomber Command took the day off. The Americans, however, did not, and VIII Bomber Command despatched 359 B-17s on Operation CADILLAC, a massive drop of arms and material to the French Resistance in the St Lô, Limoges and Vercors areas; 131 B-24s were sent to bomb two Luftwaffe airfields in northern France (Montdidier and Peronne), supported by 612 fighters. They also despatched 100 P-38 'Lightning' fighter-bombers to various rail targets to the east and south-east of Paris.

One such railway target was at Bar-le-Duc (ten miles to the south-east of Revigny) where a train carrying tanks was strafed by the American fighters. They also caught a train loaded with ammunition and petrol on the line between Longeville-en-Barrois and Silmont (just south-east of Bar-le-Duc) with very satisfying results. The entire train blew up, and completely destroyed a 30-metre stretch of the main Paris-Strasbourg line, one of the links to the great industrial area of the Ruhr in Germany.

The evidence was there for all to see — lines in eastern France were still being heavily used for the transportation of German troops and material to the Normandy front.

The night of 14/15 July was to be reasonably busy for Bomber Command. 100 (BS) Group would supply 90 aircraft; 92 and 93 Groups of Training Command another 72; 5 Group would provide the bulk of the aircraft for an attack on the railway junction at Villeneuve-St Georges to the south of Paris; 4 and 6 Groups would each send just over 50

Halifaxes to two V-1 sites at les Landes and Anderbelck, and 8 Group 42 Mosquitoes of the Light Night Striking Force to Hannover.

3 Group was required to put up only eight Stirlings to do some 'gardening' (mine-laying). Also on the bill for the night's proceedings were 132 miscellaneous aircraft from several Groups which were to create a diversion across the North Sea towards the Low Countries. This was an unglamorous but important part of operational flying, aimed at drawing enemy night-fighters away from the true raids.

The Revigny raid on 12/13 July having been a total failure, 1 Group would provide 106 Lancasters for the second attempt. The Special Duties Flight, which had tried to mark the target two nights earlier, would be replaced by eight Lancasters of 156 (PFF) Squadron and 11 of 635 (PFF) Squadron. 156 Squadron would also provide the Master and Deputy Master Bombers.

The route, too, would be almost identical — Base, Upper Heyford, Bridport (south coast), the Channel Islands, in over the French coast by St Malo and le Mont-St Michel, on to 4750°N/0000° (several miles north-west of Tours), and thence to 4715°N/0200°E, where the route swung north-east before coming in to Revigny from slightly north of west (the first raid came in from the south-west). The return journey would be almost the same as two nights previously.

5 Group would again take advantage of the deeper 1 Group thrust into France and go straight from Bridport to the French coast near Cherbourg. From position 4750°N/0000° their track would swing north-east to Villeneuve-St Georges marshalling yards, some nine miles to the south-east of Paris. 5 Group were timed to be ahead of 1 Group on the outward leg and to be back out to sea off the French coast almost an hour earlier. Their homeward route, from a position just to the north of Tours, would be the same as that of 1 Group.

12 and 13 Bases would this time supply the bulk of the aircraft for Revigny (46 and 54 respectively) with 14 Base's sole contribution being five 'ABC' Lancasters of 101 Squadron (who also provided another five for the 5 Group raid). In the event, one of the 12 Base aircraft would be cancelled before take-off. Bomb loads would be the same as before — Marks I and III Lancasters to carry seven 1,000 lb and five 500 lb bombs; 'Y' types seven 1,000 lb and four 500 lb; 'ABC' six 1,000 lb and five 500 lb bombs. Minimum fuel load would again be 1,990 gallons. Each aircraft was to carry 845 bundles of 'window' (520 more than on the first raid), but would begin throwing them out at 4840°N/0140°W, much earlier than on the previous raid. H-Hour (the time the bombing was due to start) was scheduled for 0150 hours/15 July.

At 1040 hours/14 July, RAF Elsham Wolds received the raid details on Form B. The Base was to provide 12 Lancasters from 103 Squadron and 13 from 576 Squadron for a night target. At 1415 hours the numbers required were reduced to 11 and 12 respectively, and the target was given as Revigny. Station staff informed the Base staff that the ordered bomb load (11 x 1,000 lb and five 500 lb bombs) could not be carried to Revigny. Twenty-five minutes later the load was reduced by four 1,000 lb bombs. At 1520 hours, Base HQ informed Station HQ that the requirement was now 12 aircraft from 103 Squadron and 13 from

576 Squadron. This was later changed again to 12 from each squadron!

Briefing at Elsham Wolds began at 1845 hours, after the operational crews had been fed, leaving plenty of time for them to collect their equipment and report to the assembly points. At Upwood, home of 156 Squadron, the meal was at 2000 hours, and buses left for the aircraft at 2055 hours.

Main Force were briefed that 8 Group would use controlled 'Newhaven'* to mark the target. This was the code for ground marking by visual methods, with crews aiming at the target indicators burning on the ground.

Main Force crews to Revigny were briefed to expect illuminating flares to be dropped six minutes before H-Hour and to be followed by Red and Green TI on the aiming point. The Master Bomber would assess which TI was most accurately placed and instruct Main Force to bomb accordingly. Simple as it may sound, it needed only a slight wind blowing from an unexpected direction or cloud in the wrong place to produce inaccurate bombing. In the heat of the attack, crews could also be confused as to which marker the Master Bomber was referring, or the marker could be obscured by dust or smoke, or the Master Bomber's radio could be malfunctioning. Any one of these factors, or any combination thereof, could reduce a raid to shambles.

★   ★   ★

Most of Main Force were airborne for Revigny between 2100 and 2130 hours, but the last aircraft of 460 Squadron (Binbrook) and 101 Squadron (Ludford Magna) delayed their departures until 2145 hours. The two 8 Group squadrons further to the south, 156 (Upwood) and 635 (Downham Market), left at around 2200 hours.

There was one serious incident on take-off at Kirmington where, at about 2100 hours, the first 166 Squadron Lancaster, due to take off, set a few pulses racing. ME647 (F/O G. Lewis) was gathering speed down the runway when the starboard tyre suddenly burst. 'J-Jig' swung violently to the right, detaching the offending tyre as it went. As the enormous pressure on the now tyre-less wheel increased, so the entire starboard undercarriage collapsed and the heavy aircraft ground to a halt, fortunately off the runway.

The crash-tender and ambulance were already moving and raced to the scene of the inevitable accident. Firemen quickly applied foam to the smoke now issuing from the aircraft, but there was no trade for the 'blood wagon', and the shaken, uninjured and much relieved crew watched the rest of the squadron take off past the wreck, and with the minimum of delay — the first Lancaster was airborne only a few minutes after ME647 had begun moving.

As Main Force headed for Upper Heyford they began climbing to reach their operational height of 8-10,000 feet. The weather on take-off that summer's evening was far from good. At Elsham Wolds it was reported as being 8/10ths cloud over Base. Far from getting better, the

---

* *The name 'Newhaven' had been chosen by AVM Bennett, AOC 8 Group, after he had asked his confidential WAAF clerk where she lived — Newhaven!*

further south they flew, the more the cloud increased, to 10/10ths as they neared the south coast at Bridport, but it began to break up as they ploughed on across the English Channel to the turning point near the Channel Islands. At their briefed height, Main Force were 2,000 feet or more above the cloud. The forecast given to the Air Staff at 1755 hours/14 July had promised that all bases would be fit until midnight, but that 1 and 5 Groups would 'need to watch carefully the gradual eastward spread of rain'.

The German gunners on Guernsey reminded the 1 Group crews that there was a war on, flinging up desultory flak at the passing bombers, but with no success. Unconcernedly they headed on across the Gulf of St Malo towards the French coast. LM455 (Sgt G. B. Smith, 550 Squadron), however, had not even reached Bridport, having developed a faulty generator not long after take-off. The decision was taken to return to base, where they landed at 2259 hours, having been airborne for just over one and a half hours.

5 Group crossed the French coast at 2346 hours/14 July, heading past Cherbourg and down the Carentan peninsula (no doubt giving the Americans below a welcome morale booster), but were several minutes ahead of 1 Group. The Germans were aware of the progress of both raids, and soon ten Ju88s of I/NJG 2 were under control in the Orléans area from 0035-0047 hours, ready for either the 5 Group or the 1 Group raid. The latter was plotted as it flew past St Malo at around 2355 hours.

The first 1 Group contact with the Luftwaffe was made at 2349 hours/14 July when the gunners of ND458 (F/O J. G. Evans, 100 Squadron) spotted an Me110 whilst they were still over the sea. They claimed strikes on the enemy aircraft, but the result was inconclusive, and the Me110 broke away without firing. The next interception, at 0023 hours/15 July, again involved a 100 Squadron aircraft, LM620 (P/O J. Orr), flying at 10,000 feet several miles to the north-west of Tours. The attacker was identified only as a single-engined fighter. The rear gunner opened fire but again it was not returned.

There were to be no further contacts as the stream headed on across France on its south-easterly course, until Revigny was reached.

The 128 Lancasters of 5 Group, to the east of 1 Group but on a converging course, forged on to the marshalling yards at Villeneuve-St Georges. The Bomber Command summary for the night of 14/15 July (written on 19 July) made the comment that the 'plan of operations looked somewhat similar to that of two nights previously and it may well be that the Germans did not expect that the Paris area could be approached by a force coming in so far to the S.W. of the capital'.

Two other raids on 'Crossbow' (V-1) sites were taking place well to the north, at les Landes (a few miles inland from Dieppe) and at Anderbelck (near the coast on the Franco-Belgian border). Anderbelck was attacked between 0107 and 0118 hours by 50 Halifaxes of 6 Group, with support from two Lancasters and five Mosquitoes of 8 Group, whilst the attack on les Landes was made between 0157 and 0206 hours by 49 Halifaxes of 4 Group, again supported by two Lancasters and five Mosquitoes of 8 Group.

Further north, the mixed bag of 132 aircraft from six Groups were laying on the diversionary sweep ('Bullseye') over the North Sea — 1 Group (eight Halifaxes), 3 Group (14 Stirlings and Lancasters), 4 Group (seven Halifaxes), 5 Group (31 Stirlings and Lancasters), 92 Group (32 Wellingtons) and 93 Group (40 Wellingtons). Once more, this feint was intended to draw off the night-fighters based in the north-east of France and the Low Countries. 100 (BS) Group provided a 'Mandrel' screen through which the 'Bullseye' would fly.

There is evidence to suggest that, once again, the plan worked for, as the enemy plotted the Anderbelck raid emerging from North Foreland in Kent, soon after midnight, they sent two *gruppen* of night-fighters north-west from the Brussels area between 0125 and 0140 hours. The 'Bullseye' had left the English coast via Orfordness, Suffolk, and was heading for Holland; but half-way across the aircraft turned round and scuttled back to England. By the time the Germans were on their way to intercept the threat, the 'Bullseye' crews were already on their way home. Some night-fighters followed the retreat, and one Halifax was attacked at 0144 hours off Orfordness without being damaged.

The two 'Crossbow' raids attracted a small amount of attention, with single-engined fighters attacking both the earlier Anderbelck raid and the later one at les Landes; but the only combats reported occurred at Anderbelck, between 0109 and 0115 hours, when two Halifaxes fired on enemy aircraft. No aircraft was lost from either 'Crossbow' raid, and none from the northerly 'Bullseye'.

As these raids and diversions were in progress, so 1 Group continued across France until, at 4715°N/0200°E, they swung on to the north-easterly track heading for a point 150 miles away. But a second Lancaster could go no further. The oil pressure on the port outer engine of LM439 (F/S A. D. L. Greig, 576 Squadron) fell and the engine had to be feathered. As if that were not problem enough, the starboard outer followed suit and it too had to be feathered. Now on only two engines, the bombs were jettisoned and the Lancaster managed to stagger back to Stanton Harcourt, home of No 10 OTU, at 0330 hours/15 July.

Before they reached the great River Marne, however, the rest of 1 Group (now down to 123 Lancasters) turned sharply to starboard to pass south of Châlons-sur-Marne. Revigny now lay only some 40 miles away (about 13 minutes flying time). The German controller decided that this was the moment to get the St Dizier-based night-fighters into the air. Between 0114 and 0127 hours at least 12 Me110s of I/NJG 5 took off and began orbiting in the area. Also coming to join in the action were Ju88s and single-engined day-fighters, FW190s and Me109s. As the Lancasters neared their target, the fighters began to close in.

Over Revigny it was now the turn of 8 Group to see what they could do in a standard, controlled 'Newhaven' attack. Ten 'illuminators' were to drop their flares at ten-second intervals across the Aiming Point (AP) which they had to locate using H2S. Having done that (but they were under orders not to release their flares if H2S was u/s) they were to make an oval orbit to port and bomb when directed by the controller of the attack. There was to be a reserve of four 'illuminators' from 156 Squadron who would drop two minutes later if required.

As the flares went down, the Deputy Master Bomber was to mark the

AP as early as possible with Red TI, having located it visually. He would be supported by two further Lancasters of 156 Squadron. The Master Bomber, all the while keeping a close eye on the proceedings, would drop his TI if required. Once the Red TI were in position on the AP, the Master Bomber was to call up the 'backers-up' (four Lancasters from 635 Squadron) who were to drop Green TI on the Reds at two-minute intervals from H-2 to H+4. If no Red TI were seen, then the 'backers-up' were to drop their Greens on the AP if it could be positively identified. H-Hour was 0150 hours.

At 0140 hours, the Australian Master Bomber, F/L R. C. Wiseman DFC (PB177, 156 Squadron) reached the target:

'We arrived absolutely on time. The flares were dropped right on target, absolutely on time. I felt sure when I saw it that I could see the target alright. I thought "Oh, this is good. I've got it in the bag!".'

He found that the cloud base was at 5,000 feet, and called for flares to be dropped. At 0142 hours the first illuminating flares went down, two minutes ahead of schedule and, in the eight minutes up to H-Hour, 367 hooded 7-inch flares, type 'B', were released from heights varying between 11,000 and 12,500 feet.

Sgt Jack Cuthill (ND618, 156 Squadron) arrived over the target one minute late. F/S D. R. Breeze:

'The flares were already going down, so we dropped between another two lines. As we flew around we could clearly see the target — railway lines and sheds.'

The next wave of markers, the 'backers-up', were, however, unable to make positive visual identification of the AP. On his first run over the target, once the flares had gone down, Wiseman identified the aiming point too late to mark and, making a second run over the target at 4,000 feet, found that the flares were becoming dispersed. Consequently he was again unable to identify the aiming point in time to release his markers.

He made a third run, now at only 2,000 feet, and at 0148 hours called for more illumination. At 0152 hours, two minutes after Main Force were due to commence their bombing attack, he broadcast 'Have identified target and am going down to mark'. In the event, he found that he could only identify the AP when he was directly over it and was therefore in no position to release his markers.

At 0154 hours he broadcast 'Sugar Plum' — the code to abandon the mission and return home without bombing. The raid had failed again, through no fault of the aircrews. Richard Wiseman, an extremely experienced pilot (he had already completed a tour on 50 Squadron), was naturally upset at the decision he had had to make:

'Things were getting close to being out of hand. I had no alternative but to cancel the raid. It was unbelievable. I really couldn't believe my own voice that I had to do this. I was quite sure that we were going to be successful, the reason for the failure being that we were too low.

'The fog stopped the bomb aimer [F/L Lawton, another very experienced member of the crew, and squadron bombing leader] from seeing his sighting point and we were all equipped with the Mark XIV bomb-sight, which was very good, but would have done better higher. If I'd been left to myself, I'd have chosen about 8,000 feet [bombing height], mainly because the Mark XIV sight worked so well from that height. However, the powers that be didn't want that; so . . .

'The reason for being as low as we were was we were told to go right down and make perfectly sure. As a result, having got down low, it was impossible to get up again in time. I did try giving the old Lancaster all it had but I wanted another three or four thousand feet to be any good. I had no chance of getting it. Main Force were there travelling at about three miles a minute. It just had to be ready or there was an absolute mess.'

They had been beaten by the weather once more. Officially the weather in the target area was stated to have been 10/10ths cloud, tops at 6,000 feet, with a small break over the target. But the crews of the Australian 460 Squadron were most indignant. They found Wiseman's decision to call the attack off without bombing 'surprising as several aircrew are convinced that they saw the target clearly'. No doubt they did see the railway clearly, just as Wiseman himself had done but, as on the first abortive raid, there were strict orders not to allow the bombing if there was the slightest chance of causing unnecessary civilian deaths.

There was little delay this time in calling off the attack once Wiseman was satisfied that visibility was too bad to ensure the accurate delivery of the bombs. He himself, looking straight down, could see the ground and the houses in Revigny quite clearly, but his bomb aimer peering through the bombsight at an acute angle could see only his sights 'running along the fog bank; and presumably Squadron Leader Davies [Deputy Master Bomber] was in the same position'.

Just 12 minutes elapsed between the first flares igniting and 'Sugar Plum' being broadcast. Most of the waiting Lancasters made off to the next turning point a few miles to the south-east of Revigny, but four crews spotted a clear patch where hitherto there had been thick haze and decided to bomb. P/O W. C. Kuyser (ND614, 166 Squadron) had seen the flares going down at 0145 hours and claimed to have bombed the railway junction from a height of 10,000 feet at 0152 hours, the first to do so.

The second crew to drop their bombs was that of 1/Lt F. G. Marvin (ND992, 625 Squadron). Marvin, an American, had also identified the railway by the light of the flares and bombed through a break in the clouds just before the order to return was received, and after having completed two orbits of the target.

Another 166 Squadron Lancaster, NE113 (F/S R. W. Miller), had arrived over the target only for the crew to find it covered with broken cloud. As they were unable to see any markers, they made an orbit to starboard and came round again for another try. This time they saw a Red TI (at least ten minutes late in their opinion) which, at 0158 hours and from a height of 7,500 feet, they bombed. Unfortunately, no Red TIs were dropped by any aircraft of either of the two Pathfinder squadrons (although one 635 Squadron Lancaster unloaded its cargo of four 1,000 lb bombs). It is likely that NE113's bombs fell harmlessly wide of the target, and that the bomb-aimer was aiming at either a fire started by other bombs dropped earlier or, more likely, at the burning wreck of another aircraft (possibly LL837).

A fourth crew unloaded its bombs 'in the target area'. Lancaster PD208 (550 Squadron, piloted by another American, Lt G. P. Fauman) had reached the target on three engines and was steadily losing height. In view of this, Fauman made the easy decision to release the bombs to give them a better chance of reaching home over 700 track miles away. This they were eventually able to do. Three other crews bombed 'targets of opportunity' on the way home.

P/O J. C. Hutcheson (EE139, 'The Phantom of the Ruhr', 550 Squadron*) was also flying on three engines (one had had to be feathered due to an oil leak) and dropped his bombs on a nearby airfield which had been clearly identified as such by the lighted flarepath.

P/O T. G. Page (ND326, 100 Squadron) dropped two 500 lb long-delay bombs on an enemy airfield at 0209 hours. The last to drop was F/L T. H. I. Fleming (ND707, 166 Squadron) who bombed an airfield flarepath in the Auxerre region at 0232 hours from a height of 8,500 feet.

Jack Cuthill and crew were on their 32nd operation, and it was nearly their last. They had circled the target three times waiting for something to happen, ready to drop their four 1,000-pounders, when they heard the order to return to base with bombs. As they were leaving, a fighter latched on to them, but they managed to lose it, only to run into two more. F/S Breeze again:

> 'We twisted around like eels, at one time turning right round and starting back for the target. This foxed them and they lost us . . .'

But other Lancasters, not so lucky, were now being shot down as F/S Breeze recalls:

> 'In the light of one of these our gunners saw one little bastard that was coming up below us. We dived down and he followed us for the next 30 minutes, during that time making four or five attacks, none of which were successful. We all sweated like hell and I was throwing "window" out at the rate of five a minute and sometimes throwing whole packets out hoping to confuse them; but they were still following us.
>
> 'At last we got out of their range and flew peacefully back over France. We re-crossed the French coast and reached England. I was glad to see English searchlights. Our petrol was getting low, so we came back as quickly as possible.'

---

* EE139 completed its 100th op on 5 September 1944 — Hutcheson again — and finished with a total of 121, before being scrapped in January 1946.

Even then, they were the sixth, and last, to return of the seven 156 Squadron aircraft that had taken off seven hours earlier.

★ ★ ★

It is a fact that squadron records kept at the time are frequently incomplete and inaccurate. Ron Yeulett was a rear gunner on 582 Squadron, Little Staughton. His skipper was F/O Owen Milne. Records state that the Milne crew were posted to 582 Squadron with effect from 23 July. Ron has stated that his log book indicates that they took off at 2125 hours on the night of 14/15 July 1944 in Lancaster 'L for London' bound for Revigny; 9 hours 20 minutes later they landed back at Upwood (diverted there due to bad visibility at base) with bombs still aboard. I can only presume that the Milne crew were sent on the Revigny raid to get some experience.*

* *Five months later, on the 23 December 1944 daylight raid to the Gremberg marshalling yards at Cologne, five Lancasters were lost; all were from 582 Squadron. Milne and his crew, bar Ron Yeulett, perished with Lancaster PB371. One of the other pilots lost on this raid was S/L Robert Palmer, on his 111th operation. He was posthumously awarded the VC for four years of sustained courage in the face of the enemy.*

4

The Second Raid – Homeward, 15 July 1944

As the Lancasters circled the target area, the Luftwaffe again made contact. Hitherto there had been no casualties but, at 0154 hours, a Lancaster was suddenly 'seen to burst into flames and crash to the ground' in the Revigny area. It was probably the handiwork of an FW190, as several crews reported having seen a Lancaster explode at 4,000 feet after being attacked by one.

The victim was probably LL837 'Q-Queenie', skippered by the 30-year old CO of 550 Squadron, W/C P. E. G. G. Connolly. LL837 crashed near Bussy-la-Côte, a few miles to the south-east of Revigny. Connolly and the rest of the crew (which included the Squadron Gunnery Leader, F/L K. W. L. Fuller DFC, who had only been posted from 12 Squadron on 9 July) were killed.

Connolly had joined 550 Squadron on 15 May 1944 and this was only his sixth operation with it but, in the words of the Squadron scribe, he had already 'proved himself to be a leader of men, a man of understanding and was liked by all with whom he came into contact. The squadron has lost not only an efficient commander but a very gallant gentleman.'

After nearly half a century Connolly is still remembered with respect and admiration by Tony McKernan:

'If ever I get the chance to visit France, I shall certainly say a prayer at his graveside . . . He was a very charming man, and a great leader. One example of this was a prang on take-off of "S-Sugar", always regarded as the Squadron "jinx" kite, and this was a brand spanking new "S". We were stood down, and acting "Cheer Party" at the [flying control] caravan. Les Wareham, our skipper, thought he could detect a slight "cough" from one of the engines as "S" turned on to the runway.

'However, as the engines were run up, the "cough" disappeared and on the green from the A.C.P. "S" trundled off down the runway. It hadn't got very far before it began to swing to the left on to the grass. The pilot corrected this and got it back on to the runway, but "S" had other ideas and swung right on to the grass again. By this time we were all lying flat on the deck with faces in the mud, waiting for the big bang.

'Not so the Wingco — he was in his car and haring off down the runway after "S", which eventually finished up over an air raid shelter, close to the bomb storage — back broken, one engine on fire, but fortunately all the crew away and running like hares. Wingco calmly examined the aircraft and, having satisfied himself that all the crew were safe, waited to meet the fire crews as they arrived. Had that aircraft exploded, the whole bomb storage would have gone up and us with it. A very cool man was Connolly.'

★ ★ ★

Just before the raid was called off, the Deputy Master Bomber, who had been heard discussing the location of the AP with the Master Bomber, was heard no more. At 0157 hours Lancaster PA984, 156 Squadron, carrying the Deputy Master Bomber, S/L George Geoffrey Davies DSO, and his experienced crew, crashed into high ground 15 miles or so south of Revigny, killing six of the eight-man crew.

Geoff Davies had taken PA984 down to just a few hundred feet and was making height for the homeward trip when, without any warning, a night-fighter attacked from below and port quarter astern. Geoff flung the bomber into a 'corkscrew port', but not before the fighter had raked it from stem to stern. He was hit in the left wrist and left thigh but, receiving no instructions from the rear gunner, maintained a 'corkscrew port'. The rear gunner shouted out:

'We're on fire, Skip!'

'I know we're on fire,' replied Geoff. 'I'll try to get it out. Take it easy and watch for the fighters; but prepare to jump.'

The first attack by the fighter had started a fire in the bomb-bay, which held eight Red TIs, eight hooded flares and four 1,000 lb bombs. Thick, black smoke was filling the cockpit. Geoff was unable to read his instruments:

'I suspected that one of the TIs had been hit as the fire had a pronounced red glare. I immediately opened the bomb doors and gave the bomb-aimer his instructions for jettisoning TIs and bombs. Felt them go and tested on toggle, but the aircraft was still blazing away.

'The smoke by this time was absolutely solid, suffocating. Couldn't see or breathe, turned oxygen right up and clamped mask to face, but was still unable to breathe. I therefore opened the port side window and stuck my head out. I heard the engineer gasping and told him to do the same at his side. Judging by the draught he did so. I continued corkscrewing by touch as I was still unable to see instruments.

'I closed the bomb doors as soon as the load had gone in order to cut down the draught. However, the fire was still going strong, and the smoke was filling the cockpit. The aircraft controls then went u/s completely. Tried fore, then aft, finally the rudder. The flames were coming through the floor and I was on fire personally (helmet, hair, face, silk gloves, hands, scarf).

'I then ordered the crew "Jump! Jump!" and a few seconds later "Bale out, blokes, and let me know as you go". I heard the rear gunner say "I'm going, Skip!". I felt the draught from the front as if the escape hatch had been opened. Still holding my head out of the port window (at intervals), I saw (I think) two parachutes open. I heard no more from any other crew member, although my intercom was still working.

'I therefore called up the crew but received no answers. I decided it was time to get out, the controls being u/s, and I could see the ground which was pretty close. The aircraft was, as far as I could judge, in a shallow diving turn to port (the throttles had been left open as, due to lack of control, they were the only means of attempting to keep the nose up).

'I unplugged after taking a couple of deep breaths out of the window and made for the forward escape hatch, feeling for the engineer on the way. I could not find him and presumed he had got out. By this time flames were roaring in the cockpit between me and the hatch. I sat back for a final effort and leaned out of side window for another breather. Next I found myself out of the aircraft, presumably blown through the window.

'Rather dazed by smoke, heat and burns (eyes, hands, arms and hair) and bruised, I remember feeling a blow on my left side and leg. Then I remembered to pull the rip-cord and the parachute opened immediately. I hit the ground about 60 seconds later, crashing 50 or 60 feet through trees. The aircraft appeared to hit the ground a few seconds earlier (or may have been TIs burning).'

The remains of PA984 crashed to the ground at around 0200 hours. Only Geoff Davies and the bomb aimer, F/L K. Stevens, survived. Stevens baled out when the 'nose and centre section began to fall apart'. Five of the crew were found at or near the crash site and were buried at Ancerville. The sixth body, the flight engineer's, was only found on 23 March 1945, by a hunter in Valtiermont forest. The dead man's parachute had failed to open properly.*

Many years later the daughter of the Australian wireless operator (F/L H. G. M. Robinson DFC) visited the scene of the tragedy:

'I was taken to the forest where the aircraft had crashed. Unbelievably after 40 years I could see exactly where the wreckage had been. The whole place was heavily wooded apart from the area I have described. No trees or bushes had ever grown again.'

PA984 was shot down by a Ju88, possibly of 1/NJG 2. Flying nearby was Lancaster ED888 (P/O J. S. Griffiths, 576 Squadron) 'whose rear-gunner sighted a Ju88 in the glow of a burning Lancaster which it was

---

* F/O Fernand Camille Guillaume Debrock DFC (born in Ostende on 28 December 1907) was buried alongside his comrades at Ancerville the following day. On 9 May 1950, the Chief Administrative Officer of the Imperial War Graves Commission (French District) gave permission for the body to be exhumed and returned to Belgium. On 21 August 1950 this was done.

attacking'. The hungry Ju88, not satisfied with its victory over PA984, spotted veteran ED888 and began its approach. The two gunners fired long bursts at the enemy aircraft as it attacked from the fine port quarter down. Hit many times, the Ju88 burst into flames, dived down out of control, hit the ground and exploded.

Although too late to prevent the destruction of PA984, Griffiths's crew had the satisfaction of destroying its probable executioner. It was, incidentally, a joyous crew that landed safely at Chedburgh, where it had been diverted, some hours later. They had just completed their tour of 30 operations in three months!

Enemy night-fighters followed the Lancasters as they streamed homewards from Revigny. At 0200 hours/15 July the crew of LL748 (W/O W. H. S. Ansell, 550 Squadron) received a shock when a rocket projectile shot past their nose from right to left. Seconds later they saw an Me410, at which both gunners opened fire. Neither aircraft was damaged, but the Germans were not to be denied, and two minutes later they claimed their third victim for the night. ME755 (P/O W. A. H. Vaughan, 460 Squadron, on his 19th op) was shot down near Chevillon, Haute-Marne.

Its demise was witnessed by several crews who reported seeing air-to-air tracer, following which the aircraft burst into flames, fell slowly and broke into pieces before hitting the ground and exploding. Miraculously the wireless operator and the mid-upper gunner survived (see Chapter 10). They both confirmed that they were shot down by a fighter. Their five comrades were buried in Chevillon Communal Cemetery, alongside the five from JB644 lost on the first Revigny raid.

The crew of one of 100 (BS) Group's B-17 'jammers', HB763 'T', 214 Squadron, which had been escorting the raid reported:

'At St Dizier about 12 H.F. guns were in action, and an aircraft was seen to be shot down by flak at 0202 hours — it caught fire and hit the ground.'

This may have been the end of ME755, even though the facts do not exactly fit.

At 0205 hours, three minutes after the attack on ME755, there was a brief flurry of activity when the gunners of ME839 (P/O H. A. L. Wagner, 166 Squadron) twice fired at a suspected FW190. The enemy aircraft did not return fire, and they made no claim regarding their would-be attacker who, doubtless, went off in search of easier prey.

P/O C. H. 'Denny' Ogden DFC (103 Squadron, on his 26th trip) was certainly not inexperienced, and would not have made an easy target, but there was little answer to a skilfully flown night-fighter equipped with *schräge musik*. Thirteen-year old Michel Boussel of Biencourt-sur-Orge witnessed the end of Ogden and crew in NE136:

'Two aircraft passed overhead in flames; one of them crashed one kilometre away from the village. The explosion was terrible, shattering windows. When we got to the scene early next morning, we saw that the aircraft had made a very deep crater, which probably meant that it was still carrying bombs. There was still the odd explosion for a few more days.

'It was a horrible sight. We picked up bits of body which were stuck in the trees. All but two of the crew had been blown to bits in the explosion, but not burnt. The worst for me was to find the scalp of a red haired man who had literally been skinned from head to foot.

'One crewman jumped too late for his parachute to open and he hit the ground 800 metres from the crater. I can still see him as if he were in front of me . . . He was a man with inky black hair and a tanned face, very stout. He landed on his back. It was obvious that he did not suffer.'

'Denny' Ogden and the rest of his crew were buried in Biencourt-sur-Orge Communal Cemetery, and a large crowd was present. There was even a German delegation there, which caused a few hearts to quicken for fear of maquis reprisals. But the ceremony passed peacefully as befitted the occasion. There is a fitting tribute in 'Black Swan' by Sid Finn*:

'I should like to close this account by saying what an admirable character Danny [sic] was. A leader of men, and one England could ill afford to lose . . . His loss was keenly felt on the squadron even in the days when such tragic happenings were commonplace.'

Some ten minutes after the loss of NE136, the enemy claimed their fifth victory, another 103 Squadron Lancaster — ME773 (P/O H. R. Anthony, on his 11th op). Six of the seven crew are buried in the churchyard at Magny-Fouchard, Aube, some 45 miles south-west of Revigny. Horrified villagers at Vauchonvilliers watched as ME773, heading uncontrollably towards Magny-Fouchard a mile away across the valley, crashed into a field some 400 yards from Magny-Fouchard.

Somehow the wireless operator, F/S W. H. Taylor, survived. He managed to stagger on to the main road in Magny-Fouchard (the N19) and, at Madame Moreau's house, tapped on a window. With the war apparently as good as over, it was decided to hand the Englishman over to the gendarmes at nearby Vendeuvre-sur-Barse. He was handed over to the Germans, and spent the rest of the war in Stalag Luft 7, Bankau.

⋆　⋆　⋆

The returning Lancasters had been heading south-west for some time and, to the French listening on the ground, it was clear that the raiders were straggling home. René Demongeot, a young maquisard hiding in the woods near Vitry-le-Croisé, heard the unmistakeable sound of a four-engined aircraft, off track. Then, suddenly — Thump! Thump! Thump! Just as unmistakeable was the sound of the cannons of a night-fighter. Three short bursts and it was all over. It was 0224 hours and on the receiving end of the short attack was ND994 (F/O R. E. Linklater, 576 Squadron, a Canadian on his seventh trip).

---

* *Newton Publishers, August 1989.*

Standing outside his farmhouse to the north of Loches-sur-Ource was Roland Jeanvoine. He too heard the cannon fire and then saw, to his horror, a huge explosion in the sky above him as ND994 was blown into two. The tail section fell a hundred yards or so from a small road to the north of Essoyes. The rest carried on towards Loches-sur-Ource and came to earth in a cornfield several hundred yards away. Then two massive explosions sounded down the fields. Folk at Loches thought that it was a bomber getting rid of its load. Roland knew better, but dared not get too close.

Doctor Claude Poisson was summoned, though there was nothing to be done. The bodies of the two gunners, Sgt George Robert Sims (mid-upper) and F/S William John McCollum (rear), were found in the tail section. Dr Poisson was sure that McCollum was alive for at least one hour after the impact. The gruesome task of collecting up the remains began as soon as it was light, but it was never to be completed for 'the explosion threw bodies in pieces hundreds of yards away'. On 16 July five airmen, all Canadians, were buried in one coffin, and a brass plate was placed over each set of remains. The other two men were never found.

The bomb craters are still there, now overgrown by small trees, but the field has been kept to corn as a mark of respect, and to this day small bits and pieces of torn Lancaster can still be found.

★ ★ ★

The last Lancaster to be shot down by the enemy fighters this night was ND621 (P/O S. Martin, 166 Squadron). This was a doubly tragic loss, for not only was there a 'second dickie' aboard (New Zealander F/O A. O. Rodgers, aged 21) but also the crew were on their 29th operation. Just one more, and they would have been 'tour expired', with every expectation of surviving the war. They are buried in Lusigny-sur-Barse Communal Cemetery, one and a half miles north-west of the spot where ND621 crashed. How they came to be shot down is not known, but crews reported an aircraft bursting into flames, diving to the ground and exploding at 0236 hours.

Main Force flew on unmolested for 40 minutes until, at 0316 hours, F/S Barrington, rear gunner of LM623 (P/O H. J. Mills, 460 Squadron), suddenly saw an Me410 500 yards away, silhouetted high up against a sky lit by a near half-moon.

'Corkscrew starboard,' shouted F/S Barrington, and immediately P/O Mills flung the heavy aircraft into the sickening see-saw motion. Barrington was unable to use the reflector sight because the fighter was so high up, nor could he crouch low enough in his turret. Nevertheless, both he and the mid-upper gunner (F/S Carceldine) blazed away as the fighter closed to only 400 yards. Then, at the worst possible moment, all six guns stopped. Barrington had fired off only 150 rounds when he had a servo-feed stoppage, and Carceldine only 100 when his guns stopped from over-feeding.

LM623 had been flying at 6,000 feet, but during the 'corkscrew' dropped 2,000 feet. The fighter, which had been unable to open fire, appeared to be following, waiting for a better opportunity. Providentially,

Mills was able to steer the Lancaster into welcoming cloud and lost the fighter. No damage occurred to either aircraft and the Lancaster landed safely two and a half hours later.

The remaining Lancasters from the abortive raid were now on the reverse of their outward course. Ahead of them were the Lancasters of 5 Group returning from their successful attack on Villeneuve-St Georges. Although they had had a few encounters with enemy night-fighters, none of them had proved fatal. The Luftwaffe effort for the night was almost over, and only two further inconsequential contacts were made before the Lancasters rounded Guernsey and hurried north to their crossing-in point at Bridport.

As with the raid two nights earlier, weather over England on the return was bad and diversion calls were sent out for the Lancasters to be diverted again to 3 Group airfields in East Anglia. There was some confusion amongst 460 Squadron crews when Group HQ diverted them to Waterbeach. Unfortunately, the Diversion Schedule issued by Group prior to the raid showed Waterbeach as 0011°W instead of 0011°E, and four Lancasters landed at Graveley. A fifth 460 Squadron crew landed at Mepal when the wireless operator of ME649 mis-read a number on the Diversion Schedule. At 0445 hours all 166 Squadron aircraft were diverted to Mildenhall, but one nevertheless managed to land at Wyton.

There were fun and games at Waterbeach, 33 Base Station, and at its sub-stations at Mepal and Witchford. At 0445 hours/15 July Waterbeach was alerted to the imminent arrival of 15 aircraft at each of the three airfields — 460 Squadron to Waterbeach; 100 Squadron to Witchford; and 625 Squadron to Mepal. Thirty-five minutes later a message was received from 1 Group that they had made a mistake — 625 would be going to Witchford and 100 to Mepal. At 0535 hours a Wing Commander from Grimsby telephoned Waterbeach to say that 100 Squadron should return to their own base. This was checked with 3 Group who said that Waterbeach should land the 100 Squadron Lancasters anyway. By the time this fracas had been sorted out, two 100 Squadron crews had already been told to go to Grimsby!

Aircraft were already landing. LL956 (P/O R. H. Wintle, 625 Squadron) was the first to arrive at Witchford, at 0527 hours; ND656 (P/O R. S. Stott, 460 Squadron) the first down at Waterbeach; and ND326 (P/O T. G. Page, 100 Squadron) the first at Mepal, at 0509 hours. When the count was finally made, Waterbeach had taken in nine from 460 Squadron and one each from 100 and 625 Squadrons; Witchford had landed six from 625; and Mepal four from 625, two from 100 and one from 460 Squadrons.

Moreover, despite being tired after their long and fruitless journey, they all got down in one piece, all that is except for ND392 (P/O R. W. Hofstetter, 460 Squadron) who, having just completed his 20th operation, celebrated by taxying his Lancaster into a truck! This caused a certain amount of damage to a propeller, but was nothing that could not be fixed. He returned to base some six hours after his fellow squadron members, leaving at 1550 hours, no doubt roundly cursed by the over-worked Waterbeach ground crews.

The weather later that morning of 15 July was considerably better than it had been two days previously, and at 0745 hours instructions were issued that aircraft could return to their bases as soon as they had been topped up with 1,000 gallons of fuel. They were to take all their bombs back with them, except for those fitted with long-delay fuses which were to be removed. However, by 0830 hours the fickle weather began to deteriorate and crews were ordered not to take off. But, lo and behold, a quarter of an hour later the weather cleared again, and at 0845 hours crews were instructed to return home. And so, from airfields all over East Anglia, the 1 Group strays took off on the final part of what had been just another night of operations.

The two crews of 100 Squadron who had flown back direct to Grimsby were later joined by their comrades from Lyneham, Mepal, Upwood, Waterbeach and Wyton; but Air Commodore Wray, 12 Base Commander, ordered a close enquiry into why the two early returners — P/O J. D. Rees (LM644) and P/O D. G. Mills (ND413) — had returned to base direct, contrary to their diversion instructions.

F/L Harry Guilfoyle and crew in LM227 (576 Squadron) were stooging home when they were diverted to Newmarket. George Tabner, navigator, passed on the helpful information to his skipper that there was no aerodrome there. But orders were orders and, on arrival at the famous racecourse, they saw five Spitfires (possibly of 1483 Gunnery Training Flight) dispersed on the inside of the track itself. George Tabner:

'Harry said "Anywhere a Spit can go, so can a Lanc." So, with our 9,000 pounds [of bombs] still on board, in we went.

'I remember the F/L Intelligence Officer, who had rushed all over the camp scrounging cigarettes for the visiting "operational" crews, offering them to us. Five out of seven, plus the second dickie, F/O Watts, said "No thank you, Sir, I don't smoke." Two did — Rear Gunner "I have my own Canadian", and the R/O "I prefer his Canadian, thanks". The poor fellow's face dropped a mile.

'Then he asked our Aircraft ID. I told him "I2". He said "They do not use 'I'." So I said "You go and look then!".'

P/O M. J. MacDonald brought ND381, 103 Squadron, safely back to Elsham Wolds where the flight engineer, Sgt D. E. Bell, remembers that

'. . . visibility was not at all bad, but it did seem rather quiet in the way of planes landing. We should have diverted again but our WOP/AG said that he had missed it. We had to believe him!

'As I put my bike in the rack prior to going into the briefing room for interrogation, the Station Commander, Group Captain Sheen, turned up. Fortunately, I knew from being on the station three months that it was him, for he had on an old cap without "scrambled egg", a polo-necked pullover and an old raincoat. He asked me what had happened, and when I told him we had brought our bombs back again he said "You won't go there again", and stalked off. And we did not.'

* * *

Saturday 15 July 1944 was dull and cloudy, and that must have been the mood at Bawtry Hall, 1 Group HQ, when the results of the two Revigny raids were assessed — 16 crews and 18 Lancasters lost; damage to the railway junction, if indeed there had been any, negligible. It would not have been pleasant reporting the bitter truth to Bomber Command HQ, but it had to be done, even though the two failures were attributable to the bad visibility directly over the target, which, together with the strict orders not to bomb in such circumstances, effectively guaranteed such a result.

Richard Wiseman, whose unpleasant but correct duty it had been to call off the show, has had many years in which to contemplate the events of that night:

'Well, I've been many times over and over this again in my mind of what I could have done to have altered the situation. I haven't yet come up with an answer. Anyhow, it was a very bitter moment . . . When I called "Sugar Plum" and cancelled the whole operation, I carried on towards home from about level with the target, and I presumed that everybody else would have done the same, done an about-turn and made for home. There was no point in hanging about.

'Fighters were obviously there and the only thing I find it quite hard to understand is the report from several people that there was cloud and that they bombed through holes in the cloud. As far as I could see there was no cloud. I certainly didn't see anything. It was only fog lower down.

'As regards the chappies on 460, some of them I was quite friendly with, or knew them after, and of course they more or less told me exactly that I, in their minds, was to blame for the failure. Well, you know, if I'd been there too in their shoes I'd have taken the same view.

'But it just wasn't that way!'

On 30 July 1944 Richard Wiseman and his crew were screened from operations. They had a total of 496 operations between them, Wiseman's personal tally being 70. With effect from 3 August he was promoted to Acting Squadron Leader.

5

The Third Raid – Outward, 18/19 July 1944

After several days of unseasonal weather, the British and Canadian Divisions of the Second Army stood poised to strike to the southeast of Caen, where the German Army had been resolutely defending. At dawn on 18 July 1944 there occurred what General Eisenhower described as 'the heaviest and most concentrated air assault hitherto employed in support of ground operations'*, when 927 aircraft of RAF Bomber Command and 570 B-24s of VIII Bomber Command, USAAF, dropped over 6,500 tons of bombs on a number of villages and 'fortified' factories near Caen where elements of the German's Fifth Panzer Army were dug in. Operation GOODWOOD was under way.

Eisenhower continued:

'Although only temporary in effect, the results of the bombing were decisive so far as the initial ground attack was concerned. Actual casualties to the enemy, in his foxholes, were comparatively few, but he was stunned by the weight of the bombing and a degree of confusion was caused which rendered the opposition to our advance negligible for some hours.'†

Yet within a few hours the Germans were fighting as tenaciously as before, and made the British and Canadians pay dearly for the ground gained. For a few hours the colossal weight of bombs had indeed stunned the defenders but, significantly, Bourguébus Ridge, which dominated the battlefield and which remained firmly in German hands, had not been flattened.

Adding to this carnage were crews of 5 Group, a number of whom, if they thought that they had finished for the day, were in for a surprise. Revigny railway junction had not yet been put out of action.

---

* *p45,* Report by The Supreme Commander to the Combined Chiefs of Staff on the Operations in Europe of the Allied Expeditionary Force' *(HMSO, 1946).*

† *p46, ibid.*

The third attempt had been scheduled for the night of 16/17 July, but was cancelled at 1720 hours/16 July because of poor weather. Five ABC Lancasters of 101 Squadron, also due to go on the raid, received the cancellation order at 1818 hours. Two days later the weather improved and, after GOODWOOD, the all-clear was given for the third Revigny attack.

★ ★ ★

As we have seen, on both the 1 Group operations to Revigny, the bombers had been sent well clear of Normandy — from the Dorset coast to west of the Channel Islands, followed by a long run across France south of Paris, with a turn north-east to the target. They had returned the same way. But for the third raid, by 5 Group, the route would go the shortest possible way — straight down England, east of London over Gravesend, out over the south coast at Hastings, and on south-east across the Channel until the French coast was reached just north of le Tréport. There the Somme estuary was several miles to port, though few would spare a thought for what had happened there a generation before. They would have their own more immediate aerial horrors with which to contend.

Maintaining their south-easterly track, the Lancasters were to fly between Beauvais and Montdidier, Creil and Compiègne (across the River Oise), Meaux and Château-Thierry, and over the River Marne with Paris a few dozen miles to starboard. Then, when the distinctive, twisting River Aube was reached, they would swing east-north-east straight to the target 40 miles distant. Homewards, the track ran slightly north of west before meeting the outward course and crossing over the coast again at almost the same point — out into the Channel, a gentle turn to starboard, up the Straits of Dover, north over North Foreland, on to Orfordness and home to base.

Most Lancasters would carry 10 x 1,000 lb MC and 4 x 500 lb MC GP bombs, variously long-delay fused, some for as long as 144 hours. 463 and 467 (RAAF) Squadrons had to carry one more 1,000 lb and one fewer 500 lb bomb than the others.

That was the plan. A piece of cake. But it proved to be costly and not a little unpopular.

Other raids on 18/19 July were mounted to the V-1 site at Acquet (62 sorties), and to the railway at Aulnoye, near the Belgian border (148 sorties). The oil plants at Wesseling near Cologne and Scholven (194 and 170 sorties respectively) were also visited.

In addition to these raids, six 8 Group Mosquitoes went on a 'spoof' to Cologne, and a further 22 to Berlin. A diversionary sweep across the North Sea was also laid on.[*]

100 (BS) Group provided its customary bomber support (86 aircraft on various duties). Other odds and ends made the total effort for the night an impressive 972 sorties. It was hoped that the result of the spoofs, diversions, sweeps and electronic interference would be a 'clean sheet'

---

[*] *Made up of 139 miscellaneous aircraft from the five operational Groups and the three training Groups (91, 92 and 93).*

for Bomber Command. The Luftwaffe, though, had other ideas.

★   ★   ★

By the summer of 1944 the Allies had achieved a mastery of the daylight skies over France and had caused grievous losses to the Luftwaffe's day-fighters. But their night-fighter arm continued to grow and, by December 1944, it was to have more machines than at any previous time in the war. But on 18 July 1944, throughout the whole of France, Belgium and Holland, there were only 221 twin-engined and 28 single-engined serviceable night-fighters. Few enough to go round:

> 'From May 1944 onwards, on the assumption that RAF Bomber Command would not restart its costly deep-penetration raids over Germany in the near future, the Luftwaffe had moved its night-fighter formations (except parts of JG 302) from Central Germany to the periphery of the Reich Air Defence area: the west, Northern Italy, Austria and Hungary. There remained in Germany only parts of NJG 1 and NJG 3, stationed in the north, and the replenished "Staffeln" of single-engined night-fighter "Gruppen". With its units thus deployed, the Luftwaffe command believed that it could counter any raid, from whatever direction, by means of timely interception and subsequent concentrated attacks by single-engined night-fighters near the target.'*

The deep-penetration raids over Germany that had proved so costly to Bomber Command during the winter of 1943–44 tailed off from March 1944 onwards, as targets were switched to France. The Luftwaffe reacted by transferring II and III/NJG 1 and I, II and III/NJG 5 to France, and intended, once the invasion was under way, to transfer the whole of NJG 2, III/NJG 3, II/NJG 5 and I/JG 301 to destroy the expected 'enemy bomber and transport formations'. They would be used in a daylight role. In the event, only the first two *gruppen* of the earmarked units moved to France.

Whilst the night-fighters did not suffer the high losses of the day-fighters facing American daylight raids, they steadily lost some of their top scorers. Men of such experience were not easy to replace and the only way for the tyros to learn their trade was in combat, and in a sky becoming more dangerous each passing week. The night sky over western Europe was no place for the novice.

So, by July 1944 additional Luftwaffe night-fighters were present in France and the Low Countries, moved there initially to counter the Normandy landings, their crews a blend of the skilled and the novice. But no one in Bomber Command believed for one moment that the German night-fighter arm was a spent force.

★   ★   ★

It was still light that Tuesday 18 July when the first Lancaster, ND797 (F/L G. Joblin, 630 Squadron) took off for Revigny at 2236 hours. The

---

* *Gebhard Aders,* History of the German Night Fighter Force 1917–1945, *p168 (Jane's Publishing Company, 1979).*

rest followed safely until, at 2319 hours, ND902 (F/L D. E. Stone, 61 Squadron) lifted off from Skellingthorpe, the last of the 109 Lancasters. For half an hour silence descended upon the Lincolnshire airfields.

Then, at 2347 hours, the familiar sound of Merlins at full throttle echoed across the airfield at Woodhall Spa. The first of 627's Mosquitoes (DZ611, F/L W. W. Topper at the controls) was on its way. The fifth, and final, Mosquito was clear seven minutes later. One aircraft yet remained.

W/C J. R. Jeudwine DFC had a rendezvous over Revigny at 0140 hours as the marker-controller in a single-seater P-38 'Lightning'.[*]

The first Revigny-bound Lancaster reached France at 0040 hours/19 July, though it was not the first Bomber Command aircraft to do so that night. Twenty minutes earlier the raids to Aulnoye and Acquet had crossed the 'enemy coast'. The Acquet raid by the Halifaxes of 4 Group, with Mosquito and Lancaster marking by 8 Group, was finished in eight minutes and the last aircraft left France at 0046 hours, while 5 Group were still streaming south. Two Halifaxes, however, failed to return.[†] Some of the 5 Group crews saw two aircraft shot down from 10,000 feet at around 0035 hours — cause unknown. These were almost certainly the two Halifaxes. A third Halifax, MZ788 of 78 Squadron, was luckier, but not much. Hit by cannon shells and set on fire, three of the crew baled out; two were never seen again. The fire was extinguished and the Halifax crashed at West Malling. For his heroism the flight engineer, Sgt. W. J. Bailey, later received the CGM.

Acquet was not far to port of 5 Group's track, and the blaze from the two unfortunate Halifaxes would have served as a warning to the Lancaster crews to be on their toes. Even further away to port the 3 Group raid on Aulnoye railway junction and engine sheds was taking place. This was a bigger raid than either that to Revigny or Acquet, with 124 of their Lancasters, 19 Lancasters and Mosquitoes of 8 Group, and five ABC Lancasters of 101 Squadron. The attack at Aulnoye began at 0053 hours and lasted for only eight minutes. Two Lancasters were lost.[§]

It was hoped that the Aulnoye raid, which entered France in roughly the same area as the Revigny one, albeit 25 minutes earlier, would attract the night-fighters and leave 5 Group a clear run to their target. The Luftwaffe was indeed attracted to the 3 Group raid and, in response to the early radar warning, alerted III/NJG 5 (Laon/Athies), despatching 15 Me110s to the Cambrai and Amiens area. At 0015 hours/19 July the enemy bombers were plotted over the middle of the English Channel and NJG 3 (le Culot) sent several aircraft to the Bapaume area.

I/NJG 4 (Florennes) was ordered off to the same area to attempt an interception. At 0030 hours I/NJG 3 was near Acquet, but both these units were moved to the west of Aulnoye as 3 Group continued its eastward journey. With the Aulnoye attack quickly over by 0101 hours, some of the night-fighters of I/NJG 4 and III/NJG 5 were, five minutes

---

[*] *The P-38, number 42-3482, was loaned at the beginning of July 1944 to RAF Coningsby by Maj-Gen Fred Anderson, CO of VIII Bomber Command, USAAF. It was later exchanged for a two-seater.*

[†] *LK873 (76 Squadron) and NA513 (78 Squadron).*

[§] *LL921 (75 Squadron) and LL943 (115 Squadron).*

later, sent to the west of Lille. The Lancasters of 3 Group, meanwhile, were making good their escape via the shortest route possible. By 0140 hours, the last of their aircraft was speeding north over the French coast.

With Acquet long since quiet and Aulnoye fizzling out, the Luftwaffe was able to concentrate on the bombers which were still heading south-east into France. Long-range radar had identified the separate bomber streams as they made their way over the Channel, and at 2345 hours/18 July II/NJG 4 and II/NJG 2 (Coulommiers) sent aircraft to the Dieppe area. But they were too early for 5 Group.

At 0048 hours, eight minutes after the first 5 Group Lancaster had breached French airspace, units of probably I/NJG 4 were ordered to a point a dozen miles inland from le Tréport. Fortunately for 5 Group, the order was soon countermanded. Had this not been done, the night-fighters would have been waiting precisely in the path of the incoming stream!

It was a long, almost straight run of 170 miles from the French coast before turning on to the north-east leg of some 40 miles from Revigny. It would take the Lancasters a little over an hour to cover the whole of that distance.

The Revigny raid, plotted as soon as it reached the French coast, now became the centre of Luftwaffe interest. Accurate plots were passed to the German night-fighters by R/T from as early as midnight and continued regularly up until the time when the bombing was well under way over the target itself. At 0105 hours St Dizier flying control, having correctly assessed the destination of the incoming raid, passed the information on to its resident unit — I/NJG 5. Two minutes later, that same unit was ordered to a position north of Paris and handed over to another controller. At 0135 hours, bombers were reported over St Dizier. But the hunt had already begun.

On returning to Waddington F/O R. H. Purser (LM100, 467 Squadron) reported: 'From enemy coast inward track was marked by enemy with green changing to white flares. Fighters seemed very busy all the way.'

P/O V. A. Baggott (LL789, 467 Squadron) complained: 'I think we might have been routed around south of searchlight belt south of Pas de Calais area. S/L's were very active.'

F/O L. Pederson (ND512, 49 Squadron) was coned by the lights for three minutes before managing to shake them off by 'corkscrewing', and JB701 (F/O G. M. Burns of the same squadron) was held for four minutes. It must have seemed a lifetime. The 'searchlight belt' (at approximately 4950°N/0150°E), although very disturbing, was tame in comparison to what lay ahead, even though the unexpected lights had bothered some of the crews.

JB318 (57 Squadron), for example, had no sooner crossed the French coast than it was coned by the lights. Violent evasive action by the pilot, F/L J. A. Bulcraig DFM*, had the desired effect, and the lights were 'lost', but in so doing it is possible that the Lancaster was by then outside the bomber stream and easy prey for the night-fighters.

The Luftwaffe night-fighters, following their standard procedure of

---

* *He won the DFM as a navigator on 50 Squadron in 1940.*

beacon-hopping, were able to make contact soon after the searchlights had played their part, helped to some extent by the clear skies. The first reported sighting of a night-fighter by a 5 Group Lancaster was timed at 0040 hours by the crew of LM190 (P/O G. G. Poole, 49 Squadron), who saw a Ju88. At 0045 hours an Me110 opened fire at 600 yards range on a 50 Squadron aircraft but missed. This was just as well as the rear turret was u/s. LM190 was back in action at 0046 hours when both gunners blazed away at a Ju88 as it crossed from the port beam to port quarter at 700 yards range, and missed — the Lancaster was in a 'corkscrew' at the time.

At 0056 hours, F/O A. B. Fleck and crew (ME866, 619 Squadron) watched anxiously as an unidentified twin-engined aircraft fired at them from 700 yards directly above. Neither gunner was able to get a sighting on the night-fighter, again due to a 'corkscrew', and the enemy missed.

At 0101 hours the first Lancaster, JB186 (619 Squadron), was shot down near Auger-St Vincent, Oise. The rear gunner was killed in the attack, but there was evidently time for some of the crew to escape. The bomb-aimer baled out and evaded, but the wireless operator was found with his parachute not opened properly. The navigator's body was found some distance from the aircraft.

Their loss was followed immediately by LM640 (619 Squadron) and DV304 (61 Squadron), and soon a third from 619 Squadron, LM378. The fighters were well into the stream now and combats were coming thick and fast. Upward firing was observed — *schräge musik* — as one crew laconically reported, after the raid: '0105. Lancaster caught fire and exploded on ground following fighter attack from below.'

The damage was not all one way. PB244 (F/O A. Kemp, 630 Squadron) was attacked at 0110 hours by an unidentified aircraft, after 'Fishpond' had been activated. The attack lasted for three minutes, but ended when the rear gunner loosed off his four Brownings and sent the assailant spinning to the ground. At the same time, LM226 (F/O D. B. Jeffery, 467 Squadron) suddenly came under attack, with no 'Monica' warning. The perspex on the mid-upper turret was damaged and Jeffery hurled the heavy aircraft into an immediate 'corkscrew', which ensured that the enemy was not seen again.

At 0112 hours, an unidentified fighter shot down PB245 (F/O N. W. Donnelley), 619 Squadron's fourth loss within 15 minutes, but not before its gunners had given as good as they had got. The fighter, possibly from III/NJG 5, was also seen to go down.[*]

0113 hours. No sooner had it beaten off one attack than PB244 was attacked for a second time; no damage was caused and none done to the opposition. A little way behind PB244, but at the same time as their second attack, LM582 (P/O J. Beard, 57 Squadron) was in action. An Me109 attacked from above with no warning from 'Fishpond' (there was a blind spot there, above the horizontal plane), but the gunners responded and their accurate fire set the fighter ablaze. It too was seen to crash to the ground.

[*] *Records show that, offset against the seven victories gained by III/NJG 5 on this night, the unit lost three crews — those of Unteroffiziers Busch and Busskamp and of Gefreiter Murogi.*

At 0114 hours, ND977 (F/L R. Walker, 57 Squadron), when still some way short of the target, tangled with a Ju88 which had been spotted starboard quarter down. The night-fighter got in a telling burst, causing considerable damage to the Lancaster — the rear turret, occupied by P/O W. 'Goldie' Golding, was set on fire, the intercom ceased functioning, and 'Gee' and H2S were also found to be useless. Furthermore, all external navigation lights came on. Despite losing a great deal of height during the attack, the Ju88 had no difficulty in following the Lancaster down, and as the enemy closed in for the kill both gunners (Golding and the mid-upper, F/S A. 'Red' Brown) opened fire.

They hit the fighter in the starboard engine, and it was last seen diving steeply away in flames. P/O Golding succeeded in extinguishing the flames in his turret but in so doing suffered burns to his feet and thighs, despite being 'very well protected by his flying boots and suit'.

The wireless operator, F/S R. A. 'Ginger' Hammersley DFM, recalls what happened after the Ju88 had been driven down:

'Mack [the navigator, F/O H. B. Mackinnon] went to the rear with a fire extinguisher. I tried to warn him of the need to take his 'chute but he failed to hear me. (It was years later when he realised what I tried to say). All lights — external and internal — were on. I followed Mack to the rear and helped "Goldie" out of the turret and assisted him to the rest bed. His turret was u/s. He had suffered bullet wounds as well as serious burns to his legs and feet. Mack and Essie [the flight engineer, Sgt E. Chung] managed to put out some of the lights and, as my wireless was still functioning, I was able to advise base of our problems . . .'*

The bombs were dropped and F/L Ron Walker swung ND977 on to a course for home. With P/O Golding out of his turret, Roland Hammersley was able to apply a 'Gel' dressing from the aircraft's first-aid kit to his wounds. With no further alarms, the Lancaster touched down at East Kirkby some two hours later — and burst a tyre!

When the crew visited their injured rear gunner in Rauceby hospital next day, the surgeon, whilst praising Roland for the good job he had done, regretted the use of the 'Gel' dressing as it had proved difficult to clean up Golding's wounds. Orders were soon issued throughout Bomber Command that all such dressings were to be removed from bombers' first-aid kits.[†]

* * *

There was a few minutes' lull after the attack on ND977 before, at 0121

---

* *p91, 'Up the Creek (or Five Years With the RAFVR)', Roland A. Hammersley DFM, 1989*

[†] *Hammersley and Walker had now completed 29 operations, Chung 26 and Mackinnon and Bly (bomb-aimer) 25. After debriefing the Squadron CO conferred with the Base CO, who agreed that the crew were now 'tour expired', even though none of them had completed his full quota of 30 trips. Golding was awarded an immediate and well-deserved DFC.*

hours, JB318 (57 Squadron) was hit by cannon fire from below. It will be remembered that they had already tangled with the searchlights and were possibly outside the protection of the bomber stream. The rear gunner, on only his third operation, saw nothing until the port wing exploded. But three men survived (see Chapter 15).

Six Lancasters had now been shot down and 38 aircrew were dead. Worse, much worse, was to follow.

PB236 (F/O A. J. Sargent, 630 Squadron) was lost near Neuvy. There is a report from another Lancaster that at 0121 hours two aircraft went down following air-to-air tracer, and it is certain that PB236 was caught by the rampaging night-fighters. There were no survivors. The same fate awaited ME681 (F/O N. L. Weekes, 207 Squadron, on his fourth op) which crashed to one side of track and fell into a field near Chacun, Marne. Locals heard one burst from a fighter, and that was that. The Lancaster hit the ground with bombs still aboard, the explosion forming a crater ten feet deep. The largest piece of aircraft found, the remains of one of the propellers, now adorns the graves at Margny. Some 500 people attended the funeral and every year, on 14 July and 11 November, the Mayor's wife places fresh flowers on the graves.

Eight aircraft lost; 52 dead.

The turning point at the River Aube was now coming up and a near 90-degree turn to port was required. Three more Lancasters — ND684 (F/O W. D. Appleyard, 49 Squadron), JB178 (F/O W. R. Green, 49 Squadron) and DV374 (F/O J. R. Worthington, 463 Squadron) — got no further, shot down by night-fighters. Their wreckage was strewn across the Aube and Marne départements. It was probably the demise of JB178 that was witnessed at 0130 hours by another unidentified Lancaster: 'Lanc dead astern 800 yds own height [7,800 ft] seen to burst into flames and crash. One parachute seen. Cause unknown.'

There were no survivors, and the fact that no mention was made of tracer or air-to-air firing suggests that yet again *schräge musik* had triumphed.

Eleven Lancasters lost; 73 dead.

Given that the Germans had relatively early assessed that the raid was heading for the general direction of St Dizier, it is not surprising that they were able to follow the bomber stream. The radar installations around St Dizier were as good as anywhere, comprising an arrangement of two *Giant Würzburgs* and one *Freya* radar at Chancenay, barely two miles north-east of the airfield. The W/T station for the sector was situated on the south side of the airfield itself at Valcourt — '3 masts 87 feet tall in form of isosceles triangle with small hut in centre'.

Further attacks were now mounted as the night-fighters closed in once more, picking up the bombers as they headed for Revigny after the turn on the River Aube. PB231 (F/O C. Lacy, 49 Squadron) and LL969 (F/O S. B. Morcom, 619 Squadron) (see Chapter 15) were on the short leg to the target when shot down.

Thirteen lost; 84 dead.

Then, at 0134 hours, at 10,000 feet, a Lancaster crew reported: '3 unidentified a/c seen falling with smoke coming from engines. Went down one after the other in quick succession. Positions starboard bow

8–10 miles away. All three were seen to hit the ground and explode. Cause unknown. No parachutes seen.'

These were almost certainly ME814 (F/O J. G. Dallen, 207 Squadron, on his 13th op); ME833 (F/O L. J. Wood, 9 Squadron); and LM537 (F/O P. B. Dennett, 630 Squadron). LM537 was brought down by flak, the first victim of the ground gunners that night. The other two were lost to night-fighters.

Sixteen Lancasters down; 99 dead.

Also at 0134 hours, a Ju88 with both engines on fire was seen 600 yards astern of another Lancaster, diving towards the ground, although not seen to crash; and the crew of LM100 saw a single-engined fighter by the light of burning bombers about a mile away.

At 0137 hours, F/O D. G. Bates and crew (ED860, 61 Squadron) were at 8,000 feet a few miles south-west of the target when a Ju88 appeared only 150 yards away on the starboard beam and slightly below. There was no question of the gunners being caught napping, and they both poured lead into the Ju88's port engine, main plane and fuselage. Most satisfyingly it caught alight, but they claimed only a 'damaged', as it was not seen to hit the ground. The two gunners, however, were not finished for the night.

At 0140 hours LM226, whom we have already seen in action half an hour earlier, was under attack again; this time it was an FW190, and again there was no 'Monica' warning. Another 'corkscrew' in the other direction, port, also lost the fighter. At the same time P/O T. Russell (ND647, 49 Squadron), at 8,500 feet, watched with baited breath as a Ju88 crossed from port to starboard 500 feet below them. One minute later and the crew of LL922 (F/O D. A. T. Millikin, 50 Squadron) were alerted by 'Monica'. Five hundred feet above them, at 8,500 feet, they saw a Ju88 which, thankfully, melted away into the night.

At 0142 hours, at 12,000 feet and still six miles short of the target, it was the turn of LM582 to suffer a second attack, by another Me109. There was no moon, but stars were visible; downward visibility was poor. The mid-upper gunner, Sgt Walker, was watching another Lancaster being shot down in flames (possibly ME796) when he suddenly spotted the fighter level on the port beam at a range of 300 yards. It was breaking away from its victim and was flying on a parallel course to them when it began to attack. The pilot was ordered to 'corkscrew port', and both Walker and the rear gunner, Sgt Osborn, opened up. LM582 received a hole in its port wing, but it was not serious. Walker continued firing until the Me109 had passed underneath and was lost from view. He had the satisfaction of seeing tracer from his two guns strike the fighter, which made no further attack.

At about the same time as this attack DV312 (F/O W. J. Long, 50 Squadron), was shot down. Judging by the location of its crash (at Robert Magny, 25 miles south of Revigny), it was well to starboard of track and must have been an easy target for the crew of the night-fighter, who destroyed the two starboard engines. Long gave the order to jettison the bombs and bale out. The Lancaster was by this time in a steep dive and only the bomb-aimer, with the greatest difficulty, managed to escape (see Chapter 10).

Seventeen Lancasters lost; 105 men dead.

The gunners of LM226 were really on their toes for, at 0145 hours, they were attacked for the third time that night. It was another FW190 and both gunners opened up and the enemy aircraft broke away without returning fire.

This turned out to be the last attack before the target area was reached. It had been a furious 45 minutes from the moment the first Lancaster was shot down at 0101 hours.

I/NJG 5 and III/NJG 4 (Juvincourt) were ordered to St Dizier at around 0140 hours. III/NJG 5 were told to assemble east of Cambrai, ready for the return. It was reckoned by Bomber Command Intelligence, when they came to assess this raid, that six or seven *gruppen* of night-fighters had been active against 5 Group at some point or other along their track. Each *gruppe* had a nominal strength of 30 aircraft, but the number serviceable at this time was down to between 50 and 60 per cent. Even had all available night-fighters in north-eastern France been airborne at the same time on 18/19 July, it is unlikely that they would have totalled more than a hundred or so.

However few, the Germans had experienced no difficulty in finding the bombers. They were assisted by some odd 'new' devices. Various crews reported having seen, *en route*, yellow flares being fired from the ground, which rose to about 5,000 feet and illuminated aircraft 'very brightly'. It was estimated that at one time no fewer than 50 such flares were airborne at the same moment.

Whatever these odd missiles were, there was nothing unusual about the fighter flares that were dropped along the route from the French coast to Revigny and back again. When first dropped, the flare appeared as a small pale green trace in the sky; after some ten seconds it burst into a ball of bright yellowy-orange fire which burnt for about another five seconds. Once expended, the flare drifted earthwards and burst on the ground where it gave off a column of 'black smoke resembling burning aircraft'.

Not even the dimmest, greenest, youngest Luftwaffe pilot could fail to find the bombers with such a pyrotechnical display. And if the chase was momentarily lost as the Lancasters turned to port on their run-in to Revigny, then they would soon get the scent again when the sky was illuminated for them by the 'pathfinders'.

6

The Third Raid – Homeward, 19 July 1944

Obeying orders during the long wait, the crews continued to make orbits to port. P/O T. Russell and crew (ND647, 49 Squadron) complained on their safe return to base that they had had to wait 12 minutes before they could bomb. Another crew (F/O W. Buchanan, PB250) of the same squadron had to make no fewer than four orbits to port before they too could bomb. Clearly the plan was not going according to schedule.

Simple on paper, the plan was for 83 Squadron, once they had located the target area with H2S, to illuminate it with their powerful 7-inch white 'hooded' flares, whilst the Mosquitoes of 627 Squadron went down low and located the AP visually. Once found, one of the Mosquitoes was to drop a Red Spot Fire (RSF) on to it. This in turn would be assessed for accuracy. When satisfied as to the location of the RSF, the Master Bomber could then instruct Main Force where precisely to bomb.

There was always one factor, though, quite apart from the Luftwaffe, that could ruin any raid. Bombs are subject not only to the 'laws of gravity' but also to any wind that might be blowing from whatever direction and at whatever strength. There was no easy way of finding the true wind speed and direction. Some of the more experienced navigators were therefore detailed to transmit back to England the strength and direction of the wind that each had found to be obtaining at various intervals along the route. Group's mathematicians rapidly plotted an average, and this was quickly passed back to all crews, who either believed it or chose to go by their own findings. This continued all the way to the target.

On this particular night, if no broadcast wind were received at the target, crews were briefed to use '170°/8 mph' at 8,500 feet as their data. Nine windfinders had been detailed, but three of these were missing, a fourth had a technical problem and of the five who transmitted only four messages were received. The winds, it was concluded, were too light and variable to be found with any accuracy. A broadcast was, however, made by Group HQ (using additional information supplied by DZ636 and DZ611, 627 Squadron, at 0125 hours), and it differed greatly from the original briefing. Instead of 170°/8 mph, the wind was 120°/17 mph at bombing height.

Researchers at 5 Group HQ later calculated that there was a probable vector error 'of just under 10 mph . . . On the Revigny attack . . . a large spread was experienced, two-thirds of the W/V were in the Westerly sector and one-third in the Easterly.' The analysis of all winds found by the navigators showed the average to have been 240°/5 mph. In other words, the wind was blowing from the south-west instead of south-east and at a third of the strength, although light enough to have been of little effect.

Such matters were of little concern to the crew of PB140 (F/O J. A. Kelly, 83 Squadron). At 0130 hours they flew over the target at 15,000 feet and 140 knots scanning the ground with H2S. Flares were dropped, but they were too far west of Revigny. There was still ten minutes to go to H-Hour, and there was still time to locate the AP. The remaining ten 83 Squadron Lancasters, flying at around 14–15,000 feet, had all dropped their first load of flares by 0138 hours. The five 627 Squadron Mosquitoes, below the flares, dived down to just a few hundred feet above the ground trying to locate the AP. But Main Force were not far behind, alarmed and discomfited by the ferocity and intensity of the night-fighter attacks, at 7–10,000 feet, sandwiched between the two.

Six of the 83 Squadron Lancasters made two runs over the target and dropped further flares as required. The first wave had proved 'unsuccessful' — 627 Squadron were unable to see the AP. At 0132 hours, Marker Leader called for more flares, and 'Marker 3' (F/O M. D. Gribbin and F/L R. W. Griffiths, DZ534, 627 Squadron) were at last able to identify the target area which had proved hard to find due to the low haze. They dropped a 'Wanganui' flare to call up the reserves. 'Marker 1' (F/L J. G. Grey and F/L F. W. Boyle, DZ650, 627 Squadron) were, however, able to identify the target visually and at 0134 hours, in a dive from 2,000 to 800 feet, released a 1,000 lb Red TI which, at 0139 hours, was assessed to be only 50 yards and 50 degrees from the aiming point.

Two minutes before planned H-Hour (0140 hours) the Controller, W/C Jeudwine, ordered Main Force to stand by, and the attack was put back five minutes, to 0145 hours. The crews, though, were getting impatient and the attack began before the order to bomb had been given. F/L S. Scutt (PD212, 57 Squadron) and F/O A. B. Boyle (DV373, 467 Squadron) dropped their bombs at 0140½ hours! What they actually dropped them on is a matter of conjecture, for not even the low-flying Mosquito crews were altogether convinced of the accuracy of their RSF, though Scutt's stick of bombs was afterwards plotted as having fallen across the railway. Confusion grew when Lancasters and enemy fighters that had been shot down also burned with a red glow on the ground. It was very difficult for crews who had already been through quite a battle and who had been flying round in ever-decreasing circles to be completely sure of the exact AP. They were tired and excited and, to some extent, confused.

Matters were not made any easier by the close attention of the

Luftwaffe. At 0140 hours, over the target, the crew of PB210 (F/O A. B. Neilson, 619 Squadron) saw two single-engined fighters; PB244 was attacked for the third time; P/O W. J. Davies and crew (ME813, 50 Squadron) spotted a Ju88 at 0142 hours; and one minute later LM190 (P/O G. G. Poole, 49 Squadron) encountered an FW190. Just after this the Controller gave the order to 'Attack Red Spot Flare'. It was 0143½ hours and nine Lancasters had already unloaded their bombs.

One of them, PD199 (F/O H. L. Inniss, 61 Squadron), scored a 'bullseye'. From a height of 7,600 feet, at 0143 hours, the bomb-aimer 'pressed the button' and sent the bombs on their way. The bombs, 11 x 1,000 lb MC and three 500 lb GP, were supposed to have been primed with long-delay fuses (those used this night were a mixture of ½, 12, 36, 72 or 144 hours duration). Luckily, three of PD199's fuses were faulty and the bombs exploded on impact. The bomb-aimer had sighted on a signal box 200 yards left of the RSF, and his bombs exploded right on the railway with a blinding flash. Many crews reported having seen 'one very large explosion at 0144 hours'. One crew even thought that an ammunition truck had been hit.

They were not wrong. Photographs taken on the ground soon after the raid reveal a mass of debris and twisted rolling-stock, mute testimony to the direct hit by PD199. Another crew, in old ED588 (F/O H. W. T. Enoch, 50 Squadron), reported: 'Railway junction seen complete with rolling-stock in yard. Bombed RSF. One fire observed — thought to be oil burning in marshalling yard.'

And from F/O G. M. Burns (JB701, 49 Squadron): 'One stick seen to burst on suspected factory, roofs of which were seen 300 yards on track from RSF.' Clearly other fuses were faulty.

On the other hand, the Australian F/O D. B. Jeffery again (LM226, 467 Squadron) had this to say:

'Nothing seen except flares and markers. No bombs exploding. Too much talk between controllers on VHF about marking. They didn't seem to know what to do. Somebody asked Controller where RSF was. He replied "To west of fires." At that time there were at least five fires on the ground — aircraft burning. Four aircraft were shot down over target in two–three minutes. They just went down one after another.'

Jeffery's bomb-aimer had done a good job, their bombs also plotted bang on the lines. But confusion there certainly was. The exploding ammunition wagons had caused so much smoke that the RSF was totally obscured. The Controller then ordered the fires from the blazing rolling-stock to be attacked, but during an orbit of the target he once again saw the RSF burning on the ground. He thereupon countermanded the order to bomb the fires and issued further instructions to bomb the RSF. It is easy to see why Jeffery was not happy, and he was, in fact, the third last to bomb, at 0155½ hours. Of the 84 Lancasters that actually bombed, 63 are known to have done so between 0144 and 0152 hours.

Meanwhile, ED860 (F/O Bates), after the brush with a Ju88 11 minutes earlier, was running up to bomb at 0148 hours and at the correct height of 8,500 feet when it was attacked at a range of 350 yards by an unidentified aircraft using rocket projectiles, which missed. Not so the two Lancaster gunners who set the enemy aircraft on fire, and watched it hit the ground. It would have been of little consolation to the German attacker had he known that he had, by firing at that precise second, forced ED860 to break off its bombing run at the critical moment, and that it was obliged to leave Revigny with its bombs still aboard. F/O Bates waited patiently until they had reached the English Channel when, from a height of 17,000 feet, the bombs were jettisoned as soon as they crossed the French coast.

★ ★ ★

From 0141 hours/19 July onwards the first bombers began to leave the target and head for home; it was not until 0157 hours that the last bombs were dropped.

F/O L. Pederson (ND512, 49 Squadron) had bombed at 0146 hours and was still at bombing height when, three minutes later, a Ju88 was spotted port beam up at a range of 600–700 yards. Both the gunners opened fire, the Ju88 made no reply and the gunners made no claim.

LM212 (F/L M. M. Milne, 50 Squadron) was suffering from major electrical failure as it came up to the target. W/T was u/s, the VHF radio was on the blink and the bomb-sight gyro had 'toppled', making it impossible to bomb with any degree of accuracy. At 0150 hours, therefore, F/L Milne gave the order to drop the bombs. Somewhere south of Châlons-sur-Marne a load of highly dangerous metal fell out of the sky from 12,000 feet.

Some Lancasters had not been so fortunate. ME796 (F/O G. E. Maxwell, 630 Squadron) received the order to delay the attack for five minutes but, whilst orbiting to port, was suddenly attacked by a fighter and set on fire. Three of the crew escaped. The Lancaster, with four of its crew still aboard, was finished off by flak (see Chapter 15).

The score was now 18 Lancasters and 109 men lost.

With Main Force milling about over the target waiting for the aiming point to be located, there was always the danger of a collision and, with H-Hour having been delayed, the odds of that happening further increased. There was a report from one crew, flying at 9,500 feet at 0144 hours *en route* for the target, that they saw two unidentified aircraft collide at a height of 10,000 feet and fall to the ground 200 yards apart. The sighting was made from a level distance of five to six miles on the port bow.

A report by another crew orbiting at 9,500 feet stated that at the same time they saw an unidentified aircraft two miles away on the port bow receive a direct hit from flak. The unidentified aircraft broke up in mid-air. On the scant evidence of the first report, a collision seems rather doubtful and it is probable that what the first, and indeed the second, crew saw was the demise of LM551 (463 Squadron) as it crashed on the canal bank at Revigny itself, victim of a night-fighter.

The flames from this aircraft as it burned on the ground by the canal were quite possibly one of the fires seen by F/O Jeffery. It was the 19th loss that long night.

With the night-fighters amongst the bomber stream, a third Lancaster was soon to go down near the target — PB234 (467 Squadron), caught at the precise moment it was making its straight and level bomb-run over the target. The bomb-aimer managed to get the bombs away, but the blazing Lancaster crashed in a field near Brabant-le-Roi, a short distance north of Revigny. Four of the crew escaped (see Chapter 11).

Twenty Lancasters down; 119 dead.

F/O Jeffery reported that he had seen four aircraft 'shot down over target in two–three minutes'. Whether or not the four he saw were all Lancasters is doubtful — one was probably a German night-fighter. To have seen the fourth Lancaster he would have had to have been on his own way home, for it was a few miles off to the west of Revigny that the fourth Lancaster was attacked. Another 'Australian' Lancaster, old R5485 (467 Squadron), was the victim this time, shot down at around 0200 hours when on its way back to Waddington having bombed. Five men survived (see Chapter 16).

Twenty-one Lancasters lost; 121 men dead.

Another Lancaster was very nearly lost at 0154 hours. F/O H. F. Arnold (ME787, 49 Squadron) had bombed four minutes earlier and was at 10,000 feet when, without any warning ('Fishpond' was u/s), a Ju88 opened fire. The German pilot was a poor shot as he was only 50 yards away when he opened fire! ME787 was, nevertheless, hit, the Lancaster's gunners returned the fire, and strikes were observed on the enemy aircraft. F/O Arnold managed to coax ME787 back to England but, with serious hydraulic problems, decided to land at Woodbridge, with its extra long and wide emergency runway.

One final, nervous attack was made on the retreating bombers at 0156 hours and the intended night-fighter victim was Lancaster NE165 of 54 Base flown by W/C J. Woodroffe (83 Squadron). The unidentified enemy aircraft opened fire when it was 700 yards slightly astern and to port, but the two gunners replied and the fighter broke away downwards. Both aircraft were unscathed.

The remaining Lancasters melted away into the night, as fast as they could, and the night-fighters for the most part did likewise as they were probably beginning to run short of fuel. But the slaughter was not yet over.

Two more Lancasters, PD210 (207 Squadron) and LM117 (630 Squadron), were lost at almost the same time as they made their way back over the rolling fields just south of the Champagne region. PD210 was shot down at 0204 hours, the handiwork of a night-fighter, and there was only one survivor (see Chapter 17). LM117, on the other hand, was almost certainly hit by flak at 0206 hours as it was passing to the south of Châlons-sur-Marne, but there were six survivors (see Chapter 17).

The dreadful toll was now 23 Lancasters and 128 men dead.

The final loss on this devastating night was 49 Squadron's fourth loss — JB473 (F/O R. M. Deacon) — but, again, six men survived (see Chapter 17). The evidence as to the demise of JB473 is conflicting, but it was possibly due to both flak and fighter. The mid-upper gunner was remarking on two other Lancasters going down (possibly PD210 and LM117 — it was a clear night and they were easily seen) and the navigator was about to recommend a 'corkscrew' when they were hit. The bomb-aimer reckoned that they were hit by a fighter; the flight engineer that it was flak; the Germans that it was a fighter. Whichever, the end result was the same — another Lancaster shot down in flames.

It was the 24th and final loss of the night; 129 were dead; 11 others would become prisoners-of-war; and 29 would successfully evade. But that was all in the future. What was left of Main Force meanwhile headed north-west for home.

5 Group had started out 109 Lancasters strong. Two had returned early with mechanical defects (LM624, 57 Squadron, and LM208, 207 Squadron) and a third (ND977, 57 Squadron) after being attacked by a night-fighter. The remains of a further 24 lay scattered across north-eastern France. On the other side of the balance sheet, the Luftwaffe had lost at least three fighters, with two more 'probable' and several 'damaged'. In addition, the enemy had suffered a loss, as yet unknown, on the ground at Revigny.

As the remaining 82 Lancasters headed for the French coast, near le Tréport, a few crews reported further attacks by night-fighters. These were possibly from I/NJG 3 and I/NJG 4, which had been gathering to the north of Paris from 0201 hours/19 July onwards, but were a little early for the bombers. Waiting would have used up a considerable quantity of fuel and they could not have stayed for long.

But at 0239 hours (at 5010°N/0130°E, on a course of 315°T), JB309 (F/O J. A. Giddens, 207 Squadron), was coming up to the French coast when, with no warning from 'Fishpond', the two gunners spotted a twin-engined fighter about to attack. They opened fire before the enemy, who thereupon broke away without firing. No claim was made.

Sixteen minutes later, R5868 (467 Squadron) was in trouble again (at 5020°N/0110°E) when 'Monica' gave a warning that danger was approaching fast 1,500 yards astern. The gunners were ready and suddenly saw a single-engined fighter bearing down on them from the starboard quarter. F/O Johnson followed the urgent instructions to 'Corkscrew starboard' and, as the fighter flashed past, the rear gunner gave it a quick squirt. The fighter did not bother to stay and play, and disappeared into the night. No claim was made.

The last contact with the enemy was made at 0308 hours, well over the English Channel (at 5040°N/0100°E). LM226 (467 Squadron) was flying at 13,000 feet when an Me109 was seen dead astern. A 'corkscrew starboard' lost the fighter, but two minutes later the persistent fighter was seen again on the starboard quarter down. Another 'corkscrew' to starboard and the fighter was lost for the second and final time.

Other aerial activity was seen by various crews which may well have been Mosquito-related. 100 (BS) Group had put up 34 *Serrate* Mosquitoes to cover all the night's raids, of which only 28 completed their patrols. One partial success fell to a 169 Squadron crew (F/L Dix and F/O Salmon) who damaged a Ju88 near Douai; and a 141 Squadron crew damaged an Me410 four miles west of Brussels. Between 0032 and 0341 hours, a further 28 Mosquitoes flew over all the airfields in the west (including St Dizier). They were assisted by 16 others of the Air Defence of Great Britain.[*]

As noted, 100 Group had other aircraft out and about on this night apart from the Mosquitoes. 199 Squadron had put up 16 Stirlings from North Creake for the 'Mandrel' screen, and 214 Squadron had sent two 'Flying Fortresses' (SR386 'N' and SR388 'H') to Revigny on 'ABC' patrols. They were airborne just after 2300 hours/18 July and had landed back at Oulton by 0345 hours/19 July. The receiver aboard SR386 had failed 40 minutes after take-off, 'so the operator barrage-jammed up and down, with both transmitters'. SR388, on the other hand, had no such problem and one 'persistent frequency (42.2) was jammed by the operator. Three other R/T frequencies were heard and jammed. There was considerable "ABC" jamming heard on other frequencies, but no R/T.'

For both aircraft it was otherwise a quiet night, though they both saw the numerous searchlights 'in the defence belt in the Amiens area'.

* * *

The Mosquitoes were too thinly spread to have been of much help to the Revigny crews, for which one Luftwaffe pilot in particular would have been grateful. Fahnenjunker-Oberfeldwebel Herbert Altner of III/NJG 5 claimed five victories this night in the space of 33 minutes. The first (possibly JB186) was timed at 0101 hours/19 July and the others followed at 0111, 0121 (possibly JB318), 0125 and 0134.

All his victories were gained with *schräge musik*, and all followed the same pattern. The bomber was picked up on the SN2 radar at a range of 800 to 1,000 metres. Altner dropped down below the intended victim until he made visual contact at about 400 or 500 metres range. Still keeping well below the Lancaster, he synchronised the position of his Me110 with it and then, at about 200 metres, rose like a lift, and fired. It was the same each time. With his first victim he aimed between the two port engines, closing his eyes as his cannons blazed away. His crew, though, watched the shells pumping into the Lancaster and told him that it had caught fire. Then:

'I broke off to the left down and levelled out. Because the approximate course of the formation was known to me, I pulled up again, and the other attacks were straight out of the textbook. After the fifth I'd had enough and flew home.'

Most night-fighter pilots had little desire to cause loss of life amongst the bomber crews, and Herbert Altner was one of them. Ever since he has wondered as to the fate of the crews who fell to his guns. Of his first victim he asks:

'Was the whole crew of the aircraft able to get out? As I could fly my attack so precisely not one round went into the fuselage. Because I

[*] *One 8 Group Mosquito, MM136, on the raid to Berlin, was shot down by Hauptman Strüning of III/NJG 1 in an He219.*

had to bale out twice with my crew from a burning aircraft, I thought it possible that the English crew was able to bale out.'

Although the victories had been so easily achieved, he was shaking so much when he landed back that he was unable to light a cigarette. His flight mechanic was ordered to keep him supplied until he had calmed down.

Herbert Altner ended the war as a Leutnant with 21 confirmed victories and the German Cross in Gold. His operational flying career had begun way back in September 1941 when he was posted to II/NJG 3. In May 1943, now an 'old hand', he joined III/NJG 5 and stayed with that unit until February 1945 when posted to Sonderkommando *Welter* flying the Me262 jet. This was the crowning moment of his wartime career, but his joy was tempered by the earlier loss of his radio operator, who was killed on the second occasion on which they had had to bale out of their burning Me110.

For all these years he has lived in what was once East Germany, where the strictness of the communist regime forbad contact with the West:

> 'We could not even talk about the dead. Officially there are no graves or memorials from the Second World War. But that is gone, thank God!'

★　★　★

As Altner celebrated his successes, what was left of Main Force made its way up the Channel, through the Straits of Dover, and past the Thames estuary to Orfordness (one of the three official East Coast crossing-points for the night). From there the Lancasters made their way to their bases in Lincolnshire. There was no bad weather to cause last-minute diversions as there had been on the two 1 Group raids. ME787 peeled off over Suffolk and landed safely at the Woodbridge emergency landing strip at 0351 hours/19 July.

The first Lancaster back, at 0348 hours, was ND854 (F/L A. F. McLean, 83 Squadron). The other 80 drifted home until the last (ME809, F/S W. D. Tweedle, 9 Squadron) had landed at 0446 hours. It was now that the story of the battle to and from the target would slowly have unfolded. How quiet it was at East Kirkby as they waited in vain for the five missing from the 20 despatched, and at Fiskerton where only 11 of the 15 sent out by 49 Squadron returned. At Dunholme Lodge, home of 619 Squadron, amidst scenes of utter disbelief ground crews waited in vain for the return of five of their 13 aircraft. 'A' Flight had suffered badly, losing four, and the only rear gunner from the Flight to return recorded in his diary:

> 'This was the worst trip we have done so far. We had no trouble at all but the trip was very terrifying, and I've never been so scared in all my life. This was our second trip in one day and so far, the 18th July, I did my easiest trip and my worst . . .
>
> 'We had no sooner crossed the French coast when the first kite was shot down. From there on to the target and all the way back there

were kites going down right and left . . . The majority of them were shot down by fighters, but at the time we did not know what was causing it. If ever we see a bomber going down, we tell the navigator, who writes down the time and position. After I had reported 15, the skipper said not to bother with any more. I saw about ten more go down after that.

'At the time I thought it was impossible for us to get out of there. When we got back, the few of us that did, the experienced crews said that they've never seen anything like it before . . . When we got back and went to bed I couldn't go to sleep I was still so scared . . .

'The whole crew said when we got back that they thought the same as me, that our time had come. We didn't see any fighters at all and there was very little flak over the target. But it was seeing the other aircraft going down in flames and blowing up when they hit the ground that made it so bad.'

Fred Whitfield, rear gunner of PD198 (9 Squadron), felt the same as the anonymous 619 Squadron gunner and wrote, on his safe return to Bardney:

'This is our second trip over enemy territory today, and it has to be one of the worst I've ever experienced and ever wish to encounter again.'*

5 Group's Operational Research Section were nothing if not thorough, and their statistics tell us that of the 24 crews missing on 18/19 July, eight had completed no more than five operations; four had between six and 11 under their belt; and seven between 12 and 17. Oddly enough, the highest loss for a group was amongst those crews who had completed between 24 and 29 operations. Five of the 12 who took off failed to return. None of the 12 crews on their second tour was lost. The Grim Reaper was not particular whom he chose.

As for aircraft, apart from the 24 lost, three were damaged by flak (LM214 and LM582, both of 57 Squadron, and LM226 of 467 Squadron) and another three by fighters — ME787 (49 Squadron), ND977 (57 Squadron)† and ME650 (630 Squadron).

---

* p17, "We Sat Alone": Diary of a Rear Gunner, Fred Whitfield DFM, no date.

† Although records refer to LM231, the overwhelming evidence, via Roland Hammersley, is that it was ND977.

7

Damage to the Railway

'Nous allons rendre visite à Maginot ce soir.' These words, broadcast by the BBC during the afternoon of 18 July 1944, were enough to tell the inhabitants of Revigny that they could expect another visit from the bombers of the RAF that night. It was a warning, given as one of the conditions for the continued bombing of French railway centres, approved by the Prime Minister and the War Cabinet, which would give civilians living near such targets the chance to get clear of the area. It was not difficult for the Revinéens to work out the meaning of the message — André Maginot, the French Minister for War who gave his name to the famous 'Line', had been born in Revigny.

Monsieur Goubet, head of security at Revigny station, was on duty that night of 18/19 July:

'When I arrived at work at 2000 hours everyone seemed nervous; even the telephone was unusually active. At about 2230 hours I intercepted a communication between Paris and Nancy warning of the bombing of Aulnoye and the tracking towards the east of other formations. I was in no doubt that we would be the target as I had heard the message that afternoon at a neighbour's house, and the skies were very clear . . .

'I warned the *camp des permissionaires* and, as I was frightened myself, I went home. German railway workers were already on their way along the road to Villers. As I passed the Town Hall I warned Schwaller, the country policeman and caretaker at the Town Hall, to sound the air-raid warning because we were going to have another visit that evening.'

French time was two hours earlier than in Britain. The 3 Group attack on Aulnoye had begun at 0045 hours/19 July — 2245 hours/18 July French time.

The question is, if French officials knew that an attack was heading for Revigny that night, did the German authorities also know?

★ ★ ★

Bombs had fallen in the Revigny area during the first abortive raid on

12/13 July. No damage was done to the target, but several houses in the town itself suffered damage to their roofs, though not from bombs. A milkman making his rounds early on the morning of 13 July found a 'firework' the like of which he had never before seen. It was one of the flares dropped by the Special Duties Flight. Suspended by parachute, it had drifted from the target to the south of the town on to the houses in the centre. The canister was more than a metre long and some 40 centimetres in diameter. It was quickly hidden away, for the parachute silk and cord were greatly prized.

The second raid two nights later produced no incident worthy of mention. The Revinéens, though, had not been taking any chances. Each evening for several weeks people living within a 600-yard radius of the station had evacuated their homes and stayed overnight with neighbours, or had moved into air-raid shelters in their gardens. Those with cellars made full use of them. The nearby villages of Brabant-le-Roi, Villers-aux-Vents and Contrisson welcomed the refugees.

The third raid, on 18/19 July, was altogether a different story and the locals did well to heed the warning to evacuate their homes. The attack began at 0130 hours and lasted for half an hour. The first bombs fell at $0140\frac{1}{2}$ hours, the last at 0157 hours (PB293, 207 Squadron). Around 800 x 1,000 lb and 250 x 500lb bombs were dropped, all supposedly long-delay fused from anything between 30 minutes to six days.

The Mayor of Revigny, Monsieur Dourin, kept a very detailed report of the bombing. Thirty bombs exploded on impact, and by the end of 19 July, a further 575 had erupted. On 20 July only 60 went off; ten more the next day; 29 more over the next six days; and another 19 up to 8 August, when the last one exploded. German technicians blew up nine, making a grand total of 731. It was believed that there were a further 30 still unaccounted for.

It was fortunate that some of the bombs did explode on impact, and the crew of PD199, who dropped their load of 11 x 1,000 lb and three 500 lb bombs at 0143 hours, were delighted to see some of them explode 'right on the railway with a blinding flash'. There were many other eye-witnesses to this explosion, most of whom claimed that the time was 0144 hours. One 83 Squadron crew logged the time as 0143.8 hours! By sheer chance, on the very afternoon of 18 July an ammunition train had pulled into Revigny.

Sgt Denys Teare RAF (see Chapter 11), an evader for ten months, and at the time in hiding in the home of brothers Jean and Louis Chenu at Revigny, witnessed the night's events:

'Shortly after we had gone to bed that evening the air raid warning sounded. Louis and I sat up and looked across at each other, wondering if perhaps the bombers were coming for yet a third time . . .

'During the afternoon an ammunition train had come into the sidings. The news soon spread round the streets, and people started speculating regarding the possibility of an RAF visit that evening.

'We all stood at the window listening. Soon we heard the drone of the bombers approaching; the sound came nearer and nearer; they were heading straight towards us, and the ammunition train was only a few hundred yards away from the back of the house. We decided the time had come to evacuate as quickly as possible . . .

'By now the aircraft were overhead, and suddenly white flares started dropping and the whole little town became lit up. Everyone was running from their houses with the same idea as ourselves, regardless of the curfew.

'As we ran the air overhead seemed absolutely filled with aircraft . . . and the whole town seemed to tremble with the roar of the engines . . . Everyone was running in the same direction, men, women, children. Suddenly I became aware of a uniformed figure running at my side. I turned and saw it was a German soldier, probably from the nearby barracks. It was then I realised for the first time that I was haring along in the bright light of dozens of flares. There was nothing to do but keep running . . .'

The attack was under way and Denys and the rest had had but 11 minutes in which to scurry for safety, their way lit by the flares dropped by 83 Squadron, the first of which had gone down at 0130 hours precisely (PB140). Even as Denys reached his goal, a dried-up canal bed, he heard a 'horrible whistling sound' as the first bombs dropped:

'Glancing round as I went down the grassy side into the canal, I saw the most amazing sight. The first bomb had dropped right on the ammunition train, and in the enormous sheet of orange flame I could actually see the wagons blown about 50 feet into the air . . .

'Bomb after bomb came down screaming to earth, and the ground shook at every explosion. The ammunition train was blazing away from end to end, and wagons exploding every minute. The light from the flares and the glow from the ground fires were so bright that occasionally I could see the aircraft silhouetted above their target.

'The aircraft were all making their bombing runs from the south, which meant that they carried on right over our heads, and I knew that a bomb-aimer had only got to make an error of judgement . . .

'Each time an aircraft made its run over the target I lay there perspiring, listening to the screech of the bombs . . . Every minute seemed a lifetime as hundreds of tons of explosives rained down upon us. The women and children were praying aloud for the bombardment to cease . . .

'Gradually the roar of engines overhead died down, and eventually the last aircraft was on its homeward journey. Explosions still continued from the railway sidings as the ammunition train burned, but it was essential that we should get back to the house as soon as possible . . .

'Just as we entered the house a terrific explosion shook all the shutters and we heard pieces of earth falling in the garden and on the roof. It was apparently a delayed-action bomb that had gone off in the field behind the house.

'We lay on the beds resting, but the explosions of delayed bombs kept shaking us every half-hour. The idea was obviously to keep repair workers away from the railway as long as possible.

'In the morning we went to the bottom of the garden in twos and threes to watch the explosions. A pall of smoke hung over the twisted masses of steel that had been railway lines only a few hours previously. Then suddenly the ground would heave and up would come a fountain of earth; then came the deafening bang as the noise of the explosion reached our ears, followed by a rushing sound, something like a waterfall, as all the rubble poured back to earth. This went on throughout the day and following night . . .'

Twenty of the ammunition train wagons were destroyed and the West sidings were indeed a mess but, unfortunately, so too were several buildings in the vicinity. All the lines through Revigny, except for a section of the track to Bar-le-Duc, were damaged and the marshalling yards were devastated. The area most heavily hit was that in which the transit camp for French forced workers (the *camp des permissionaires*), the Vuillaume iron works and the Clavey tile factory were situated.

At 1130 hours/19 July F/O K. Durbridge flew over Revigny in his PRU Spitfire (SR397, 542 Squadron), its camera clicking. The provisional assessment of the damage was made the next day from his photographs by the Central Interpretation Unit (CIU) at Medmenham:

'At the junction of the Paris and Hirson lines two concentrations of craters are seen, one directly at the point of junction and one within sidings directly east of junction. All through lines are cut with the exception of the track between Paris and Bar-le-Duc which remains open. The line running North and South between Hirson and Troyes also remains open. In addition 10 tracks were cut within the sidings, and 18–20 goods wagons destroyed or damaged.

'A large concentration of bombs fell just south of sidings gutting one large factory-type building, and damaging at least 36 small buildings, the majority of which are hutments and barrack-type buildings.

'The highway leading Southwest to Sermaize-les-Bains is cut at eleven points.'

The 5 Group assessment, based on Durbridge's photos, was equally sanguine. The 'large factory-type building' (the Vuillaume iron works, 'la boulonnerie') was situated 'about 200 yds South-East of the Aiming Point' and it appeared 'to have blown up and to have been damaged by fire. It is highly probable that this attracted the attention, and was probably the AP of some bomb-aimers. It seems fairly clear that the majority of crews did in fact bomb something which was about 200 yds SE of the AP . . . Only a few sticks of bombs have actually straddled the railway lines themselves.'

Three sources of light were plotted from the night photographs — at '66°, 400 yards' from the AP; at '50°, 50 yards'; and at '148°, 830 yards'. The first two were both red and it was thought that the 1,000 lb marker 'skipped and broke up on hitting the ground'. Crews also reported that the two reds 'faded and re-illuminated through the attack'. The cause of this was attributed to the candles from the red marker which had different fusings and which would have spilled out along the line of the

PLOT OF NIGHT PHOTOGRAPHS Nº 458
TAKEN: 18/19 JULY 1944
TARGET: **REVIGNY SUR ORNAIN** (FRANCE)
(RAILWAY JUNCTION)
MADE UP TO 09·00 hrs. 20-7-44
SCALE:- 1:20,000 (APPROX)

| GROUP SYMBOL | Nº OF A/C REPORTING ATTACK | RESULTS RECEIVED | FAILURES & NON-EMPLOYMENT | FLOWN OR SMOKE PHOTOS | T.I. PHOTOS | PLOTTABLE GROUND DETAIL PHOTOS | | | | % SHOWING T/A | % FIRE PHOTOS ADDED |
						TOTAL	SHOWING T/A	NOT SHOWING T/A	EMPLOYED		
◇ 5 GROUP	77	69	11	–	20	38	24	13	1	63%	76%

ZERO HOUR = 01·40 HRS.
AIMING POINT = ⊙
RAILWAY = ┼┼┼┼┼┼
A/C HEADING = →

N·B THIS TABLE INCLUDES A/C WHICH PHOTOGRAPHED
WITH BOMBING ALTHOUGH NOT CARRYING FLASHES

NB AS ALL CAMERAS HAVE A FORWARD TILT
THE SYMBOLS INDICATE THE APPROXIMATE
POSITION OF THE FIRST BOMB IN THE STICK.

P/O MORRISON 9 H
8475 YDS. 2.62°

P/O PULGAR 489 E
3555 YDS. 197°

P/O WHYTE 50 M
8475 YDS. 2.62°

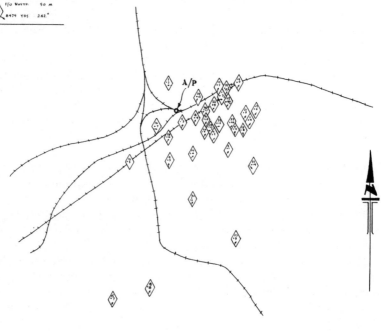

broken marker. The colour of the third light was orange and was thought to be either a crashed aircraft, a scrub fire or decoy markers.

On 28 July 1944, the CIU had issued a brief report based on the study of 68 films, six of which were in colour. These enabled the interpreter to 'determine the colour of the three lights assessed as markers'. One of the 'lights' was plotted at Alliancelles, four and a half miles to the west of Revigny, and a second on the edge of the canal well to the south of the town. Both were considered to be orange rather than red. The CIU had little enough on which to go, even though the weather over the target was clear and good photographs were obtained, and the best that they could come up with for the 'lights' was that one (plotted on the rail tracks) was a 'possible', but that the other two rated only a 'TI possible'.

Judging by their colour and position, the inescapable conclusion is that these were not markers but the burning remains of Lancasters ME796 and LM551, the former crashing near Alliancelles and the latter on the edge of the Marne au Rhin Canal, in what was known as the 'arrière champ'. This would be confirmed by the sighting of the orange light at '148°, 830 yards' from the AP.

The CIU were nothing if not thorough, and after further work on the films taken by the Lancasters they were able to plot 14 photographs. The nearest to the AP was measured at 250 yards and at 45 degrees from it. First prize to F/O R. W. Pettigrew and crew (DV326, 619 Squadron)! Two others were plotted at 400 yards, and the two worst at 1,500! Most of the 14 had been heading north or north-east, but two, F/O E. Y. O'Neill (LL778, 619 Squadron) and F/O R. W. Leonard (LM536, 619 Squadron), were heading west, and a third, F/O R. F. Adams (PD198, 9 Squadron), who had already made two orbits of the target, was going south-east! (Off on his holidays perhaps?)

It was the turn of 544 Squadron to take the next photographs of Revigny. At 1315 hours/25 July, S/L David Douglas-Hamilton[*] and F/O Philip Edwin Gatehouse DFM[†] in Mosquito MM285 took further shots of the damaged marshalling yards 28,500 feet below. An 'Immediate Interpretation Report' was produced next day by the CIU:

'There are at least 85 fresh craters visible in vicinity of target. There are also eight new craters two miles NE of Railway junction.

'Four tracks are freshly cut at East end of siding.

'Four hutments South of Railway Junction, one of which had been previously damaged, are now destroyed by new bursts. A small square building in the same area is also destroyed.

'Five unidentified buildings SE of Railway Siding, all previously damaged, are now destroyed, and two others are damaged.

'The Paris–Hirson line is still cut, but the Paris–Bar-le-Duc line remains open and a goods train is seen moving East through siding on this line.'

---

[*] *He was the youngest of four brothers, each of whom became an RAF squadron commander.*

[†] *The decoration was won in 248 Squadron when he navigated a successful attack on Sardinia in August 1942.*

That report was only provisional, and the day after, 27 July, the CIU produced the full picture:

'LOADING. Loading in the South sorting sidings is light and in the West marshalling sidings exceptionally light.

'LOCOMOTIVES. At least 7 locos are seen near the loco sheds, probably temporarily cut off because of damaged tracks.

'FLATS.   (a) A train length of open wagons and including 13 long flats (unloaded) is seen passing the West marshalling sidings in a Westerly direction.

(b) 3 flats loaded with objects resembling aircraft wings are seen in a length in the East marshalling sidings. On 1.7.44 2 flats loaded with Ju188 wings were seen in the West sidings of REVIGNY. 2 light flak wagons are also seen in this length.

(c) A number of flats loaded with unidentified objects are seen in the East sidings, in various lengths.

'MILITARY FORMATION. A probable military formation is seen moving out of the East marshalling sidings in an Easterly direction. The formation is made up as follows: Locomotive — 18 mixed unloaded flats — 2 box — 6 unloaded flats — 2 box — 2 flats — 1 flak wagon (high sider) — 10 unloaded flats — 25 box wagons.

'HOSPITAL TRAIN. An engine-headed hospital train of 13 coaches is seen moving through the East sidings in a Westerly direction. A probable light flak wagon is seen at the rear of the train.

'DAMAGE. Since 19.7.44 3 further craters have damaged lines in the West sidings.

'REPAIRS. Since 19.7.44 almost no repairs have been effected in the West sidings. All undamaged rolling stock has been cleared from the yard. 100% unserviceable.

'THROUGH RUNNING LINES. The main line through the West sidings is now serviceable and in use . . .'

It is clear from this extraordinary piece of detection (it was run-of-the-mill to the CIU) that Revigny's usefulness as a marshalling yard had considerably diminished but that it was still open for through traffic.

At 1015 hours on 2 August Douglas-Hamilton and Gatehouse took off in Mosquito MM240 to cover, amongst other areas, Dijon and St Dizier. At 1215 hours they photographed Revigny once more. They were almost back at base (RAF Benson, Oxfordshire) after a flight of five and a half hours when, at South Moreton, 'the Mosquito crashed into a line of trees, obviously while attempting to reach open land beyond'. According to eye-witnesses, both engines were stopped. The Mosquito did not catch fire, which suggests that they were out of fuel, hence the dead engines. The film was rescued from the wreck but, sadly, there was nothing to be done for the crew.

A further report was made from the new photographs. Apart from the through lines all tracks in the West sidings were still cut, but the undamaged East sidings were only lightly loaded, and only three locomotives were noticed in the depot. Twenty-two loaded flats and a 'rake' of 67 wagons, the majority unloaded flats, were seen in the East sidings. Last but not least, a hospital train of 19 coaches was seen moving eastwards through the undamaged station.

The hutments noted in the PRU photographs were those of the transit camp, and photographs taken on the ground soon after the raid show the extent of the damage — scarcely a window or roof left intact. The Clavey tile factory, on the banks of the canal, was also badly damaged. The town itself did not escape unscathed, with rue Général Sarrail, rue Joffre and rue Jean Jaurès all receiving considerable damage. A plot of all the bomb craters superimposed on a plan of the area was drawn up by various organisations (including the SNCF and the Highways Department), and it is clear that as the bombers came in on their bomb run most of them undershot the railway lines and planted their bombs in the open ground between the canal and the town. As 5 Group thought, they had indeed been aiming at the fires of the burning factories to the south of the railway.

It was thought that the only casualty had been a badly wounded woman, Madame Jeanne Peninguy, 39, who died of her injuries on 21 July on arrival at the hospital in Langres. But when the delayed-action bombs permitted clearing up, five bodies were found under the wreckage: two railway workers, a woman and her son, aged 7, killed in the yard of the Clavey tile works, and an old woman. Three others were slightly injured.

The Germans were extremely efficient at repairing bomb damage, and Revigny was to be no exception; more than 2,000 men were press-ganged to help clear up the mess. On the morning of 20 July the town crier passed the house where Denys Teare was in hiding:

'Louis went out into the road to listen and came back with the information that every man in the village had to report to the Town Hall carrying a spade to work on the damaged railway.

'The two brothers had no alternative but to obey the order, and they set off reluctantly towards the town centre . . .

'At midday they returned, neither of them having moved a spadeful of earth in a useful direction if they could avoid it. They told us that the damage at the junction was unimaginable; the whole area was covered with immense craters which would require hundreds of tons of earth to fill. Already squads of German Pioneer Corps were hard at work, together with groups of French prisoners.'

These prisoners were from the Bar-le-Duc jail, and the Germans had gone so far as to promise them their freedom if they assisted in the removal of unexploded bombs and in clearing up the mess — amazingly they kept their promise. So efficiently had the Germans organised repairs that within a few hours the line was passable to through traffic*. The Allies, on the other hand, had gained a delay of two days at most — at a cost of 43 Lancasters and the lives of 231 men.

The damage overall to the railway could have had little effect on events

* *A 'Flash Report' timed at 0100 hours on 21 July noted: 'Through working possible'.*

in Normandy. Collectively, the Revigny raids were a failure. The target was a small one and for that reason alone would always be difficult to destroy. With the hopeless weather conditions on the first two raids and the severe attacks of the Luftwaffe on the third, the chances of success were further reduced.

5 Group did manage to destroy the Vuillaume iron works. It never went into operation again; all its machinery was reduced to scrap-iron. Other bombs had burst on the canal bank between the Chapelle and the brickwork locks. Water flooded out causing a little damage. The depressions in the tow-path where the bombs fell can still be seen to this day. Bombs also fell on the French military cemetery of 1914–18, soon to receive the remains of the seven men whose Lancaster crashed on the canal banks.

Fifty-nine men were fortunate enough to bale out of their doomed Lancasters. Wounded or not, evader or prisoner, each one had good cause to remember the events of those three black nights in July 1944. For those others who survived the Revigny raids and flew back to base, there was the prospect of further raids on Germany, and a good many would be dead before the end of August. In the six weeks from 19 July to 31 August 1944 Bomber Command was to lose some 300 Lancasters on operations.

For the evaders, however, a journey into the darkness of an occupied, albeit friendly, country awaited them.

PART TWO

8

Out of the Frying-pan

In the book *Rendez-vous 127, The Diary of Anne Brusselmans**, ACM Sir Basil Embry wrote:

'It is perhaps difficult for anyone who has not lived under the oppression of German occupation and witnessed first-hand the frightful evil of Gestapo police methods to appreciate fully what it meant to work in direct opposition to them . . .

'The married man or woman caught harbouring an Allied airman brought reprisals on the whole family — even small children were put to death. This was the price for patriotism, and as the Gestapo held most of the cards, the odds were strongly in their favour . . .

'Their peril was far greater than that of the airman whom they helped, because if the evader was caught, he would merely become a prisoner of war, but if they were found helping or sheltering him they were tortured and shot.'

As the war progressed, so more and more evidence fell into the hands of RAF Intelligence as to what happened to aircrew who were shot down in enemy-occupied territory. Airmen were duly given thorough briefings into how best to avoid being captured and, with the help of the friendly inhabitants, to get back home. Before the invasion on 6 June 1944 the most commonly used route had been through France and Spain to Gibraltar but, after that date, if shot down over France the best option was to stay put until the area was overrun by the advancing Allies. MI9 even arranged, in the aptly if unoriginally named plan Operation SHERWOOD, to set up a camp in Fréteval Forest to the south-east of Paris to which evading aircrew could go for onward transmission through the Allied lines and hence to safety. Over 150 men took advantage of this.

General 'Tooey' Spaatz, commander of the USStAF in Europe, was also to write in *Rendez-vous 127*:

* *Published in May 1954 by Ernest Benn.*

'Thousands of airmen were shot out of the skies over Europe while engaged in operations against the Third Reich on targets in occupied territory . . . but a very large number successfully evaded capture . . .

'An airman who gets away from his wrecked aircraft in enemy territory finds himself in a position which is unique among fighting men. To continue his type of fighting against the enemy, he must first return home, and to do this he usually begins his travels alone; often in a state of shock, and sometimes wounded. He knows that the alternative to a long, difficult and nerve-racking evasion will be captivity, interrogation and possibly death. Above all, he wants, and is constantly looking for, help.'

In France, where the great majority of people were friendly, help was never far away, but a fallen airman had perforce to find it before he was himself found by the enemy. The French countryside where most of the Revigny aircrews were shot down was predominantly agricultural and wooded and hence sparsely populated; but the evaders were fortunate to have been shot down after D-Day, when thousands of young Frenchmen, the *attentistes*, flocked to join the maquis. It was almost impossible not to come into contact with the maquis. But let the reader be in no doubt that evasion, even in a country whose population was violently opposed to the invader, was no picnic. If an airman was caught in plain clothes and in hiding, the Gestapo were given 'first go', and they were not too careful as to how they discovered the captor's identity. Once the Gestapo thugs had found out the truth, the airman would be passed on to the Luftwaffe. Only one of the Revigny survivors is known definitely to have suffered at the hands of the Gestapo, and that was Geoff Davies, Deputy Master Bomber on the second Revigny raid.

Before falling into the clutches of the Gestapo, however, he first had to survive being blown up by his own bombs. When we last saw him he had been blown out of his blazing Lancaster. He landed safely. It was now early in the morning of July 15th:

'I was unconscious for a period. Discovered I was in a wood of some sort — thick undergrowth and tall trees close together. My face was burned, left eye very bad (thought I was blind). My right eye was half closed with burned eye-lids; left leg suspected broken shin bone; flesh wound in left thigh; had lost one tooth and had small flesh wound in left wrist. Hair was burnt off to within one and a half inches or so of scalp. Nose and mouth burned. Back badly bruised and altogether shaken and knocked about.

'It was then half-light and I calculated it to be about 0330 or 0400 hours. Set watch. It went but stopped later. Hid my chute and Mae West, opened my emergency rations and escape kit and stowed it about my person. Had a swig of brandy. [He had had the foresight to take a hip-flask with him!]. I then transferred all my socks and stocking to my left leg and stuffed the bottom with kapok from my Mae West, and cut up part of the chute canopy for bandages.

'I found it not possible to bear my weight on my left leg so I lopped off a stout branch for a crutch. I had another small swig of brandy and started off to try and find a way out of the wood.

'Heading south in the direction of St Dizier, it took me about 30 minutes to find any sort of track through the trees, and a further two to two and a half hours to get to the edge of the wood (after retracing my steps three or four times).

'By this time I could hardly see at all and I had to hold the compass about two inches away from my eye and blink rapidly in order to see at all. At the edge of the wood I could see a road running NE–SW. At approximately 0600 hours I headed south on the road (not being able to make rough going over the fields). There was a dyke about three to four feet on the left side of the road. I walked along the left side as continental traffic drives on the right-hand side. So I imagined locals would walk on the left in order to face oncoming traffic. I headed south by west, intending to keep to the road until I sighted some civilization.

'I stopped at the bottom of a hill for a rest. A Hun lorry coasting down the hill, which I didn't hear. It contained one officer and five men who covered me with pistols and invited me to enter, which I did after being relieved of my knife and stick. Apparently it was a guard ration lorry. They then turned the lorry round and took me to St Dizier.

'I sat for four hours in an office and then was moved to the Town Hall. There I was questioned and searched. I gave regulation answers. I was given a receipt for articles taken from me during the search.'

Geoff was taken from the Town Hall to the Luftwaffe *lazaret* where he received attention to his wounds. The Americans frequently flew over the area of St Dizier and, at the first sound of a raid, the Germans took to the shelters. And they took Geoff with them. One day, as he was being frog-marched through the town, he heard a commotion and saw that his escort — one *feldwebel* and one private — were being 'taken care of'. He soon found himself in the care of the maquis.

Spirited away, possibly as far away as the Belgian border (he never knew where he was), plans were made to move him 'down the line' of one of the Underground escape organisations. But something went wrong, and he and five or six other RAF types were betrayed to the dreaded Gestapo, who asked him a few questions in their own inimitable way.

Surviving their attentions, he was then sent via Dulag Luft to Stalag Luft 1, Barth, where he remained until the Russians arrived in the spring of 1945. Eventually the Americans were allowed to take the POWs away in their B-17s. Home at last.

* * *

After an uneventful journey, Lancaster LM388 (166 Squadron) had reached Revigny when the wireless operator, F/S R. F. Scott, heard the order to abandon the mission and go home; F/S Tom Millett, navigator, gave P/O D. C. Gibbons the course. Some 20 minutes later, on the long south-westerly leg, they spotted in the clear moonlight an Me110 flying parallel to them and just out of range of their machine guns. F/S Cosmo Rose, bomb-aimer: 'This we well knew meant his pal was about to attack from the rear. This he did before we could open fire or take evasive action.'*

The rear gunner, 19-year old Sgt Edwin Ashton, was mortally wounded in the attack and called out that he had been hit. The attack was momentarily broken off and Gibbons told Scott to go back and see if he could do anything for Ashton. The attack was soon resumed, however, and despite Gibbons's furious 'corkscrew' the German pilot finished off his prey. The sky was almost cloudless, but Les Lewis remembers that there was 'one small cloud, about the size of a pair of houses' into which Gibbons gratefully dived the Lancaster. The fighter was not seen again, but the damage had been done.

Both inner engines had to be feathered and, with its four-ton bomb load still aboard, LM388 was unable to maintain height. Hydraulic power to operate the mid and rear gun turrets and, more importantly, to open the bomb doors was lost. But it was still possible to open the doors by hand. Gibbons told Cosmo Rose to give it a try. With LM388 steadily losing height, Cosmo knew that he would never be able to crank the doors open before they hit the ground. He told Gibbons that the bombs could not be dropped. There was no alternative but to bale out.

At around 0200 hours, five of the crew parachuted safely into the Bois de Moriémont, to the east of Vitry-le-Croisé. The first to leave was Cosmo Rose who had wasted no time in making his way forward to the nose escape hatch. He hurriedly baled out and landed safely. With parachute, Mae West and flying suit hidden in thick gorse, he had been making his way gingerly through the dark countryside for half an hour or so when he heard someone whistling.

Meanwhile, Les Lewis (or 'Mick' as he was known) had opened the roof escape hatch behind the astrodome before he followed Rose out of the nose without too much difficulty. But as he descended gently beneath his billowing canopy, a problem far greater than how or where he would land presented itself. To his horror, the damaged Lancaster began to circle, pilotless, and with each orbit flew nearer and nearer to him. Gibbons would almost certainly have trimmed the aircraft to fly straight and level before he jumped, but as it passed Les yet again he could see quite clearly that one of the tailplanes, almost completely severed, was flapping up and down; it was this that was causing the Lancaster to fly in circles. So close in fact did the bomber pass that Les thought it would hit him.

His prayers were answered, and the 30-ton monster missed him by a whisker. Swinging gently beneath his parachute he watched as it crashed some distance away. LM388 had come down in the Bois de Vitry, one and a half miles south of Vitry-le-Croisé. Despite the damage to the tail,

---

* In his interview after the war with two RAF Bomber Command gunners, Major Schnaufer said that, so far as his own group (NJG 4) was concerned, 'no co-ordinated night attacks were ever carried out', and he 'thought that if a bomber was attacked by two aircraft at the same time it was merely coincidence. He pointed out that it was most difficult to formate with another fighter at night, and they would invariably lose contact with each other.' It was a common belief that German night-fighters hunted in pairs, or even in threes as one crew reported. Clearly, such a feat of airmanship was impossible in the almost pitch-dark. It was, as Major Schnaufer said, a coincidence and nothing more.

Above left *S/L H. F. Breakspear DSO DFC, CO of the Special Duties Flight at the time of the first raid.* (Mrs L. Breakspear)

Above right *F/O E. J. Welchman, pilot of PD202, one of the ten Lancasters lost on the first raid of 12/13 July 1944.* (B. Bertin)

Revigny: a photographic record

F/O Welchman and his crew. All were killed. (B. Bertin)

This page *Wreckage of Welchman's Lancaster PD202. (B. Bertin)*

Top right *One of the dead of PD202. (B. Bertin)*

Middle right *Crew of PB177, the Australian Master Bomber's aircraft for the second raid, 14/15 July 1944.* Left to right: *Sgt Loader, F/S Gilman, F/L Lawton, F/L Wiseman (Master Bomber), F/O Hudson, F/O Birch, W/O Birch (they were brothers) and W/O Jackson. (R. C. Wiseman)*

Bottom right *The tail section of ND994, one of the second raid's casualties. All the crew were killed. (R. Jeanvoine)*

Top and above *The funeral procession for the crew of ND994, at Loches-sur-Ource.* (B. Bertin)

Left *P/O C. H. 'Denny' Ogden DFC, pilot of NE136. He and all his crew perished on the second raid.* (Mrs E. O'Collard)

Above left *Lost on the third raid, 18/19 July 1944 — the crew of DV312. Standing, left to right: Maltais, Long, Jones (not on that raid), Lunnin; kneeling, left to right: Whiteley, Thomas, Desautels.* (B. Bertin)

Above right *Bob Desautels, the only survivor of DV312.* (via B. Bertin)

Below *Fahnenjunker-Oberfeldwebel Herbert Altner of III/NJG 5 claimed five victories that night in the space of 33 minutes. He is seen here* (centre) *with the crew of his Me110.* (H. Altner)

This page *Revigny rail yards after the third raid.* (B. Parisse)

Above *The* camp des permissionaires, *Revigny, after the third raid.* (B. Parisse)

Below and bottom *Bomb craters, Revigny, after the third raid.* (B Parisse)

Another bomb crater in Revigny after the third raid, with the boulonnerie *(nut and bolt factory) beyond.* (B. Parisse)

The road south-west out of Revigny after the third raid. (B. Parisse)

PRU (542 Squadron) photo of Revigny, 19 July 1944. The AP was at the point where the railway lines diverge on the left. (Public Record Office)

PRU (544 Squadron) photo of Revigny, 25 July 1944. Note the many new bomb craters, caused by delayed action bombs, compared with the above photograph taken six days earlier. (Public Record Office)

Above left *Eric Ashton, rear gunner of LM388 on the first raid. He and the wireless operator, F/S Scott, were killed in the crash.* (C. T. Rose)

Above right *Mike Walsh of LM388, who survived to evade.* (C. T. Rose)

Below *Wreckage of LM388.* (B. Bertin)

Top *The FFI at the funeral of Ashton and Scott* (B. Bertin)

Above *Les 'Mick' Lewis and Cosmo Rose of LM388 were taken to the house of 'Tante Louise' Dreano in Essoyes.* (B. Bertin)

Below *A recent photograph of the Ferme de la Motte, where Rose and Lewis also stayed.*

Above left *Mick Lewis* (second from the left), *Roger Mariotte* (third from the left) *and Cosmo Rose* (right) *at the Ferme de la Motte.* (C. T. Rose)

Above right *Shot down during the second raid in PA984 was its pilot, S/L Geoff Davies DSO, seen here* (left) *as best man at F/L H. G. M. Robinson DFC's wedding. Davies was eventually captured and taken to Stalag Luft 1; Robinson died in the crash.* (Mrs B. H. Carroll)

Below *The crew of LM638, 44 Squadron, which took part in the 5 Group raid to the dual target of Culmont/Chalindrey on the night of 12/13 July.* Left to right: *Arnold, Royle, Green, Lamb, Bray, Wharton, Brooks. Arnold, Lamb, Wharton and Brooks shared a maquisards' camp with Revigny evaders.* (L. Wharton)

Top *F/S Ian Innes had been shot down on the raid to the Laon railway yards on the night of 22/23 June 1944, and is seen here with Mr and Mrs Goustille at Mailly-le-Camp. He also shared the Lévigny maquisards' camp with the Revigny evaders.* (B. Bertin)

Above *At Aigremont Farm.* Left to right: *Brian Raftery, David Wade, 'Buzz' Summers and Stephen Broad (see chapter 10).* (L. Moulun and B. Bertin)

Right *At Lévigny. Larosée with an unknown pillion passenger.* (B. Bertin)

At Lévigny. Left to right: *James Reid, Danny Merrill (all 2 metres of him!) and John Waugh.* (B. Bertin)

At Vernonvilliers. The maquis 'M' with Commandant Yvan (seated centre). (Collection Jacquelin, B. Bertin)

A group photo taken at Lévigny after the liberation: Thibeault (left), *Taschereau* (second left), *John Waugh* (fifth left), *Brian Raftery* (sixth), *Larosée* (seventh, in white), *Danny Merrill* (behind Larosée), *Elliott Annon* (second from right) *and Jack Threlkeld* (right). *The latter two had taken off from Tarrant Rushton on the night of 5/6 August 1944 on Operation DIPLOMAT 9, a routine supply drop for the SOE in the Haute-Marne (see chapter 9).* (B. Bertin)

John Waugh celebrating the liberation of Sommevoire, 31 August 1944. (J. Waugh)

Top *Dave Beharrie's crew of PB234, a casualty of the third raid. Left to right, front row: Eric Brownhall, F/O D. Beharrie and F/S K. J. Schott; back row: John Brown, 'Buck' Rogers and Bob Rust, who was replaced on the raid by Fred White (see chapter 11). Brownhall, Brown, Johnson and White survived.* (J. T. Brown)

Above *The tail section of PB234 at Brabant-le-Roi.* (J. T. Brown)

Left *Red Banville, pilot of LL896 lost on the first raid.* (Mrs D. Banville)

Above left *John 'Nicky' Nicholson, LL896's flight engineer.* (C. H. Kroschel)

Above right *Bill Watkins, the rear gunner.* (C. H. Kroschel)

Below *Ken Hoyle, the mid-upper gunner* (left) *and his brother.* (C. H. Kroschel)

Above *Bill Watkins* (left) *with Ken Hoyle.* (C. H. Kroschel)

Below left *Australian Charlie Kroschel, LL896's bomb-aimer.* (C. H. Kroschel)

Below right *In the Forêt de Morley, July 1944. Nicky Nicholson* (left) *and Red Banville.* (B. Bertin)

Above left *One of the early casualties of the third raid was Lancaster JB318. Rear gunner Len Manning evaded, and is pictured with Mesdemoiselles Beaujard at le Trétoire.* (L. E. S. Manning)

Above right *Another shot of Len Manning* (second from right) *at le Trétoire.* (L. E. S. Manning)

Below left *A little later LL969 went down. Its rear gunner was Canadian F/S Charles Ratchford.* (B. Bertin)

Below right *Ratchford* (left) *with Lt W. Reese USAAF, another evader.* (B. Bertin)

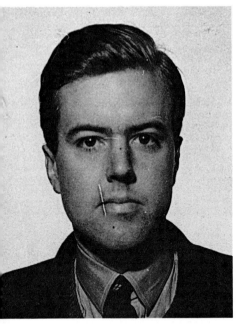

Above left *At about the same time, German flak gunners claimed LM537. Its pilot was F/O P. B. Dennett, who died in the crash.* (R. A. Hilborne)

Above right *Another of the three casualties was wireless operator Sgt W. J. Jarman.* (R. A. Hilborne)

Below left *A mugshot of LM537's Canadian bomb-aimer, F/S H. P. Ritchie.* (B. Bertin)

Below right *Sgt J. Stones, the rear gunner.* (R. A. Hilborne)

Right *Reg Hilborne* (left) *was the mid-upper gunner; he, Ritchie and Stones successfully evaded. Hilborne is photographed with Len Aitken, sole survivor of the crash of ME814, at the de Moslains farm in early August 1944.* (R. A. Hilborne)

Below left *Sgt G. A. Alexander, LM537's flight engineer, was taken prisoner and sent to Stalag Luft 7.* (R. A. Hilborne)

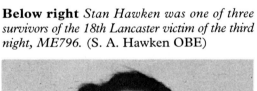

Below right *Stan Hawken was one of three survivors of the 18th Lancaster victim of the third night, ME796.* (S. A. Hawken OBE)

Left *Bill Fortune, navigator of the last of the third night's losses, JB473, was discovered in a cornfield by Gilbert Lachasse, and sheltered by him and his family.* (W. Fortune)

Below *Gilbert's sisters,* (left to right) *Suzanne, Rolande and Andrée Lachasse, at their farm at le Mesnil.* (W. Fortune)

Right Left to right: *Gilbert Lachasse, Bill Fortune and an unknown third person.* (W. Fortune)

Far right *John Diley, wireless operator of JB473.* (J. A. Diley)

Below right *A recent photograph of Maltournée Farm, from where John Diley would first have seen it.*

F/S Norman Oates, the navigator, was the sole survivor of ME833. Taken prisoner, he was taken to Stalag Luft 7, then with 1,500 other POWs undertook a nightmare walk with his German captors through freezing conditions as the Russians advanced from the east. (N. F. Oates)

'Homage aux aviateurs de la RAF tombés ici le 13-7-1944'. Henri Février stands by the memorial to the crew of ND859 at Giey-sur-Aujon.

the Lancaster descended in a shallow dive until it hit some trees, slicing off the tops over a distance of 200–300 yards before running out of momentum. Turning over on to its back, it broke into two pieces. The locals still refer to this incident as the 'coup de l'avion'.

Les landed in the middle of a cornfield and lit a cigarette. He too began walking, and after half an hour or so suddenly saw the silhouette of a man walking in his direction. So far as he could tell in the near darkness the man appeared to be unarmed and was therefore probably 'friendly', but Les was taking no chances. He kept low and started whistling.

There was an answering whistle, closer now. Then Les recognised the other man — Cosmo Rose!

As it was still dark they decided to wait until sunrise before planning their next move. When the sun rose they were able to distinguish the outlines of the houses at Vitry-le-Croisé, and gingerly made their way towards a house on the outskirts, where a man answered their knock. In his best schoolboy French, Cosmo Rose explained who they were.

The startled man, M Ferré, led them across the road to another building and up a flight of stairs to a loft — which was deep in bird droppings. Any port in a storm! Some while later M Ferré returned with food and drink. If their host seemed a trifle nervous, he had good reason to be, for his wife was in hospital and due to give birth at any moment. Sensing his anxiety, the two airmen decided to leave at the earliest possible opportunity. Cosmo Rose had twisted his knee on landing, so it was not until the night of 14/15 July that they slipped quietly away to the south.

They walked for two thirsty nights. At long last they heard the sound of tumbling water. Their joy was short-lived when they discovered that there was a steep bank down to the river and no way down. There was nothing to do but carry on and follow the river. After several more weary minutes they came to a watermill. Les:

'There we found a well with a bucket on a chain which we lowered into the well and, while we were having a good drink, a door opened and Cosmo had to explain who we were. One of the family went off and after a while returned and told us to go into the village and we would see a lady leaning on her gate. She would go into her house and we were to follow her.'

It was now dawn on Sunday 16 July, and the two tired travellers had reached the small town of Essoyes. Following their instructions Les and Cosmo soon found the house and saw, as they had been told, a middle-aged woman at the gate. Cosmo approached and told her their story. She seemed to believe it and invited the two men indoors. Introductions were made to the woman's elderly parents, and she introduced herself as 'Tante Louise', though her surname was Dreano — 'Tante Louise' was a cover, just in case! The two tired visitors 'were given a meal and packed off to a lovely clean bed'.

Around midday (16 July), they woke up to find a two-man reception committee waiting for them. 'Tante Louise' explained that the men were maquisards, there to ensure that they were genuine RAF. Cosmo Rose:

'After many questions and "Pardonnez-moi's" I convinced them we
were British airmen (Sgt Lewis had no French). They came back later
and took us to their *maquis* [camp] in a heavily wooded area where
we were to stay until August 2nd.'

They were now in the hands of the well-organised 'Mussy-Grancey'
maquis, which was 'based' on several farms in the area. The maquis
derived its name from the two villages of Mussy-sur-Seine and Grancey-
sur-Ource, lying either side of a large, wooded hillside which was soon
to figure prominently in the lives of the two evaders. The Mussy-Grancey
maquis was commanded by 'Montcalm' (real name Emile Alagiraude),
a French army career officer appointed by the Free French as the FFI
regional commander. When Lewis and Rose joined, it was some 600
men strong, but within a couple of weeks it had doubled its strength.

Soon after their arrival at the camp, Rose and Lewis were ordered into
a car without being told where they were going. Their escorts, unusually
subdued, drove for some time before they finally pulled up by a wood.
The Frenchmen were saying little as they led the two airmen through
the trees. Suddenly they came to a clearing.

There, amongst the broken branches and splintered tree trunks, lay
the wreckage of LM388, almost unrecognisable amongst the debris. To
their horror they found Scott's body lying in the rear doorway of the
Lancaster, clutching his parachute, his legs dangling out. And then they
discovered the rear gunner, Ashton, in his turret. Two witnesses — René
Demongeot (then a 22-year old maquisard) and Pierre Martinot* — are
sure that Scott survived the landing, because he could not possibly have
been killed in the position in which he was found. His parachute had
apparently been successfully used.

Despite the destruction, the maquisards were able to salvage one of
the Lancaster's machine guns and hundreds of rounds of belted
ammunition. The gun was mounted on a tripod on the roof of a lorry
for use against the enemy. Maybe the crew of LM388 had some revenge
after all. Cosmo Rose:

'The bodies were removed to the nearby village of Vitry-le-Croisé.
The following day Sgt Lewis and I with some of the maquis drove to
the village and stopped beside a garage (doors removed). The coffins
containing the remains of Scott and Ashton were sitting on trestles
and the whole beautifully bedecked with flowers. The maquis and
Mick and I stood alongside and between the coffins for some time
until they were removed to the nearby church. After the service the
whole village, young and old, filed past the remains paying their respects
to two boys they didn't even know — a truly moving experience for
Mick and I. They were buried in a graveyard alongside the church.'

The 'garage' was, in fact, the local fire-station. A guard of honour for
the sad occasion was provided by the 3rd Company, 2nd Battalion, 131st
Infantry Regiment, FFI, who were determined to put on a good show,

---

* *Mayor of Vitry-le-Croisé in 1990.*

not only for their two dead allies but also for the local population, whether they liked it or not:

'In the morning we made our preparations: cleaning weapons, brushing clothes, shaving, etc. Each did his best to look presentable. None forgot that this was our first daylight expedition since we joined the maquis. We would be seen by the civilian population — we must not give them the impression that we are "Terrorists". On the other hand, our bearing and conduct ought to silence collaborators and rally hesitators to our cause.

'After a quick inspection and a few words of encouragement, we got into the lorries. We passed through Grancey, Verpillières, Essoyes. At the sound of our engines people came to their doors and gave us a cheer. Some who were a bit more excited shouted: "Vive le maquis! Vive la France! Vive de Gaulle!" etc. Others were more reserved, but all were surprised by this maquisard expedition and were moved to see for the first time in four years Frenchmen openly bearing arms against the Boche.

'At last, about half an hour before the ceremony, we arrived. The lorries were parked on the square and look-outs quickly positioned. Our arrival had not gone unnoticed; soon the more curious began to gather . . .

'Wreaths bearing the inscriptions "To our Allies. To our Liberators" and simple bouquets of flowers tied with a red, white and blue ribbon were placed around the coffins. There were many flowers, each picked as a mark of respect. We arranged ourselves on either side, weapons under our arms, barrels pointing downwards . . .

'When the funeral service was over, the dead were taken to their last resting place. The crowd passed slowly in front of the coffins, each person blessing them. We left the cemetery and went back to our lorries.

'It was four pm . . .'

Rose and Lewis returned to the Mussy-Grancey camp, in the Forêt de Val du Puits, to find that in their absence their Canadian mid-upper gunner, Sgt Mike Walsh, had been brought in. He had landed in a tree from which he had been unable to disentangle his parachute and, with the sound of dogs barking in the distance, had had no choice but to leave it hanging there. Burying his Mae West and flying suit he left the area as quickly as possible in the circumstances — his boots had come off when he baled out. He spent what was left of the night in the woods and at sunrise (about 0500 hours) started slowly and painfully to walk to Switzerland.

With nothing but socks on his feet he made little progress, and decided to stop at the first house he found to ask for a pair of shoes. He stumbled upon Fontarce farm where he was given shelter by M Martinot (Pierre's father), who sent for a doctor. That evening (13 July) Dr Claude Poisson arrived to check that Walsh was indeed an airman and not a German spy. Despite the language barrier, Dr Poisson was satisfied that Walsh was telling the truth.

Three days later, 16 July, Dr Poisson returned with a young female interpreter, and that afternoon three maquisards took him by car 'to the house of a man who was a captain in the Resistance'. Very early the following morning, wearing another pair of shoes, he was taken to Dr Poisson's house in nearby Essoyes. Two hours later he was led to 'the headquarters of the Resistance', and from there to the Mussy-Grancey maquis camp and to Cosmo Rose and Les Lewis.

★   ★   ★

Three further stragglers were brought in over the next few days — F/O T. W. Munro, Sgt F. Stormont, and 2nd/Lt Childs (USAAF).

Tom Munro and Frank Stormont were the special operator and wireless operator respectively of the nine-man crew of a Mark III Halifax (MZ570, 192 (SD) Squadron, 100 (BS) Group) which had taken off from Foulsham at 2209 hours on the evening of 3 May 1944 to support the ill-fated Lancaster raid on Mailly-le-Camp. Despite bristling with guns (it carried four gunners — front, mid-upper, mid-under and rear), MZ570 was shot down over the Forêt de Soulaines. Seven men baled out, but two, the rear and mid-under gunners, did not and were buried in the churchyard of la Ville-aux-Bois.

Munro and Stormont separately made contact with the maquis in the Lévigny area; they were passed on to 'Tante Louise' in Essoyes, and from there to the Mussy-Grancey maquis in the Forêt de Val du Puits some time in the middle of July 1944. It is not known how Childs was shot down and brought in, but he brought the number of evaders to an even six.

★   ★   ★

Life at the camp was trouble-free for the next fortnight, until news was received that the Germans were set to attack them in force. Although formed some two months earlier, the Mussy-Grancey maquis had not been able to cause serious trouble for the enemy until 7 July 1944, when eight tons of arms had been parachuted in. By the beginning of August the Germans considered it was high time that this thorn in their side was removed.

The attack began at 0700 hours on Wednesday 2 August, with a strong force of 4–5,000 Germans, including a company of marines from Chaumont, two security regiments from Troyes, sundry units from Châtillon-sur-Seine, and White Russians from St Dizier and Tonnerre, all under the command of a General Schramm. They attacked simultaneously from five or six directions and one group surrounded the maquis stronghold at Réveillon Farm. The maquisards, though, were made of stern stuff and, in the afternoon, repulsed the Germans with a series of strong counter-attacks. Rose and Lewis had each been given an American carbine, but their sector was not attacked and so they never had the chance to prove their marksmanship.

The Germans, however, had not given up and a second attack was launched the following day, augmented by several armoured units which, passing the area, had been delayed when the road had been cut. The Germans by now were uncertain of the exact location of the main body of the maquis, and Montcalm took advantage of their hesitation to effect a tactical withdrawal to the south, thereby saving the great majority of his men — and the six evaders.

On the third day, Friday 4 August, the Germans finally managed to close the net, but by then nearly all the birds had flown. All they had to show for their endeavours were 51 dead maquisards out of a total of over 1,100. Some of them were shot out of hand after they had been captured. The rest of the maquisards dispersed into small groups and laid low for a fortnight, the Germans' only real success.

On the second day of the attack, 3 August, the six evaders were advised to split up into pairs and make good their escape. Rose with Lewis, Munro with Stormont, and Walsh with Childs slipped away for pastures new.

Rose and Lewis headed west until they 'eventually spotted a walled farm on top of a mound', where they were welcomed by Roger and Marcelle Mariotte and their family who lived at the farm 'de la Motte'. The farm, near the village of Villedieu (10 miles north-west of Châtillon-sur-Seine), was only a few hundred yards from a road (today the D 953) which was being used extensively by German troops heading towards the battle zone, but who were soon leaving rapidly in the other direction!

Rose and Lewis were advised by the maquis to stay put until the Americans arrived, whenever that might be. In the meantime they helped on the farm as best they could, and were well cared for by the Mariottes.

It was nearly four weeks before elements of XX Corps of Patton's US Third Army overran the farm 'de la Motte' and liberated its occupants. Rose and Lewis were sent back via Troyes (where they met a 'British captain (Civil Affairs)' — probably Captain P. Fleetwood-Hesketh, the British Liaison Officer in the Côte d'Or), Sens and Paris (being briefly interrogated at the Hôtel Meurice), before being flown back to England aboard a Dakota on 7 September.

Munro and Stormont had escaped to the north-west and were hidden in the Château de Polisy (4 miles south of Bar-sur-Seine) until they too were 'liberated' by the Americans on 29 August. They had not, however, been living in luxury at the château, and it was not through choice that they had been obliged to stay hidden in the attic — for a while the château had also been occupied by the Germans! All was well, and they remained undiscovered until the Americans arrived and sent them back to Paris, and thence to Hendon on 4 September.

★ ★ ★

Walsh and his American companion, Childs, were the last pair to leave and walked westwards to the village of les Riceys (barely five miles north of 'de la Motte'), where they too met some maquisards. The following day they were taken on a long and dangerous journey by lorry to Ligny-le-Châtel (30 miles west). Despite advice to stay put, the two North Americans were unable to curb their impatience and set off north on 5 August, crossing the Armançon river and the Canal de Bourgogne until they came to Neuvy-Sautour.

Fortunately they met a Frenchman who volunteered to act as their guide and interpreter and who proved invaluable in procuring food. Ever westward the intrepid trio travelled, through Dilo to Dixmont, where a change of direction was required when they reached the River Yonne; on south-east to Brion, and down to Laroche on the edge of the Yonne*. The problem now facing Walsh and Childs was how to cross the river.

This was easily solved by their resourceful guide who found a rowing boat; they crossed without incident. South-west through Champlay they came to la Ferté-Loupière and spent the night in the luxury of a hotel. The journey so far had taken about six days.

Next day, 11 August, they were off again. At St Martin-sur-Ouarre a doctor advised them to head north to Melleroy, where they were put in touch with the chief of the local Resistance. He sent them to stay at a small farm.

After two days they were taken by cart to yet another farm near Châteaurenard. Two days later again, they were moved to Thimory, a further 15 miles west, which was a French maquis base and which had been used once or twice by the SAS. They stayed there for four more days, during which time they met four more evaders.

Two of these were the crew of Mosquito NT138 of 464 (RAAF) Squadron, shot down on the night of 25/26 July 1944. F/O John Robert Crossley Walton, RAAF (pilot), and F/O Charles Henry Harper (navigator) had taken off at 2318 hours on an offensive patrol over France. At around 0215 hours on 26 July, when over Gien (near Orléans), light flak scored a direct hit on the flares in the bomb bay. The fire blazed out of control and they baled out. Walton sprained his right ankle and lost one of his shoes.

The other RAF man was F/L Dennis Barry Mason, mid-upper gunner of Lancaster LL885, 622 Squadron. He and his crew (pilot F/L R. G. Allen) were *en route* for Stuttgart on 28/29 July 1944 when they were attacked by a night-fighter in the Orléans area. At around 0015 hours (29 July) there was an explosion in the aircraft and Mason heard the pilot say 'Parachutes!'. He baled out quickly, as they were down to 3,000 feet. He was the only one to do so, landing half a mile north of Monteresson, near Montargis.

The American was Lt Evans, but it is not known how he came to be parted from his aircraft.

On Thursday 17 August units of XII Corps, US Third Army, reached Orléans, and the maquis chief left Thimory at once to inform the Americans of his wards. Arrangements were made the following day for the evaders to be handed over to the Allies, and from Orléans they were sent to Le Mans. All bar Walsh flew over to Northolt on 23 August; he continued to Bayeux where, after a brief interrogation, he left for England on Friday 25 August. He had travelled a long way in six weeks.

---

* *On 31 July 1944 127 Lancasters and four Mosquitoes of 1 and 5 Groups carried out an accurate daylight raid on the marshalling yards at Joigny and Laroche four miles east. One Lancaster (ND954, 57 Squadron) was lost.*

9

To the Woods!
To the Woods!

Tom Millett, navigator of LM388, baled out over the Bois de Moriémont in the early hours of 13 July 1944. His parachute snagged in the trees — in the darkness he had no idea how far he was off the ground, but, clinging desperately to the tree, he managed to release himself from his harness. So began his perilous descent — of six inches! There his feet touched terra firma, and he promptly set off through the forest in the direction of Switzerland.

On the evening of the second day (14 July) he found an unattended bicycle in a sawmill yard. 'Appropriating' the handy transport, he pedalled furiously away to the south for some 30 miles until reaching Pavillon-les-Grancey, where a chink of light from a café door caught his eye. He stopped. Suddenly he noticed a man approaching, with a sten-gun draped over his shoulder. The man knocked on the café door and was let in. Plucking up courage, Tom did likewise and was immediately confronted by several armed men. He had found a maquis meeting place.

The café was run by Paul and Jeanne Minot who, after feeding Tom, showed him to a bed where he could catch up on his sleep. The maquisards meanwhile kept a careful watch. They were taking no chances. When he woke up Tom was rigorously cross-examined, but was able to prove his bona fides to the maquisards' satisfaction. Had he not been able to do so, he would have been shot.

Tom was taken to their camp in the woods near Grancey-le-Château. There he remained until 20 July when he was moved south to yet another camp, at Mortière farmhouse in the Bois de Mortière a dozen miles north of Dijon. The house was well situated in a clearing in the middle of the woods, and well off the beaten track. With guards posted, no one could get close without being spotted a long way off. Tom stayed there for several weeks, enjoying the rough life of the maquis, but always well fed and with a sound roof over his head. His bed was largely made up of parachute silk from supply drops, which made good sheets.

Occasionally he assisted in these drops (when stooks of corn were set alight to mark the Drop Zone), but they were never bothered by the local German garrison who were content to adopt a 'laissez-faire' policy.

But the maquisards could not afford to relax for one moment. One day a spy was caught. The wretched man was given a brief trial and sentenced to be shot the following day. In the maquis ranks was a German deserter and, as a test of his integrity, he was included in the firing squad. He did his duty alongside the Frenchmen.

★ ★ ★

On 5 August four further evaders were brought to the Mortière camp — F/O Ralph Arnold (pilot), Sgt Lloyd Brooks (bomb-aimer), Sgt Bill Lamb (mid-upper gunner), and Sgt Leslie Wharton (navigator). They were on the 5 Group raid to the dual target of Culmont/Chalindrey on the night of 12/13 July when their 44 Squadron Lancaster (LM638) probably collided with ND859 (see Chapter 2). It crashed near Recey-sur-Ource, a dozen miles north-west of Mortière.

The rear gunner, F/S Jim Bray, thought that they were hit by flak, but Canadian Lloyd Brooks reported after the war to his home-town newspaper, *The Paris Star*, that 'suddenly a plane rose out of the darkness and crashed into us'.

All seven of the crew baled out and survived. Sergeants Ron Royle (flight engineer) and Ken Green (wireless operator) were taken prisoner, Ron ending up at Stalag Luft 7. Jim Bray managed to reach England on 13 September via Paris and Spain.

Lloyd Brooks: 'Luck was with me . . . I dropped into the ditch at the side of a road, not ten feet away from the trees. There was no wind and the silk settled on top of me.'

He soon made contact with the maquis and on 14 July was taken to their camp near Recey-sur-Ource where he met his navigator, Leslie Wharton:

'A few minutes later a maquis guide arrived accompanied by our mid-upper gunner who had arrived in the afternoon. It was quite a reunion.'

The skipper, Ralph Arnold, had baled out over Auberive and landed in a thick bush. After wandering about for a while he was met by two girls on bicycles. They told him that their brother had been watching him through his binoculars from their 'château', and invited him back with them. He stayed the night there but, whilst he was asleep, the maquis were summoned. After interrogation, he was taken to Recey-sur-Ource.

There the four men had one sad duty to perform. It was 16 July 1944. Lloyd Brooks:

'On Sunday night the maquis leader took us to a cemetery on the outskirts of Recey. There seven members of a Halifax crew were buried. Their plane had been shot down a year previously and the Germans had left them there. The villagers took the men from the plane, buried them decently and erected a white cross bearing the regimental numbers, names and rank of the men. They also erected a little white picket fence around the plot. The villagers brought wreaths and we placed them on the graves and observed a few minutes of silent respect while standing at attention.'*

After a week they were moved to Grancey-le-Château, and ten days later an Intelligence Officer came for them. Lloyd Brooks:

'He had a small covered truck and three men. We loaded up. A Frenchman in the front seat carried a Tommy gun. At the back of the truck, the navigator [Wharton] stood guard with a Sten gun, supported by two of the Frenchmen with rifles. The rest of us carried revolvers. We travelled in the daylight, using gasoline captured from the Germans.

'We arrived presently at our destination, a large 50-acre farm within a few miles of Dijon. The farm was in the centre of the woods, the buildings being used for headquarters and the sleeping huts being hidden in the edge of the woods. For the first time we could take off our clothes and we slept under silk sheets made from parachutes. The camp was called "Surcouf", after the French submarine . . .'

It was now 5 August, and they had arrived at Mortière farm, where Tom Millett had been in residence since 20 July.

A few days later a British officer appeared at the camp and announced that there was a detachment of 'Air Commandos' not far away, and that he would try to get them together. He succeeded, and on 14 August Captain John Wiseman and his men of 'A' Squadron, 1st Special Air Service Regiment, arrived by jeep from their camp south-west of Dijon, proudly flying the Union Jack. 'They gave us English cigarettes, chocolate bars and boiled sweets. The same day two British planes dropped supplies . . .'

* * *

Wiseman's 1 SAS party had been in France since the night of 21/22 June 1944 and were equipped with a small number of heavily-armed Jeeps. They had made their way to a camp near the village of Rolle which was described by their travelling padré, Fraser McLuskey, as 'the most dangerously placed of all the camps I visited'.†

Wiseman had second thoughts:

'As our position was always precarious and as we were immobile with only one jeep and as it was difficult to do jobs and guard ourselves at the same time, as our party was so small, we decided to move into a Maquis [camp] and to arm them so that we could be protected while we continued on our main task of cutting the railways.'

On 23 July they moved to Urcy, a few miles to the north. An arms drop was arranged, and in the nick of time. On 31 July they were 'attacked by Milice and on the same night we moved back to our old camp glad to be rid of the Maquis' (Milice, see page 244). They heard later, and with

* *The crew were from a 10 Squadron Halifax (JB961) shot down on the Montbéliard raid on the night of 15/16 July 1943.*

† *'Parachute Padré' (SCM Press, 1951).*

much enjoyment, that soon after they had slipped away from Urcy a German force, bent upon their destruction, had encountered the Milice (see Appendix IV) attacking from the opposite direction. With both sides believing the other to be their enemy, a fierce battle ensued and, so the story went, 22 Germans and Milice were killed!

Wiseman was still not happy with the military qualities of the local maquis and made 'contact with a much better *Maquis* North of Dijon about 15 miles, in the Bois de Mortière'. On 15 August they moved to this maquis which was, of course, the one based at Mortière farmhouse!

Two more RAF evaders were brought to Mortière on 25 August. P/O Elliott Annon (navigator) and F/S Jack Threlkeld (bomb-aimer) were members of the crew of Halifax LL334, 298 Squadron. F/O Charles Edward Anderson (RCAF) had taken off from Tarrant Rushton at 2345 hours on the night of 5/6 August 1944 on Operation DIPLOMAT 9, a routine supply drop for the SOE in the Haute-Marne. Two hours later an Me110 night-fighter attacked them.[*]

Anderson took the burning Halifax down to the deck and managed to keep the nose up sufficiently to make a good crash landing. In so doing he lost his life, the only one of the six crew to perish.

The rear turret, with the rear gunner, P/O Ronald Frederick Reader (NZ), still inside, was torn off in the landing. He was badly wounded, and was soon found by the Germans.[†] The other four survivors escaped through the gap left by the rear turret and ran like hell. Threlkeld cut his hand badly on jagged metal as he was leaving, but otherwise they were miraculously in good shape.

The Halifax had come down a couple of miles north-east of Essoyes at about 0200 hours on 6 August. The four buried their equipment and set off together 'in a South Westerly direction to reach the edge of the wood. We heard the clock of a town striking, and crossed a small valley to reach a wooded hill, from which to observe the town[§].' But in crossing the valley Annon and Threlkeld lost contact with F/S David Lewis (wireless operator) and Sgt Cyril Moskin (flight engineer).

By 9 August Threlkeld's injured hand began to give serious cause for concern. They had seen only one lorry on the road all day and at about 1800 hours, when a girl came along on her bicycle, they decided to ask her for help. Having established that there were no Germans in the vicinity, she directed them to a farmer at Neuvelle-les-Grancey who did what he could for Threlkeld's hand, and the maquis were summoned.

On 24 August they were at Mortière Farm, where they met Captain Wiseman, his 1 SAS troop and the other five evaders — Millett, Arnold, Brooks, Lamb and Wharton.

That same day, 24 August, Ralph Arnold and Bill Lamb decided to try and reach the Allied lines. After a couple of setbacks they were

---

[*] *Exactly two months earlier the crew were shot down on the D-Day Operation TONGA, but returned safely to their squadron.*

[†] *He was in hospital for only four days before he was liberated by the Americans. On 18 September 1944 he was shipped to Southampton, and then sent to a hospital in Chichester.*

[§] *Essoyes.*

eventually flown out of France on 8 September.

For Tom Millett and the other evaders who had stayed behind at Mortière farm, life was relatively tranquil; they were kept well away from any action. Then, on Wednesday 30 August, the SAS were ordered to return to England. Fraser McLuskey:

'Johnny Wiseman was responsible for the marshalling of the convoy and was shooting all over the place in his jeep, arranging the troops and sections in his usual business-like way . . . superintending the despatch of the convoy . . . Workers in the field turned to wave and gave them a cheer. The whole village was out to see them off. Of course they were glad to be going home, but . . . parting was not without regrets. "Partir c'est un peu mourir."'

On 6 September the 'great move home started. The convoy consisted of 18 civilian cars, 2 German heavy trucks and 6 jeeps as protection. We expected to meet German convoys moving east but got through to Joigny without any mishap . . .'

Tom Millett, Leslie Wharton and Lloyd Brooks, with the SAS, made their way to Orléans airfield some five miles out of the town where, on 8 September, 48 USAAF B-24 'Liberators' landed:

'Our party was divided into tens and placed in the first ten Liberators ready to return to England. After a 2-hour trip during which we passed over the Cherbourg peninsula and the ravaged battlefields of Normandy, we arrived at Middle Wallop.'

Elliott Annon and Jack Threlkeld, on the other hand, chose not to go with the SAS convoy and instead, on 3 September, were taken away by car. They were eventually flown back to England on 13 September, five days after the three who had returned with the SAS!

Little is known of what happened to David Lewis and Cyril Moskin after they became separated from Annon and Threlkeld near Essoyes on that first morning. But they were sheltered, as Rose and Lewis had been, by 'Tante Louise' Dreano in her house in Essoyes. Records suggest that David Lewis became a prisoner of war at Mühlberg. It is likely, therefore, that both were captured, though Moskin's fate is unknown. Happily, Madame Dreano survived the war.

* * *

The pilot of LM388, P/O Dudley Charles Gibbons, landed safely in the woods near Vitry-le-Croisé. Having hidden his parachute, harness and Mae West in the dense undergrowth, he chose to remain in the forest for the rest of that day, 13 July. In the evening he went into Vitry-le-Croisé and contacted a man who hid him for two nights before introducing him to a 'member of the FFI'. On the 15th he was escorted by a French Army officer and a member of the FFI to a house in Essoyes, ten miles to the south.

On the evening of the following day he was moved by the maquis to their camp near the village of Courban, where he spent the best part of 12 days. Then he was moved to another camp near Layer-sur-Roche, where he stayed for a fortnight until on '13 Aug I was escorted on a bicycle to the village of Faverolles'. He and his escort cycled some ten miles through the woods to the hamlet of Faverolles-les-Lucey, where the maquisards had established contact with Captain Grant Hibbert of 2 SAS engaged in Operation HARDY. Captain Hibbert agreed to take the airman off their hands.

Operation HARDY had begun on the night of 26/27 July 1944, Captain Hibbert's orders being to 'cause maximum interference with enemy attempts to withdraw towards Germany through north-east France: area of operations — Plateau de Langres'. By 0530 hours on Saturday 5 August the SAS had reached a suitable 'lying-up' area near Arbot (to the north of Dijon). During routine reconnaissance patrols contact was made with various maquis bands, which handed over Gibbons and four other evaders — F/S I. R. C. Innes (RAAF), Lt G. S. Call (USAAF), F/S L. Aitken and Sgt R. A. Hilborne.

F/S Ian Russell Caple Innes had been shot down on the raid to the Laon railway yards on the night of 22/23 June 1944 in Halifax MZ692, 78 Squadron. He was in the nose manning a Vickers gas-operated machine gun when flak set the port engines on fire. The bomber was soon well ablaze and the pilot ordered them to bale out. Innes lost his flying boots when the parachute snapped open, and landed in his socks about three feet from a barbed wire fence on the outskirts of Cuvilly, near Compiègne.

He decided to go south to Switzerland, eventually reaching Mailly-le-Camp, where he stayed for a fortnight with the Goustille family. There he was put in touch with the maquis and with a US pilot, Lt Glen Sterling Call, who had been shot down in his P-47 near Allibaudières (some six miles from Mailly) where he was sheltered by the Truchot family. The two evaders were taken to Troyes where they met 'a British Intelligence agent' who passed them on to the camp at Lévigny. They stayed there for five days until, on Sunday 30 July, they decided to make for the Swiss border.

They gave up at Montarlot-les-Champlittes, where they stayed with Lucien Lamarche until Sunday 13 August, when they were handed over to Captain Hibbert. At 1420 hours on the same day Hibbert was able to radio to SAS HQ in England that Innes and Call were with him and that both were well.

At 1440 hours on 15 August, Hibbert radioed: 'Following RAF personnel with us. All well. Gibbons, Hilborne, Aitken.' Hilborne and Aitken were shot down on the third Revigny raid, and their adventures before meeting the SAS are related in Chapter 15.

Hibbert also signalled on the same day that 'P/O Gibbons reports Ju 288 seen this area last week at 300 feet with small aeroplane possibly flying bomb fixed on top.' This was almost certainly a Ju88 with an Me109 supported on its back, an extraordinary combination known as 'Mistel 1'. The Mistel 'composites' were part of the German programme to use worn-out Ju88 air frames as pilotless guided missiles. The single-seat fighter was attached to the top of the bomber whose nose was filled with a hollow charge.

The Allies maintained a close watch on all German airfields and St Dizier was no exception. Me109s and Ju88s there were nothing out of the ordinary. The first suggestions of activity connected with a 'composite' aircraft were seen on 25 June 1944 when 12 Me109s and three Ju88s were spotted. It was not until 17 July that the USAAF were able to get a clear photograph of a 'composite' in a shelter in the south dispersal area. Hitherto, 'composites' had only been identified at Peenemünde and Kolberg.

In the spring of 1944 pilots of the *Einsatz-Staffel* of IV/KG 101 received conversion training for the Mistel from Junkers test pilots. Warheads (which contained 8,380 lbs of charge) were finally tested at Peenemünde in April and May, and in June the *Einsatz-Staffel*, with five Mistel 1, was sent to St Dizier airfield to carry out operations against the Allied invasion in Normandy. Commanded by Hauptmann Horst Rudat, the *staffel* carried out its first operation on the night of 24/25 June, but the pilot of the '*Huckepack*' ('piggy-back') was forced to drop the Ju88 prematurely. The four remaining 'bombs' were dropped shortly after against Allied invasion shipping in the Baie de la Seine but, even though each found its target, no ship was sunk as a result of the attack. Earlier, on the night of 14/15 June, two aircraft fitting the description of a Mistel were destroyed by Mosquitoes.

Other prying eyes also saw the Mistel. Word had filtered through to the local maquis that there was an unusual aeroplane at 'Robinson' airfield (St Dizier), and they were ordered to photograph one of these 'avions doubles'. Jean Perrin managed to get close enough to the airfield to take a photograph of a Mistel 1. The evidence was sent to England by another member of the group, Doctor Vesselle, who also sent a coded wireless message each time one of the Misteln took-off from 'Robinson' airfield.

★ ★ ★

There is a rotten apple in every barrel and, on 18 August, Hibbert was informed by a maquis agent who worked at the German HQ at Langres that 'two spies who were in hiding in a windmill' had given away the location of their base. The SAS and the five evaders — Hilborne, Aitken, Gibbons, Innes and Call — rapidly moved to a new site 'where a clearing in the wood to the North promised to be a useful D.Z.'.

Aware of his orders to 'cause maximum interference' to the Germans, Hibbert intended to make full use of his jeeps' enormous machine gun fire-power. Each usually mounted a pair of Vickers machine guns on the front and a single gun to the rear, although it was not uncommon for more guns to be carried. Innes and Call were keen to fight with the SAS and were found gainful employment as front and rear gunners. In his book *Winged Dagger**, Major Roy Farran, commander of Operation WALLACE, launched to link-up with Hibbert's Operation HARDY, mentioned that Hibbert 'had picked up a delightful American pilot called Glen Stirling[†] . . . His Texas drawl was beautiful to our alien ears and I shall never forget that he once reported having shot two Germans "way out in the cow pastures".'

---

* *Published by Collins in 1948.*

[†] *'Glen Stirling' was of course Lt Glen Sterling Call.*

It was during the afternoon of Thursday 24 August, whilst lunching with Colonel Claude Monod, head of the local maquis, that Captain Hibbert had made contact with Major Farran:

'The re-union with Grant was a great moment. He was quite astonished at the rate at which we had crossed France. Belittling my worry at our depleted numbers, he led me with his long strides into a cunningly concealed camp under the trees. Explaining it all in a dry voice, he showed me the dumps of stores, the tents made from khaki parachutes draped between the branches, and the brushwood barriers which protected the main exits. He certainly had not wasted his month in enemy territory. The rude shelters were impossible to detect except at the shortest range, and inside they were furnished comfortably with bits of parachute equipage. Most of the men wore beards and their red berets were beginning to fade, but their morale was high.'*

Farran and his men of 'C' Squadron, 2 SAS, were to be flown from RAF Broadwell, Oxfordshire, during the afternoon of 19 August aboard 40 Dakotas, 20 each from 512 and 575 Squadrons. Due to atrocious weather and mechanical difficulties only 35 Dakotas, each carrying a jeep and a few a trailer as well, landed at Rennes airfield in the late afternoon. Ahead of 'C' Squadron lay a journey of some 400 miles. Farran wrote:

'I suppose that of all the operations carried out by the 2nd Special Air Service Regiment, the jeep operation "Wallace" was the one in which the greatest distance behind the enemy lines was covered.'†

Farran started out with 20 jeeps but, due to enemy action along the way, only seven arrived at the rendezvous. The strength of both the HARDY and WALLACE parties, therefore, amounted to only 'ten jeeps, one civilian lorry and 60 men'.

Farran also brought with him Ralph Arnold and Bill Lamb who had set out that same day from Captain Wiseman's 1 SAS camp at Mortière in an effort to reach the Allied lines. Arnold and Lamb, however, stayed for only two days, before leaving on Saturday, 26 August.

Farran and his now united team began operations in earnest against the retreating Germans on 27 August and minor skirmishes and ambushes continued over the next few days. Farran, though, decided to unburden himself of the five evaders and tried to get an aircraft sent to pick them up. At 1850 hours on 25 August he radioed: 'What news plane to evacuate RAF? Propose moving further east within week so essential receive reply within four days.'

At the end of the four days, with no sign of an aircraft, Len Aitken and Reg Hilborne:

---

* *Farran, ibid.*

† *Farran, ibid.*

'. . . decided to break through to the American lines and started off in a jeep to cross the Route Nationale [RN71] at Aisey [Aisey-sur-Seine]. On the way we were ambushed by the Germans but managed to return to Aignay-le-Duc which was held by the maquis. They furnished us with guides and after two days we reached the American lines at Bar-sur-Seine. From here we were sent to the beach head and left France on 7 Sep 44.'

Len and Reg left the beach-head in a landing craft and on reaching England were met by the RAF, who promptly put them on to a train and locked them in!

On 31 August the three remaining evaders — Gibbons, Innes and Call — also decided to leave the SAS, who provided them with uniforms for their journey. They headed west on foot for two days towards the American lines* before they met the maquis at Bouix. The French took them back to their camp for the night, and the following day, 2 September, they were driven by car north to Mussy-sur-Seine, recently captured by the FFI, before finally reaching the American lines at Bar-sur-Seine.

On 27 August 1945, safely back in the USA, Sterling Call wrote to Madame Truchot, who had sheltered him at Allibaudières, explaining what happened next:

'An American lorry was taking German prisoners to Mailly via Troyes and Arcis, and it was then that we stopped to see you. I am sorry that we were unable to come to dinner that night but the person in charge of the prisoners said that there were still a number of them to be taken to Paris, and so we left with the lorries.

'The lorries went via Vitry-le-François, Bar-le-Duc, and then to Ligny-en-Barrois, and from there by car taken directly to Paris. From Paris we went to London by plane.'

They were flown back to England on 6 September, and went their separate ways — Innes back to Australia and Call to San Francisco in the far west of the United States. Gibbons had a shorter journey back to Slough.

The SAS stayed on in France harassing the Germans until ordered to return to the UK on 17 September. With the help of the two impromptu gunners, Innes and Call, the joint HARDY/WALLACE operation cost the enemy some 500 killed or wounded, 23 Staff cars, six motorcycles, 36 miscellaneous vehicles, 100,000 gallons of petrol, which had been stored in a dump, and one goods train. In return they lost seven SAS killed, two wounded, one missing and two prisoners-of-war (one of whom later escaped).

---

* *The flying divisions of Patton's US Third Army had swung south of Paris and then headed on a broad front for Troyes and Châlons-sur-Marne. As General Patton himself claimed: 'As of August 14 the Third Army had advanced farther and faster than any army in history . . .' (War As I Knew It, published by Houghton Mifflin, 1947).*

10

Dawn Raid

'Lysol' — 'return to base without bombing' — and P/O John McLaren turned Lancaster JB644 away from Revigny. Six minutes later, with no warning, a night-fighter attacked and the Lancaster burst into flames. McLaren ordered the crew to bale out.

In the nose, bomb-aimer F/O Stephen Broad could only get one of the two parachute clips on to its harness hook. It would have to do. Wrenching open the forward escape hatch he pushed it and himself out with great difficulty: 'I seemed to somersault backwards along the fuselage through a lot of flames and then my mind is a complete blank.'

The slipstream had probably swept him against the dome of the H2S scanner. Regaining his senses some time later, he found himself hanging by his parachute in a tree. Hacking away the tough straps with his penknife he hit the ground heavily, losing consciousness once more. Coming round, but still groggy, he staggered to a nearby farm:

'I decided to . . . watch the house until it was light. From then onwards my mind is a blank, but the people of the house told me later that I walked into the kitchen where Madame and her daughter were, stated that I was "un aviateur Anglais" and wanted food. They gave me some and I immediately went away into the woods.'

He walked until he came to Grignoncourt Farm, home of the Moulun family. More food. As he was eating, he glanced out of the window and saw two German soldiers. Gaston Moulun jumped to his feet and hurried out while Madame hid the Flying Officer in 'a very large wardrobe which was in the next room to the kitchen'.

The two soldiers, who were looking for food, were given a glass of wine in the kitchen. They soon left, and Stephen remained undiscovered. He continued to suffer with concussion and stayed in bed for the next three days.

News of his crew arrived. 'Jumbo', the navigator, was found hanging from a tree, strangled by his parachute lines. The only survivor was Sergeant Duncan Roy 'Buzz' Summers, flight engineer. He went to the church in Chevillon, where a service was in progress and, when it was over, managed to make the curé understand who he was. Given a set of 'civvies' he was taken to a house in the village before being taken to Grignoncourt Farm.

* * *

In the early hours of 15 July, Lancaster ME755 (P/O W. A. H. Vaughan, 460 (RAAF) Squadron) was homeward-bound from Revigny when it was caught by a night-fighter. The rear gunner was killed in the attack, which was so swift and fierce that only F/S Brian Francis Raftery RAAF (wireless operator) and Sgt David Wade (mid-upper gunner) succeeded in baling out.

Brian Raftery buried his equipment and started walking towards Switzerland. Some time later that morning (15 July), he met Gaston Moulun who took him to a small stone building nearby. He did not take him direct to Grignoncourt Farm, just in case he was not what he appeared to be. He fetched the Australian some food and a change of clothes.

Satisfied that Brian was not a spy, Gaston fetched Stephen Broad, now almost recovered, and took him to meet the Australian. It was unwise for the two airmen to stay at the farmhouse as the Germans were combing the area, so they were taken to a hut in the Forêt de Morley. It had only two rooms, one up and one down, but all things considered it was comfortable enough, and Madame Moulun brought them food regularly.

Summers and Wade were rounded up and taken to join their friends in the woods near Grignoncourt Farm. Gaston gave them food for thought one day when he told them that an aircraft was coming to pick them up. But, as so often happened, it failed to materialise, and the dispirited airmen spent three more days in the woods.

On 22 July the four of them (Broad, Summers, Raftery and Wade) were moved to the Franquets' remote home at Aigremont farm. They stayed there until 27 July when they were moved to the 'Jedburgh' camp (of which more in a moment) near Lévigny, five miles north of Bar-sur-Aube. Here they would meet eight more evaders. The destinies of these 12 airmen were to become closely linked in a way that none of them could ever have imagined.

* * *

On 28/29 June 1944, Halifax MZ644 (102 Squadron) was still some way short of the target — Blainville-sur-l'Eau, near Nancy — when tragedy struck from an unexpected quarter. Sgt John Waugh (rear gunner):

'The flak was fairly light with one or two searchlights flashing about . . . Suddenly tracers were flying in a thick stream past the rear turret, and they were coming from in front of the kite! I knew that it was very rarely that an attack came from in front, so I thought it must be some kind of super kite. Just then the skipper and the bomb-aimer began shouting and swearing, to quote: "Them bastards in front are firing at us and it's a bloody Hali".'

The aircraft began losing height and the pilot, P/O B. R. Jardine, told the crew to bale out. Only John Waugh, Sergeants Bert Crayden (wireless operator), James 'Charlie' Reid (bomb-aimer) and Danny Merrill (navigator) survived.

Crayden was re-united with Reid during the evening of 30 June. On 1 July it was arranged for them to go to a maquis camp in the Forêt de Lentilles, near the village of Anglus. Danny Merrill was already there; John Waugh parachuted into the pitch-dark woods, found shelter at a farmhouse, and was taken to meet his three fellow survivors. They stayed at this camp for a fortnight or so until, on or about 16 July, they were taken southwards by Claudia Bertin, a member of the local 'underground', to a camp near Lévigny, some 15 miles away. Here they met the shadowy figures of 'two French Canadian officers and a US Naval Lieutenant', a 'Jedburgh' team who had been dropped into France on the night of 12/13 June by a USAAF B-24 'Liberator'.

These 'Jedburgh' teams were dropped behind enemy lines in France in the summer of 1944. They were all trained in guerrilla tactics and were experts in demolition. Their role was to co-ordinate the 'resistance' in their area and to arrange arms for the maquisards if thought appropriate.

The three men in the Lévigny team were Captain Jacques Taschereau, leader; Paul-Emile Thibeault; and Richard Larosée, radio operator. Taschereau and Thibeault were French-Canadians, Larosée a US Navy lieutenant whose grandparents had been French-Canadian. They were joined by Gustav Duclos, a French deserter from the Vichy armed forces.

* * *

On 21 July, five days after the 102 Squadron men arrived at the Lévigny camp, Len Aitken, Reg Hilborne, 'Geordie' Stones and Bob Desautels were brought in.

Bob Desautels was the bomb-aimer of DV312 (50 Squadron) which had been attacked by a night-fighter when a few miles short of Revigny. It had been spotted on 'visual Monica', and the pilot, F/O William James Long (who although in the RCAF was an American), took the standard evasive 'corkscrew' action. The fighter, a Ju88, missed DV312 on its first attempt but managed eventually to get in a telling burst. Desautels heard the pilot ordering the bombs to be jettisoned and reluctantly pressed the release button.

On its fourth attack, the night-fighter managed to hit the starboard engines, and fuel from ruptured tanks was soon alight. Bob heard the order to 'Bale out!' as the Lancaster turned over on its back and went into a steep dive. Only with the greatest difficulty was he able to open the floor escape hatch and pull himself out of the almost inverted aircraft. He was the only one to escape. Just as Stephen Broad had done, he banged his head on the way out:

'I lost consciousness on the way down and came to in a wood SW of Wassy. I hid my parachute and Mae West and set out at once in a westerly direction. At daybreak I hid in a wood till noon and then continued on my way. A short while later I met a woman and declared myself to her. She brought me some food and told me to remain in hiding where I was.

'About 2230 hours (19 July) the woman's husband came for me and took me to his farm where I spent the night.'

He set off again the following day (20 July) heading almost due south though intending to reach Switzerland to the south-east, and walked until the early afternoon when he approached an isolated farm near the village of Sommevoire. Here he was invited in for a meal. The farmer told him that a few miles away he could contact a 'Resistance organisation'.

He walked until 2200 hours (20 July) when he reached another farmhouse, where again he was given a meal. Suddenly the kitchen door burst open. A bunch of heavily armed, rough-looking Frenchmen, guns pointed menacingly, were scavenging for food. They cared little how they came by it. Two ruffians remained on guard in the kitchen while the rest plundered the farm. When about to leave, one of them waved his gun at Bob and asked who he was. The farmer explained. Bob knew better than to argue, thanked the farmer and followed the men into the forest.

These men, possibly from the maquis 'Garnier', commanded by the very shady character of Georges Debert, took him west 'to their camp somewhere in the Sauvage Magny area, where I met F/Lt Stevens who was also evading'. Stevens was one of the survivors from the Deputy Master Bomber's Lancaster shot down on the second Revigny raid.

Next day, 21 July, Bob Desautels was taken to the Lévigny camp, probably with Stevens (Stephen Broad remembers that when he got there he met 'a F/Lt — Steve — on his last operational trip as a master bomber'), where they joined Crayden, Merrill, Reid, Waugh, Aitken, Hilborne, and Stones. On 26 July Ian Innes and Sterling Call arrived. The total reached 15 when Broad, Summers, Raftery and Wade arrived on 27 July from Aigremont Farm.

The days passed, but not always pleasantly, as John Waugh recalls. On 28 July

'. . . a Frenchman was brought to the camp and kept under constant guard. We were told that he had been posing as the leader of a Resistance group a few miles away, but was no more than a gangster. He and his band had been robbing local people and had in fact turned a couple of RAF evaders over to the Germans for the reward of, I think, 25,000 francs.

'He was to be court-martialled, with the Captain [Jacques Taschereau] and Lieutenant [Larosée] acting as "Watch" and "Brief" of the proceedings. The maquisards found him guilty on an overall vote. He was sentenced to death. Everyone was present when he was shot a few feet from where I was standing. It was a horrible sensation, but it showed me the true French feelings towards traitors.'

Stephen Broad was asleep in his tent when he was 'woken up by a couple of shots. I went out to find they had shot the bloke right in the forehead and he was lying in a pool of his own blood. Not a very nice sight.'

Brian Raftery reported that the 'Jedburgh' team and the maquis 'kept the railway line from Bar-sur-Aube to Troyes continually inoperative'. It was now becoming too dangerous to stay any longer at the camp. The Germans certainly knew about it as the 'Jed' team frequently used a radio transmitter (to order supplies and suchlike), and it was only a matter of time before its exact location was pin-pointed.

On the night of 30/31 July Aitken, Hilborne, Innes and Call decided that it was high time they left for Switzerland. Stevens probably left at the same time. He had intended to reach Switzerland, but failed to get there. Stephen Broad remembers that 'Steve' left with an American fighter pilot 'who had been shooting up a munition train which exploded when he was a little too close so he had had to crash land'. Presumably the American was Sterling Call.

That left just the ten. Broad:

'On the Friday, August 4th, [we] got word that we might be attacked so it was decided that we should shift camp. In the meantime our sentries were doubled and we put a few Bren guns round the camp and always had some arms handy.'

The next morning they moved, their three-hour trek covered by a fortuitously heavy mist, to a site barely half a dozen miles north of Lévigny, to the far side of Vernonvilliers. The new camp was not, however, universally popular. Broad:

'This site was completely flat and there were a lot of paths through the woods which it was quite impossible to cover with only our small band to supply sentries. We placed a sentry at the junction of four paths close to our camp and left it at that. The nearest place we could get water was about ten minutes' walk away.'

The water was not too pure, and this may have been the cause of the awful stomach pains and diarrhoea that plagued a few of them, later diagnosed as dysentery.

To break the monotony Bob Desautels, who spoke good French, got a job with a local farmer pretending to be his nephew from Toulouse, where the accent was similar to his own. For the others, they could look forward to the occasional arms distribution to the maquis. Stephen Broad again:

'One of the partisans was the local curé and it looked very strange to me to see this oldish chap wearing gaiters and a dog collar with a couple of Marlins* and a couple of Stens on his back, a bandolier round his shoulders and a rifle in his hands.'

Then, late on 12 August, word was received that two maquisards had been captured. Bob decided to return to camp, just in case. It appeared

---

* A basic type of sub-machine gun.

that that evening five maquisards had set out to commit sabotage; but two were caught red-handed on the D18 road by the Milice (see Appendix IV). The alarm was immediately raised by those who had escaped. The other maquisards were taken for questioning to the Milice HQ at Troyes 30 miles away. The camp's location was now known. With German approval, the Milice decided to attack it early the following morning. Seventy-five heavily armed men de-bussed near 'Quatre Frères' farm on the D18 road and headed for the camp. At the head of the column were the captured *résistants*.

Back at the camp the night passed without alarm and at about 0730 hours in the early morning stillness Summers crept out of the tent, taking care not to wake the others. He was due to begin his watch at 0800 hours. Stephen Broad was dozing:

'At quarter to eight exactly there was the noise of firing quite close. Paul [Thibeault] leapt out of bed, put a few clothes on and rushed out with a Sten gun. Bob and I jumped up and started to get dressed . . . I lifted up the edge of the [tent] and asked Bob if we should make a dash for it. He stuttered "No". We were both scared stiff . . . Our tent seemed to be right between two lines of fire. I saw a hole appear in the tent a few inches above my head . . . Bob said a grenade bounced into the tent about two feet from my body. He waited for it to explode, but it didn't . . .

'A few minutes later the firing ceased and I felt a blow on my posterior as somebody hit me with a rifle butt. I was told to get up . . .'

John Waugh was lying on his bed of parachute silk when he was startled by someone shouting excitedly. Then came the gunfire:

'A few dozen holes appeared in the roof of the tent just above my head. I moved quickly on to the floor and under the tent flap into the wood. I saw someone lying in the bushes firing a gun. I moved over and lay beside him to see what he was shooting at. I gave him a nudge to ask what was going on. He turned towards me. JESUS! It was one of Laval's Milice; he was pointing his gun at me . . . I was wondering where I might get some new pants from . . . I put my arms in the air and shouted "RAF, RAF". A few more of the bastards came and then a German NCO. They escorted me away.'

The attack was soon over. Four of the ten airmen were captured, and were still in grave danger — Broad, Crayden, Desautels and Summers. The other six — Reid, Merrill, Raftery, Wade, Stones and Waugh (despite his apparent capture just described) — managed to escape in the confusion.

David Wade located Merrill, Raftery and Stones and all four were taken by the maquis to Nully-Tremilly for the night (13/14 August). The following day they went to Beurville and spent the night there. Wade and Stones went off together to a farm at Curmont on 15 August, where they stayed until they met the Americans on 3 September. They were sent to Paris via Colombey-les-Belles, and flown back to England on 6

September. Brian Raftery and Danny Merrill stayed with Gaston Cartier in Beurville.

John Waugh had been guarded by four Milice when suddenly a burst of gunfire from the Canadians forced his captors to the ground. John seized the opportunity to escape into the woods and joined up with the Canadians who took him by car to Anglus. But a hasty evacuation was required three days later when the village was occupied by the Germans. He stayed for four days at another camp before he was also taken to Nully, where he stayed with the Harmand family at the café Royale. A week later he was taken to the home of Maurice Comte at Sommevoire: 'Here I lived in luxury until the Americans came and we were liberated. Believe me, there were some great parties.'

John went round to all the places where he had been given shelter, celebrating each time. The fun ended temporarily when Paul Thibeault decided to get one of the maquisards to drive them to Paris. They were not short of cash as there was a surplus from the funds dropped for their use during hostilities:

'What a time we had in Paris, a beautiful city even though there was no electricity. We were there a few days then reported to the British Authority that we had JUST been liberated. We were put aboard a Dakota from Paris airport to London, then interrogated at Air Ministry by M.I.9.'

When the Americans arrived on 31 August, Raftery discovered that they were only 'forward units' and decided to make his way towards the rear of their lines. This was arranged by the FFI who escorted him to Bar-sur-Aube, where he met Elliott Annon and Jack Threlkeld (see Chapter 9) who had arrived there on 4 September.

★ ★ ★

Back at the Vernonvilliers camp that morning of 13 August the Milice were taking no chances. The four prisoners were forced to kneel with their hands above their heads. The airmen were anxious to be recognised as prisoners-of-war and Stephen Broad kept repeating to the Milice commander 'Je suis Anglais. Je suis un aviateur'; but this only provoked the deranged man who smashed him over the head with the butt of his gun. For good measure he dealt each prisoner a violent blow to some part of his anatomy — Summers in the stomach from the gun butt, Bert Crayden a boot in the groin. When he had finished he stepped back and pointed his sub-machine gun at the kneeling group. It needed just one squeeze . . . Stephen had both his wrist watches and precious penknife stolen. Then:

'One of the maquis chaps now crawled up to join us dragging a wounded leg. He was made to sit down by us. One or two of the attackers were injured and Bob suggested to someone who seemed to be in charge that he give them some first aid. They agreed. He attended to their wounds first and was then allowed to attend to our poor maquis chap who was in great pain with a bullet in his leg.

'A fair-headed chap in civilian clothes came along and wanted to shoot us all . . . somebody stopped him.'

Reid, who had been hiding in the woods all the while, heard voices speaking in French and thought that the camp had been re-taken by the maquis. He was soon captured! One maquisard, Melaye, who had been wounded, was finished off on the spot. A second, Reux, died on 27 November 1944 of wounds received that day.

Their job done, the Milice wrecked the camp. Then, Stephen Broad recalls:

'We were all made to carry stuff along to a lorry which had been backed up to where our sentry used to stand. We carried our own supplies of food along, our parachutes, medical stores and ammunition. This they found with the help of the two ex-saboteurs whom we began to see must have been the cause of our unhappy position. Later it came out that these two lads on the previous evening were just crossing a field in sight of a road [the D18], wearing their British battledress, when a van drew up and someone shouted to them to go to it. Like bloody fools they went to it. The chaps in the van recognised their Free French shoulder flashes, said they were patriots and told our chaps to jump in. They did, were immediately made prisoners and taken into Troyes.'

The lorry set off down the track to 'Quatre Frères' farm on the D18 road and the prisoners, now five in number — Broad, Desautels, Summers, Crayden and Reid — tagged along behind lugging two very heavy ex-RAF 'hampers'. At the farm an old bus was waiting and the hampers were heaved on to its roof. It was a hot day and they stopped for a drink: 'At last we all got in the coach with the exception of one or two, including the fair-headed bastard, who had a car.'

Accompanying the airmen to Troyes were the bodies of two dead Milice 'covered by a sheet through which blood was soaking', and two other wounded Milice, who were soon complaining of the bumps on the terrible roads. *En route* they stopped at a village where a camouflaged German convoy was laagered, to see if there was a doctor amongst it. One was found, one of the wounded was handed over to his care, and the bus proceeded to Troyes, to the intense relief of the RAF prisoners who had visions of being handed over as terrorists and, inevitably, being shot.

The journey ended, as Broad recalls, when

'. . . the coach pulled up beside a canal, opposite a severe-looking building surrounded by a high brick wall with iron gates and a Milice sentry on duty.

'We were escorted across the courtyard, around the house, down some stone steps into the basement and then into a foul-smelling stone cellar with two little barred windows looking on to the courtyard at the front . . . The furnishings of our new home were three boards and a paint tin full of urine.'

This house, in the Rue du Cloître Saint-Etienne, was the Milice HQ in

Troyes which, in 1940, had been the RASC HQ for the area. Some of the doors still had English names on them. The prisoners found themselves in 'Signals B'!

With their future in some doubt, the airmen were anxious to make the commandant of the prison, the Comte de Percin, understand that RAF aircrew were entitled to be treated under the Geneva Convention. Bob Desautels did the talking, to such good effect that an identification parade of the Milice was held one afternoon so that those who had robbed the prisoners could be identified, and the goods restored to their rightful owners!

Bob was also told that the Germans were to be told of their whereabouts, but that the Milice intended to exchange them for some of their own number who were prisoners of the Americans. Apparently the Germans refused to believe that the Milice were holding five RAF prisoners, so Bob was chosen to go to the German HQ as proof.

There was no doubting the evidence of their eyes, and the Germans agreed to take the men in a few days time. Right now, though, they were rather busy. It would have to wait.

Back in their cell, the prisoners convened a council of war. Bob, Stephen and 'Buzz' were happy to go off on their own when the time came, but Bert Crayden and James Reid could not speak French. The best time to go was just before the Americans arrived. They knew that the Milice planned to slip away to Dijon before the Americans got to Troyes (other Milice had already arrived from Rheims), and it was agreed that in the confusion of the Miliciens' departure they would slip over the wall. The problem was what to do after that.

Bob Desautels, a Catholic, had been allowed to celebrate mass at Troyes cathedral on Sunday 20 August and had been able to get an idea of the lie of the land. He also learned that in a nearby convent the Holy Cross nuns were sympathetic, so a message was duly passed via the prison cook to the Mother Superior telling her to be prepared to receive some male visitors in the near future. Stephen also gave the cook a postcard to send to England. It reached the Broad household on 8 February 1945!

With each passing day XII Corps, US Third Army, was forcing its way nearer and nearer to Troyes. On the morning of Tuesday 22 August, to the distant sound of the guns of XII Corps, the Milice were getting ready to leave. The prisoners were informed that they would all be leaving for Dijon at 1500 hours that very afternoon. A second council of war was held and it was decided to split up and escape singly. Stephen said that he would hide within the prison confines, in the old stables to the rear of the house, and wait for the Milice to clear off before attempting his escape.

Then the Milice held a roll-call. This was the moment to go, before they were counted and taken to Dijon. Stephen Broad slipped quickly and unnoticed into the prison stables. Although animals were no longer kept there (the prison had in happier times been a school), there was a pile of straw and rubbish in the loft and he buried himself in it. The other four, conveniently standing at the back of the assembled throng, seized their opportunity when the guards' attention was distracted and scaled the wall.

The four men split into pairs — Desautels with Summers, Crayden with Reid. The Anglo/Canadian pair headed for the cathedral and mingled with the few people kneeling at prayer. A priest refused to help. So Bob spoke to a woman. She agreed to help and the two fugitives were taken to the convent 'des Clarisses', 26 rue Mitantier, barely 200 yards from the cathedral.

The nuns of the Order of St Vincent and St Paul were vowed to silence, but no less a person than Monsignor Julien le Couédic, the Bishop of Troyes himself, was summoned. When the bishop was satisfied that the men were 'genuine', arrangements were made for them to stay at the convent.

Crayden and Reid had managed to find safety in a hostel run by a Mademoiselle Babé.

Meanwhile, in the straw-filled loft, Stephen Broad had been watching the Milice packing-up in the armoury underneath him:

'About four o'clock . . . someone came up the stairs . . . 'Est ce qu'il y a quelqu'un la?' he shouted as he reached the top. I tried to smother my breathing as he strode towards the straw . . . As he passed he gave it a hefty kick which finished with his boot about an inch from my face.'

Undiscovered, he stayed put until dusk. Cautiously he climbed over the wall and jumped into the garden of the Holy Cross convent. He met a nun coming out of a chapel. He explained who he was and asked to stay the night there. The Mother Superior was summoned, but she said that he would have to stay in the laundry which was in a house across the road: 'There they brought me a meal which I ate by the light of a candle.'

He spent the night on a pile of old blankets. After a breakfast of coffee and bread a priest took him to Mademoiselle Babé's hostel where he found Bert Crayden and 'Charlie' Reid. They were delighted to see him 'not because of myself, but because I could speak a little French for them'. Mlle Babé told them to talk quietly as the woman next door was pro-German.

Next day the Germans ordered the hostel to be evacuated by 1400 hours, as they were setting up a field gun nearby. A plan was hastily devised with the help of the priest to move the men through Troyes in broad daylight, with Stephen pushing a barrow:

'We were held up at the first main road we had to cross by a short German convoy . . . We reached the large square in front of the Cathedral. The priest traversed it diagonally. Bert and Charlie wanted to go one way and I, seeing that there was an "entrance forbidden, one way only" sign up, pushed the barrow the other way . . . we then pushed it to the other side of the square close to the cathedral . . .'

Soon they reached the house of Madame Thomassin, who gave them her two attic rooms. Then Stephen found 'a real water closet fitted with a comfortable and clean wooden seat! After six weeks in the country, this was indeed bliss!'

At lunchtime on the following day, 24 August, as they were about to devour a delicious omelette, a massive explosion rocked the house and shattered the windows; for the rest of the day the air was filled with the sound of explosions as the Germans blew the bridges into Troyes.

That evening they heard a different sound. American artillery shells! The duel of the heavy guns finally ceased around midnight. On the morning of 25 August, the tempo of the battle picked up. Shelling, mortaring and machine-gunning continued. By the afternoon, American armour was knocking on the town's gates.

Madame Thomassin decided to spend the night in the vault of a nearby chapel, but the RAF boys decided to stay put in the cellar. There was to be little sleep that night as the last Germans were driven from the city. By dawn American armoured columns were rumbling through the outskirts blazing away at the German guns. They got the range of the gun outside Madame Thomassin's house and a shell burst in the street. Rubble blocked the exit from the cellar. Stephen Broad 'tried the trap door but it would not move, so decided to leave it till the town was freed. We hadn't long to wait, for the firing suddenly ceased and bursts of machine gun fire [became] shorter and fewer.'

Passers-by finally heard their cries for help and pulled away the rubble. They rushed out into the road and found a great crowd of Troyens surging in the direction of the American tanks. Caught up in the euphoria they joined the throng and, quite by chance, spotted Bob Desautels and Summers.

The brief battle for Troyes was over. It cost the lives of 74 civilians, 17 FFI, 15 Americans and between 50 and 60 Germans. A further 572 Germans (including an SS General) were taken prisoner. The capture of Troyes by the American 4th Armored Division was called by General Patton 'a very magnificent feat of arms'*. The officer responsible, Colonel (later General) Bruce Clark,

'. . . brought his combat command up north of the town, where a gully or depression gave him cover, at about three thousand yards from the town. The edge of the town was full of German guns and Germans. Clark lined up one medium tank company, backed it with two armored infantry companies, all mounted, and charged with all guns blazing . . .'†

★ ★ ★

The five evaders — Broad, Desautels, Summers, Crayden and Reid — reported their presence to the American authorities, were given 200 cigarettes each and then hitched a lift in US Army trucks to Orléans. At 1210 hours on Monday 28 August an RAF Dakota took them back to RAF Lyneham where they landed at 1630. The following day, after interrogation, they were sent on leave whilst the RAF and RCAF decided what to do with them.

---

* War As I Knew It *(Houghton Mifflin, New York, 1947)*.

† *Ibid.*

11

A Pain in the Backside

Cannon shells ripped into the low-flying Lancaster as it approached Revigny in the early hours of 13 July 1944. In an instant PA999 was on fire and went into a steep dive. Only the bomb-aimer, F/S Dick Greenwood, 'baled out with difficulty'. He landed safely near the villages of Mussey and Véel, about six miles south-east of the target. In the mistaken belief that the blazing wreck of PA999 below was their target, other crews began to unload their bombs. Dick ran to the woods as fast as his legs could carry him, away from the lethal rain. He reached Trémont-sur-Saulx after 'about six hours not knowing where I was going. I had lost my escape box when I baled out.'

His escape kit contained a compass and a map, which would have told him that in all his six hours of wandering he had travelled barely three or four miles from the spot where he had landed. The unfortunate Greenwood had also lost his flying boots when baling out, an experience shared by many aircrew. Dick, barefoot, was understandably in some discomfort when he reached Trémont:

'I crossed the road and hid in some woods. Eventually a woodcutter came along and I spoke to him, explaining who I was. He told me to remain in the woods, and fetched me some food and a pair of shoes.'

The Frenchman could do no more than advise him to go to the village of Robert-Espagne a mile or so away and then on into the Forêt de Trois-Fontaines, where the maquis would take care of him. But so much did his feet hurt by the time he reached Robert-Espagne that he found he could walk no further. There he spotted a farm and, after watching for half an hour to make sure that the coast was clear, approached the farmer, who agreed that Dick could spend the night in his barn. For everyone's safety he would have to hide in the woods during the day, until such time as arrangements could be made for him to be properly looked after. On 16 July the farmer told him that in a few days an aircraft would be taking him back to England.

No aircraft, but a charcoal-burning van duly arrived. Dick found himself conveyed to No 1, Avenue de Paris, Revigny-sur-Ornain, home of the two brothers Louis and Jean Chenu, and in which nine men were already hiding. Driving the van was a Monsieur Colombo, its owner, accompanied by Louis Chenu. The aircraft, as ever, was but a dream.

Monsieur Colombo was reputedly a black-marketeer, and lived in the nearby village of Neuville-sur-Ornain*. When the Germans came he saw no reason why they should not part with as much of their money as he could arrange. He was so successful (it was wrongly thought that he must have been a collaborator) that the Germans allowed him to use his van for 'business' purposes, one of which was transporting evaders and maquisards!

One of the nine men being hidden by the Chenu brothers when Dick Greenwood arrived was another RAF evader, Sgt T. D. G. Teare[†]. Denys Teare had been in hiding ever since baling out into the Forêt des Koeurs, some 30 miles south of Verdun. He had entertained hopes of being passed 'down the line' to Spain and home, but, after many disappointments, his progress was minimal. On 10 February 1944 he was moved to Revigny and to the Chenus' house, where he had been ever since (see Chapter 7).

Denys Teare was there to welcome Dick Greenwood on his arrival:

'Through the slits between the wooden shutters I saw [Louis] enter the courtyard and beckon our new companion to follow him into the house. Louis burst into the room and shouted excitedly, "Denis, Voilà! L'Anglais!".'

It was an emotional moment, for Dick Greenwood was the first Englishman whom Denys had seen for ten months:

'I stepped forward and shook his hand, grinned and tried to say something, but I had spoken French for so many months that I could not summon up my English. I eventually stammered out "I too am an aviateur Anglais", and went on to tell him that I had been in France since the previous summer, then suddenly realised that I was speaking in French again. The boys standing round saw what was happening and they laughed and told me that I'd better start learning English.'

Denys would have plenty of opportunity to practise speaking English again when, over the next few days, another six evaders were brought to the Chenus' house. The first of these was F/S F. K. White, rear gunner of Lancaster PB234 (F/O D. Beharrie, 467 Squadron). Fred White had already done one trip on 18 July, to Caen, and was planning an evening off at the cinema in Lincoln with his mid-upper gunner:

'Before leaving the Base we were intercepted by someone from "A" Flight who said that a volunteer was required to replace a sick gunner in the crew of F/O Beharrie. As a rear-gunner I volunteered to take his place.'

Beharrie's usual rear gunner, Bob Rust, had been unable to fly that day, 18 July, due to sickness. Bob later joined F/S Ian Cowan's crew as Fred's replacement and completed a tour of ops with them. So Fred found himself doing two ops in one day, Caen and now Revigny.

* *Near Vassincourt airfield where No 1 (Fighter) Squadron, RAF, had been based in 1940.*

† *Shot down on the way back from Mannheim on the night of 5/6 September 1943.*

At around 0200 hours on 19 July, an Me110 night-fighter attacked PB234 a few seconds after the bombs had been released on the aiming-point. The starboard wing fuel tanks were set on fire and, efforts to extinguish them having failed, the pilot gave the order to bale out. A few moments later the tanks exploded and blew the wing off. The Lancaster turned over and plummeted earthwards, taking all seven of the crew with it. Fred White:

'No problems arose on the outward trip, but on arriving at the target I can remember that the ground was well lit and I held my turret steady for the bombing run. I heard the bomb-aimer to the point where he said "bombs gone" and then in a matter of possibly ten seconds nothing happened until someone said that we had been hit and that our port-inner engine had been hit and was on fire. The pilot called me asking if I had seen anything, to which I replied "No" and at this point resumed my searching. I can also remember to my concern that obviously German fighter pilots had been dropping night flares above us and that the sky was like daylight. Our aircraft was on fire and we were a sitting duck. I asked the mid-upper gunner if he had seen anything and he replied "No". The pilot was unable to stop the fire and at this stage I can't recall any inter-com conversation and on testing I found that I had no response on my inter-com and that it was dead.

'It seemed like an eternity but a lot appeared to be happening and everything seemed to be alight with flames passing my turret; and at this stage I quickly left the turret and had just crossed the rear spar when I noticed that my mate and mid-upper gunner (Frank Rogers) was hanging half way out of his turret. Frank and myself trained on the same courses. I made an attempt to help Frank but then found that I was forced down into the side of the fuselage as a result of the "g" factor, and I can only assume that we were diving, possibly in an attempt to douse the fire in our aircraft.

'I found it impossible to move and then there was a shocking explosion in my ammunition racks and I was blown from the plane.

'I would have jumped without any doubt, but I was unable to do so and the next thing I can remember is a smell of burning aircraft, losing my boots in mid air and a rush of cold air and a pain in my arse. I remember floating down and there were voices which I think belonged to my engineer and bomb-aimer.

'I must have hit the ground with a thud and apparently laid there unconscious. It was around 6.30 to 7 am that I remember being aroused by a Frenchman, and I will always remember the first two words that he spoke which were "allez" and "boches". I had sprained my ankle, had pains in my chest (which made it difficult to move) and a gash in my backside in addition to torn clothing which did not worry me. I hobbled across a road and tried to bury my parachute in the woods. I think that the Frenchman may have taken my chute, but I then started walking away from the area as quickly as possible . . . My aircraft hit the ground a couple of hundred yards from where I lay, was in two pieces and destroyed by fire.'

Fred staggered along for a couple of miles until he reached the farmhouse

of M and Mme Cohrot near Laheycourt, who cleaned him up, fed him
and made a bed for him in the garden shed. He was in hiding for three
days before word reached Louis Chenu that there was yet another RAF
survivor from a crashed aircraft in hiding a couple of miles away. Louis
at once telephoned Colombo who, ever-obliging, agreed to take Louis
with him in his van to collect the airman. Denys Teare again:

'I was in the workshop when I heard Mr Colombo's "charcoal-burning"
vehicle come to a standstill. Peeping across the courtyard through the
cobweb-covered windows hanging heavy with sawdust, I heard the
lock being turned, then the iron door opened.

'Louis stepped out into the courtyard, glanced round to ensure that
everything was in order, then beckoned to someone behind him to
follow. It was then that I had my first view of Flight-Sergt Fred White.'

Word was soon received that three of the crew of PB234 had been killed
in the crash (they are buried at Brabant-le-Roi, a mile or so north of
Revigny) and that a fourth had been badly wounded and captured by
the Germans.

This was Sgt Eric Brownhall who had broken his collar-bone on landing
and suffered other minor cuts and bruises. He had managed to reach a
nearby farm and a doctor was summoned, but, from his examination of
the airman, he could not be sure that Eric was not suffering from internal
injuries, and recommended that he be handed over to the Germans for
proper attention. He was taken to the hospital in Revigny where he
received a visit from a Luftwaffe pilot who claimed that he had shot
down their Lancaster. The German apologised for the inconvenience
and produced chocolate and cigarettes, and added, cryptically: 'Of course,
we knew you were coming!'

At Dulag Luft Eric got the shock of his life. He is to this day convinced
that the German who interrogated him there was the same man who,
six months earlier at No 17 OTU Silverstone, had lectured him on escape
and evasion! He was transferred to the hospital attached to Stalag 9c,
Mulhausen, and then on to Stalag Luft 7, Bankau.

The other two survivors were Sgt William George Johnson and F/S
John Trevor Brown, flight engineer and bomb-aimer respectively. John
Brown:

'The pilot gave the order to "jump out" so we clipped our parachutes
on to our chests and just as I went to release the catch on the escape
hatch cover the starboard wing fell away and the Lancaster "flipped
over" and went screaming down to earth in a spin still in flames — a
fantastic sight I was told by a watching Frenchman some time later.
Once a Lancaster gets into a spin there is no way of escaping from it
because the gravitational forces hold you in a vice-like grip; so we
knew that very shortly we would all be killed. The next thing I
remember is hearing whistling noises. I opened my eyes and saw the
stars in the sky above. I quickly realised that the Lancaster had blown
up and that I was flying through the air. My parachute was still clipped
on to my chest, so I pulled the release handle (rip cord). The canopy
billowed out and my rate of descent was abruptly reduced. It was a

wonderful change of experience, from being in a very noisy four-engined blazing bomber diving down to your death one moment and then to find yourself dangling on the end of a parachute in the cool, quiet mid-summer night air the next moment.

'My next worry then was where am I going to land? I always had a fear that if I had to use my parachute I would probably land down a factory chimney stack with a very large furnace at the bottom, or on a church spire! I looked down but, as it was about 2 am, I could not see the ground, just a grey haze. My parachute had hardly opened before I hit the ground quite hard, breaking a bone in my left foot. I released my parachute and sat up to find I had landed in a field [on the farm of Bellefontaine, owned by Monsieur Paul Thomas] expecting to be surrounded by a large number of Germans. But all was quiet, so I gathered up my 'chute and hid it in a hedgerow surrounding the field. As I did so I could see that there was a cart track on the other side so I climbed over the hedge and, looking to my right, I could see the track was blocked by the large tail-plane of our Lancaster. So I began to walk in the opposite direction.

'I had not gone far when I came to a T-junction and there I met a Frenchman pushing a bicycle. As I had been told in my RAF lectures to try and contact a priest if you land in France by parachute, I said to the Frenchman, Monsieur Georges Mandet, that I was an aviator with the RAF and asked if he could direct me to the nearest church; but I said it in English as I could not speak French, so I was not sure if he understood me. Just then I heard footsteps coming down the track and turning I saw that it was my flight-engineer, Bill Johnson. He had been thrown out of the Lancaster as I had.

'M Mandet made signs for us to follow him, and soon we came upon his cottage and he invited us to go inside. When I got inside the living room I could see about six wooden boxes placed around the room and, to my surprise, each one had a child in it, aged from about a few months to five or six years old. So I said to Bill Johnson "We must not stay here because if the Germans find us they might kill all of this family."

'Madame Mandet was not very pleased when we refused the food she offered us, but we just wanted to be directed to the nearest church. M Mandet told us how to get to the church in the village of Laheycourt and also gave us a map of the area. We set off up the road towards a T-junction where we had to turn right. Just before we got to the junction we heard a motor-cycle approaching from the left. We hid in the ditch at the roadside and, peeping through the long grass, we saw the motor-cycle stop at the junction. The German had a good look round, then rode off in the direction from whence we had come. We started off again and eventually found the church. It was a large church and very dark inside. I walked into a row of chairs which made a dreadful noise scraping along the floor and woke up hundreds of birds which were roosting in the roof. They flew down, screeching all around us, which was quite frightening, as being dark we could not see them. So we decided to sit on the floor just inside the door and await the arrival of the dawn and, hopefully, the priest.

'The dawn arrived but, unfortunately, the priest did not. During the afternoon we began making plans to walk down through France, Spain and on to Gibraltar, but about 5 pm the door of the church opened and an elderly lady came in to pray. Whilst she was praying we decided to ask her if she could contact the priest for us; when she had finished we approached her but she was not surprised to see us — it was almost as if she was expecting us. We asked her about the priest, using our hands and our RAF escape card (French/English), and she made signs for us to remain in the church and off she went.

'About 20 minutes later a very pretty girl, aged about 17 or 18 years, came into the church with her boyfriend of a similar age and she could speak very good English. We told her we were RAF aviators and would like to speak with the priest. She said he would arrive at 7.30 pm for choir practice and she would arrange for us to see him afterwards. Her name was Antoinette. She had brought a bottle of champagne with her which she gave to us, and her boyfriend gave us some chocolate. We thanked them and off they went.

'We had found a table and chairs in a store room to one side of the altar, so we went in there and drank the champagne and ate the chocolate and felt quite merry as the choir started their singing. When the practice had finished, the priest, Antoinette and her boyfriend came into the room and, with the help of Antoinette, we asked the priest, Roger Guillemin, if he could help us contact the Resistance. Of course the priest would not commit himself because we might have been Germans trying to trap him. He said we could stay the night with him in his house at the far end of the village; so the four of us and the priest walked back through the village. Bill and I were still in our RAF uniforms. The priest's housekeeper prepared a meal for us, but we were disturbed by a knock on the front-door.

'It was one of the villagers enquiring about the arrangements for celebrating the liberation of the village. Apparently several villagers had recognised our RAF uniforms as we walked through the village, thought they had been liberated and started hanging the flags out! The flags were hastily removed and we finished our meal and went to bed. The next day, 20 July 1944, a drummer appeared in the village shouting out the news. The main item was to warn the villagers that there were some RAF aviators on the run in the area, and if anyone was caught helping them they would be shot. The next day a car arrived and two men came into the house and asked us questions.'

The two men were the ubiquitous Colombo in his 'charcoal-burning' van and Louis Chenu. A rumour had been circulating in Laheycourt 'that a certain carpenter in Revigny was known to help Allied airmen return to England', and in due course the priest's message had been passed to Louis Chenu, who was indeed the carpenter (he and his brother Jean ran a small furniture-making business on the premises). Louis contacted Colombo, and off they went, on 21 July, to pick up two more 'strays'.

The Chenus' house now held six Frenchmen — including four deserters from the hated Vichy Garde Mobile de Réserve (GMR), who brought with them their rifles and as much ammunition as they could carry — two Russian prisoners-of-war who had escaped from a working party and the five RAF evaders — Denys Teare, Dick Greenwood, Fred White, John Brown and Bill Johnson.

It was against this background of fear, hatred and hostility that life continued for the occupants of No 1, Avenue de Paris, Revigny. They managed to keep their presence hidden from the Germans even when units of an armoured division rolled into town one night on their way to Normandy. A troop-carrier parked in their courtyard and stayed there all day, camouflaged against the prying eyes of Allied fighters, before eventually moving off that night.

Apart from the obvious difficulty of remaining undiscovered by the Germans, several of whom were billeted next door, the real problem was how to feed all the extra mouths. Only the two Chenu brothers were drawing official rations, which were barely adequate to feed two men, let alone 13. The daily ration for all was usually 'just one slice of bread, a couple of boiled potatoes and lots of cupfuls of water to fill us up'. They managed to augment this poor diet from time to time by stealing food and vegetables and fruit when ripe. Denys Teare:

'We had acquired some small cheeses which were allocated in little pieces to each man with some meals. The last to be eaten were absolutely heaving with maggots, so I used to mash my small ration up with my potatoes before eating it.'

They lived mainly on stolen potatoes and bread. But they had a rare treat one day when a horse, pulling a cart driven by a German, collapsed and died outside their house. No sooner had the driver gone to report the incident than the French rushed out with knives and meat cleavers and in no time at all had removed the entire mortal remains of the unfortunate beast. When the Germans returned to the scene minutes later, only the cart and the horse's trappings remained!

Louis Chenu chopped off the horse's head, which he lugged back unseen by his 'lodgers'. He asked Denys to come into the kitchen:

'No one can realise the size of a horse's head until confronted face to face with a specimen on a table. It would have to be divided into four pieces and each cooked separately in a bucket . . . The task of dividing the skull into four quarters was far easier said than done, but after wrestling with the bony, blood-stained object for half an hour and bringing into use two wood chisels, an axe and a hacksaw, I finally succeeded. The brain was removed and then fried, the rest, boiled with potatoes, making an excellent soup. The following day chunks of bony skull were boiled again, and once more we enjoyed a savoury soup, but when boiled for a third time someone said the soup was 99 per cent potato water, and hoped that another horse would die soon, so we decided to change the menu back once more to mashed potatoes, a slice of bread and a glass of cold water.'

Denys himself was beginning to suffer from malnutrition; the other recently arrived RAF evaders had not had time to feel the effects of such a poor diet although, by the time the Americans had 'liberated' Fred White after six weeks' evading, he too was in a bad way.

12

The Tears Rolled Down

Leaving the Chenus' hungry guests for the time being, we go back to the night of the first raid, 12/13 July 1944, and pick up LL896 again as it flew deeper into France. It was now that it was imperative for those of the crew not otherwise engaged to keep a good lookout — John 'Nicky' Nicholson (flight engineer) was busy shovelling 'window' out of the Lancaster and Ted Julier (navigator) was curtained off in his 'office'. But Harry Kidd (wireless operator) had his head in the astrodome, and the two gunners' eyes were out on stalks — Bill Watkins (rear) and Ken Hoyle (mid-upper). And Charlie Kroschel (bomb-aimer), too, was looking for the turning point, a lake.

Red Banville (pilot):

'Charlie spotted the lake OK and we turned on to the final course about three minutes ahead of time. Ted advised me to cut speed down as much as possible to avoid arriving too early, so I reduced my throttle settings to set the airspeed at 135 — which at that altitude and a full load was just above stalling speed. Another 30 miles to go, and I could feel a wave of excitement welling up inside.

'The Met boys certainly had the right dope, because about 7 or 8 minutes before the target we ran into cloud — not too thick, no rain in it — but it meant going down in a hurry as only about three minutes remained until ETA. I pulled the throttle back and shoved the nose down. We dropped at 3,000 feet per minute, which would give us an altitude of 2,000 feet in two minutes. Here's hoping we don't have to go down that far!

'Charlie was busy now doing his final check on his bomb-sight and his bombing panel. He called back to me that everything was all set to bomb — all we had to do was await word from the M.C.

'Blast the M.C. Where in hell was he? I'd switched the R/T on some ten minutes ago, but all I could pick up was a terrific din of static. It was so bad that I couldn't leave the radio on, because the noise completely drowned out the voices of my crew members. The only thing I could do was manipulate the key back and forth trying to keep in touch with the crew, and then a few seconds on the R/T — just in case there was a message coming from the Master Bomber.

'Not a word came over, and we were still dropping down. The altimeter showed 2,700 feet — would we never break cloud? — would we never hear from the Master Bomber? — had he got lost? — was he shot down? — what in hell will we do?

'Aloud to the navigator: "I'm going down to 2,000 feet and no further. If we don't break cloud, I'll circle to port and await instructions."

'"Roger," answered Ted. And the altimeter read 2,200 feet and — at last! — we broke clear. The odd light could be seen down below — too close for comfort, too — the black-out was never very well kept in France. There was a Lanc a couple of hundred yards to starboard and he was in a bank to port. I looked at my clock — a minute past ETA.

'I opened the throttles and told the crew to stand by — we were going to circle too — but I wanted a good margin of speed as I intended to hug the base of the cloud and zoom up into safety in case of trouble.

'"Will that M.C. never show up?" I kept thinking, and even if he did we could never make out a word he might say owing to the deafening static. We just kept circling. Lancs were all over the place, and then about 0150 what we had feared materialised.

'White fighter flares were coming down by the dozen, and the whole area was beginning to light up with a ghastly light — St Dizier's Ju88s! The Jerry night-fighters were in amongst us — God, where is that Master Bomber? I tried the radio again, and the static was still deafening. That was the last straw. I switched the damn thing off.

'I called out to Charlie: "If we don't see a Bombing Flare in 5 minutes (the time was now 0155) we're packing up for home."

'"Roger," said Charlie, and then "Look. Off to port, Red — a red marker. Turn on to it." Sure enough there was a marker, and I commenced my turn.

'"Running up on target," I called, as soon as I set the new course.

'"Running up," Charlie repeated.

'Silence now, for what seemed like an hour, as we ran up on the marker, and we were running 185 indicated speed. We seemed to be all alone — no S/Ls, no flak, not another a/c seen for two to three minutes.

'Then "Bomb doors open" from Charlie.

'"Bomb doors open," I repeated, selecting the door lever.'

Then at long last, after the customary sequence of 'Left — left — steady' from the bomb-aimer, came 'Bombs gone'. R-Robert lurched with the loss of the 9,000 lb bomb load, still on course while the camera recorded the scene below as the flash went off.

'Course for home, 185 degrees,' Ted called, and Banville climbed through 10/10ths cloud to 6,500 feet, breaking clear with flak ahead.

'Keep your eye on that stream of fire,' Banville called to Kroschel, 'and steer me around it if you can. He may just be hosepiping — hoping to hit someone.'

'Enemy fighter on starboard quarter' — Watkins, rear gunner.

152 MASSACRE OVER THE MARNE

'Keep me posted, Bill, if you see him again' — Banville.
The flak was getting closer.
'90 degrees around to starboard' — Kroschel.
'New course 275 degrees till we clear this gun' — Banville.
'Roger' — Julier.
'Levelling at 8,000 feet, Ted. Air speed 175 mph.'
Red Banville:

'I never heard Ted's answer, and never saw him again. I shall never forget the next few minutes . . . One minute we were flying along, everything under control, and then WHAM — WHAM — two terrific blasts — seemed right beside me, and two blinding flashes of fire, and everything went mad inside me. Fire broke out everywhere — it seemed to be dropping in great blobs from the roof. I remember thinking: "Phosphorus shells!"'

Then over the intercom came an anguished cry from Ken Hoyle:
'Red! Red!'
There was no point in staying in the aircraft, and Red gave the order to leave:
'Get out! Everybody bale out. We're going down.'
Only Ken Hoyle responded, once again calling his name. It was time for Red to go:

'I heaved myself out of the seat — the kite was lurching badly to starboard — I caught a glimpse of both starboard engines and the wing — it seemed to be on fire from leading to trailing edges, and clean to the wingtip.'

But as he tried to heave his legs over the throttle boxes, his harness caught in the levers; somehow he worked himself loose and stepped down into the bomb-aimer's space. He looked back for the navigator. The compartment was a mass of flames. There was no sign of Ted Julier.
Then Red's left foot jammed. The 'window' that was ready for use on the return journey was now on fire, as was the de-icing fluid, which was pouring past him and down the steps:

'I was getting weaker all the time — guess the flames were consuming all the oxygen — little enough at that altitude — we must be dropping at a fearful rate now. If I don't hurry up it'll be too late. At last I felt my foot slide out of my tightly laced flying boot — the special escape boots I had gone to so much trouble to procure.'

Red lunged for the escape hatch, only to find that he was caught somewhere else and could not move any further. He twisted round and saw John Nicholson down over the hatch — it was open:

'And there was Charlie sitting forward facing me — his face seemed white as chalk — I was sure he was dead — there was no expression on his face, yet his eyes seemed very large and unblinking.

'I struggled to free myself, but very weakly.

'"This is it," I said to myself. "I just can't make it."'

His thoughts turned to his wife and parents, and he resigned himself to his death. Suddenly he came to his senses — he was still wearing his helmet and the wire from the earphones to the intercom was still plugged in! He whipped it off and dived for the hatch:

'God, now what's that? It's Nicky. He's jammed in the hatch, the long-legged bugger. I hit him with my head and he's through ahead of me. So am I. The noise, the flames all gone. The rip cord. I grope for my right breast and yank the ring. Will it open? A terrific jerk nearly split me in two, but I'm safe, free. My life is saved.'

Charlie Kroschel was not dead as Red had imagined. He was very much alive and left after the other two.

Ken Hoyle had heard Bill Watkins telling Red that he had sighted an enemy fighter but, because he was searching the area above the Lancaster, he, Ken, had not seen it:

'I continued to sweep that area while Charlie was guiding us around the flak up forward when, suddenly, out of the corner of my eye I saw and heard shells pass right through the rear turret. I am sure Bill never saw or felt what hit him. There were several other explosions, one or two just behind me, and they must be the ones that got Harry's equipment, and most likely Harry and Ted as well. At once flames were shooting into my turret from the fuselage, and I called out to Red, but got no answer.

'By this time my clothes were beginning to catch fire, and I could see that the whole aircraft seemed to be on fire from one end to the other, and the starboard wing and engines also. I figured out that I had better get out or I would be a dead duck!'

It was never easy getting in or out of the mid-upper turret at the best of times. As he tried amidst the flames, Ken's clothing caught on every jagged point:

'I finally got down to the floor of the fuselage after what seemed an age. My flying suit had caught fire while I backed down out of the turret, and I used my big flying gauntlets to extinguish the flames. With the light from the fire, I could see right down to the rear of the aircraft, and where Bill's turret used to be was just a mass of wreckage. As I made my way further aft I could see that there was no hope for Bill, or of getting him out of that maze of twisted steel. Besides, the turret was a mass of flames and smoke, evidently caused by the oil in the hydraulic lines. It's a wonder the lead-in racks of ammunition didn't start popping, but I guess it takes a tremendous amount of heat to start them going off.

'I really expected the ammo would start going off, and I figured I had better get out as quickly as possible. I took my parachute out of its rack on my way aft, but to snap it on I had to remove my mitts. I suppose that that is when my hands got burned. The chute seemed to be okay, but even if it hadn't been I think I would have jumped without it.

'I mounted the two steps to the rear door, and jettisoned it. Without thinking of our training in abandoning ship, I simply jumped out. Imagine my surprise when I found myself flung back in again and ended up in a heap by the port wall. On my next attempt, I attacked this business of getting out the way we were taught. I climbed the steps once more, with a firm grasp with each hand on the side of the doorway and, putting my feet and legs out over the bottom of the doorway, gave a supreme pull. Presto! I was out and, fumbling for the rip cord, pulled the cord. The chute opened with a terrific jerk, but I was okay.'

Red, meanwhile, landed gently enough and was gathering up his parachute when he 'saw a tongue of flame reach heavenwards and a few seconds later a terrific crash'. The tongue of flame subsided, but he could still hear the fire crackling in the distance, the end of R-Robert. Then he became fully aware of the awful pain from his burnt hands, at which he was too scared to look, and in which there was scarcely any strength left. But he managed to stuff his paraphernalia into a bush, and began walking away from the crashed aircraft:

'I had not gone 25 yards when I came to a wire fence with a small woodcutter's road on the other side. I then realised how lucky I was. I was really in a dense wood, and the clearing I had landed in couldn't have been more than 25 or 30 yards across!'

Climbing over the fence he set off along the path, when suddenly he heard someone call out. A tall, slim figure loomed out of the darkness, and to his intense relief he recognised John Nicholson. Asking him how he felt, John was unable to answer. Red:

'I could see that his face had been burned, and when he held out his hands I could see that they had been burned too.

'Without a word, we continued walking — we knew not in what direction, but away from the aircraft.

'It was only then that I realised that I only had one boot — I then looked at Nicky and saw that he had no boots on at all.

'"What happened to your boots, Nicky?" I asked.

'"Boots?" he answered, looking down at his feet in astonishment. "They must have come off when my chute opened."'

Red lit two cigarettes and handed one to Nicky. As they smoked they realised how incredibly thirsty they were:

'Not even the morning after a very bad night before could compare with my present thirst . . . Nicky was feeling the same way. Our first objective was a drink of water, muddy or otherwise.'

The pain from their burns became unbearable, and they agreed to find a doctor as soon as possible. After a further 40 minutes of agony they found a pond, and Nicky filled the drinking bag from his escape kit. What a drink! Looking round they made out the dim outlines of houses, barns and a church not too far away. The village, Morley as they discovered later, was deathly quiet; Red looked at his watch — 0330 hours!

Still in intense pain, they wandered through the village, but could find no one to help them. Panic was setting in when they decided to bang on the door of what they took to be the curé's house. Red:

'What a racket. I'm sure Der Führer must have heard it on der Wilhelmstrasse!'

But he hadn't. Someone else had, though, and started shouting. But that was all. The two desperate men continued walking round the village, trying all the doors until at last they found one that was open. Red:

'Without further thought, we pushed it open and stepped inside — very gingerly — because it was inky black inside. I flicked my lighter on and saw we were in a stable with a couple of sleepy horses eyeing us.'

They found a second door, unlocked, and in they went, into a kitchen. But they had been heard, and a frightened female voice challenged them. Red replied that they were English, shot down a couple of hours ago. More voices and soon a woman, Madame Marie Guillemin, appeared holding a lamp, followed by her parents, Monsieur and Madame Albert Renard:

'It was the first time I had seen my hands under a light — they were just a mass of huge blisters, right from the wrists up to my finger tips. Nick's wrists were OK, but the fingers on his left hand were burned horribly.'

The French did what they could for the men. The pain subsided.

With the dawn not long in breaking, it was decided to take the two airmen to a farm a couple of miles away, dressed as forestry workers, but Nick had no footwear and Red just one boot. Madame Guillemin could find only one pair of slippers, which were given to Nicky. Red had to make do with his one flying boot.

In their sorry condition the walk took nearly two hours of painful effort, not helped by Nick's slippers continually coming off in the mud. It was about 0700 hours when, breasting a hill, they saw farm buildings ahead — and a large, fierce dog that barked loudly. A man came to the door and shouted at the beast which, to the airmen's relief, stopped growling. The tired men were invited in and given a breakfast of two fried eggs and salt pork. One of the family was then sent to fetch a doctor, and the two replete evaders were put to bed. Red:

'By now it was about 8.30 and although dog tired neither of us could sleep. We lay there without talking, but I'm sure both Nick and myself were thinking of our terrifying experience, and of the shock to our folks at home when they heard we were missing.

'Try as I might, every time I closed my eyes I was back in that burning aircraft . . . over and over again the whole panorama passed before me. Soon I commenced to sob and shake and the tears rolled down my face and on to the pillow; but I just couldn't stop.'

But they did get some sleep and when they had woken up the doctor was ready to start treating them. This was their first sight of Jean de Sartigues, also on the run from the Germans. Although not yet qualified, he knew how to treat burns. He cut away the burnt skin and pierced the blisters, and in no time both men were feeling much better.

Again it was agreed to move the airmen to another farm, when it was dark. Jean would meet them there and take them to his hideout in the woods. Just then the dog started barking, and a stranger was brought in. Red:

'I gathered from bits of conversation that another RAF type was in the vicinity and needed medical attention, and when I told Nick what they were talking about we both commenced to speculate on who it might be.'

The stranger was unable to describe the man, whose face was burnt as black as charcoal, and whose lips were so charred that he was unable to utter a word. But he was being cared for in a house in Morley. Red asked what the man was wearing, and the reply that they were dreading was given — a flying suit. Red and Nicky guessed that the man was their mid-upper, Ken Hoyle. At that, Jean left to go and attend to the wounded man in Morley, taking with him a written message for Ken, if he indeed it was.

At around midnight they were on the move again, a pair of shoes having been found for each of the two airmen. Red left his one flying boot as a souvenir.

It took them an hour or so to get to the next farm. Then they heard the creak of wagon wheels in the farmyard. Blowing out the candle, the farmer opened the door and two men pushed a two-wheeled cart into the room. On it there was a man, curled up. Jean de Sartigues followed, together with his elder brother. When the candle had been relit, the man was lifted off the cart and moved gently into the light. Red: 'Neither Nicky nor I recognised who it was, his face was so black and disfigured.'

Red asked the man what his squadron was. There was no answer, but the man unbuttoned his jacket and produced his 'passport' photograph, which he gave to Red:

'A surge of pity swept through me — this was Ken Hoyle, and look what the dirty Hun had done to him. How Nicky and I cursed the Germans at that moment. Poor Ken. He couldn't stand unassisted, he was so weak.'

Despite Ken's condition, the three airmen had to be moved there and then to Jean's hideout. A carbide lamp was lit, and the procession set off into the night, through the woods and along narrow, slippery and steep paths. It was agony for Ken on the cart, but he made no sound. After an hour and a half they came to a halt; Red thought that it was journey's end:

'We seemed to be on the edge of a fairly steep hill. Two ropes were taken out of the wagon and made fast to each wheel; and the descent began. One man held each rope and the rest of the party, excluding Nick and myself, eased the wagon downwards. We followed as best we could, slipping and sliding, half the time on our rear ends.'

From the little available light Red could see that they were in a disused quarry. Ken was lifted off the cart and carried into a well-hidden cave in the side. This was Jean de Sartigues's bolt-hole. It was not big as caves go, measuring some seven feet by seven and about ten feet to the roof, but it had the merit, apart from its inaccessibility and remoteness, of being dry. Refuge and hospital, it was to provide the shelter that the airmen so badly needed:

'There wasn't a stick of furniture in the place — simply odd bits of the doctor's kit suspended from wooden pegs driven into crevices in the walls, and his bed roll and haversack in one corner.'

It was on to Jean's bedding that Ken was gently laid. Red:

'With great difficulty the doctor and his elder brother undressed Ken down to his underwear and somehow managed to get him into the sleeping bag. During all this Ken never said a word, and I knew he must be very sick indeed.'

The Frenchmen thereupon left to fetch bedding for the others and, if possible, a proper bed for Ken. Red heard them as they returned some hours later:

'They brought in a cot first of all, and lifted Ken up into the bed and covered him with some blankets that they had also brought along. The poor lad said not a word, nor showed any feeling whatsoever. I could see by the look on the young doctor's face that he was really worried about Ken's condition.'

In the afternoon, Jean checked Ken again, and it was clear from the thermometer reading that he was running a high temperature. Jean was worried and told his brother to fetch their father, Raoul, who was a fully qualified doctor. Jean, in the meantime, would do what he could for them. He began with Nicky. The whole of his left hand was a red mass, dead skin hanging down everywhere. Jean cut off the loose skin and poured alcohol on to the raw flesh. From the expression on Nicky's face there was no doubting how much it hurt. Red was next:

'I felt the liquid on my wrist and no pain for a second, but then it felt as if a red-hot poker had been laid on it. With a howl I jerked my hand away, and my senses reeled so that I thought I was going to faint.'

Jean managed to complete Red's treatment, but decided not to do anything with Ken until his father had arrived. In the evening Jean cooked them a superb meal, and around midnight they tried to sleep. Lying on the hard ground, even in the sleeping bags with which they were all now supplied, sleep did not come easily. In the morning, to their delight, they found that Ken was able to speak, albeit with difficulty, and was as hungry as a bear. Red asked him whether he thought that Bill Watkins had managed to bale out:

'His face told me the answer, and my heart fell. I could also see that the question brought a lump into Ken's throat, because he and Bill had been very close, having been together practically from the day they both joined up.'

Then Ken told them how he escaped. After he had managed to jump from the blazing rear door, he landed safely in a field, minus his flying boots. In the distance he could see the burning remains of R-Robert. His hands were hurting badly and it was all he could do to remove his parachute harness. He did not have the strength to hide it, so he just walked away:

'How long I walked I don't really know. I seemed to be going around in circles, and was beginning to feel sort of woozy. I rested a lot as my feet were getting pretty sore from walking in the wet grass and undergrowth without boots.'

It was beginning to get light when he reached Morley after some three hours. He was ready to drop. Even in his semi-conscious state he was aware that the few people who were already out and about were avoiding him:

'The next thing I seem to remember I was being helped into a house on the outskirts of town by a woman and her daughter. They must have undressed me, and dressed my burns, because the next thing I remember I was nice and cosy in a warm bed, and this woman was feeding me some hot soup out of a bowl.'

He may have been guided to Morley by a light hung out at the back of their house by the Pionnier family, who had been woken up by R-Robert passing overhead before it crashed into the woods on the far hillside. They had hung a lantern out in the hope that any survivors would be guided to them. Some while later there was a knock on the door and there before them was the sorry figure of Ken Hoyle. An interpreter had to be found. Two doors away lived Madame Geneste whose daughter was able to speak some English; so he was moved to their house, and from there to the farm where he met Red and Nicky again.

13

Full House at Revigny

It was on or about 18 July that Red, John and Ken received news of their crew. The mutilated bodies of two of them had been discovered in the broken remains of the Lancaster; the third was found about half a mile away. Had he tried to use his parachute? The informant did not know. They were told that Charlie Kroschel was on his way to Switzerland on foot. Although they had feared the worst about the three who died, finally being sure made them all feel very low. Red:

> 'I had met Ted's wife and little nipper (as he called his youngster) on our last leave in London. And being captain of the aircraft, naturally I felt at the time that I should have paid more attention to Bill's initial warning of the enemy fighter on our tail than I did.'

It was no secret that there were three RAF airmen hiding in the cave, and there was no shortage of visitors, but they were in for another surprise soon afterwards, when one particular visitor was brought to the cave. Red again:

> 'He arrived along with the Game Warden. As he came towards us, he looked like any other Frenchman, but when he got real close I recognised Stephen Broad, the bomb-aimer from McLaren's crew. We were naturally all very pleased to see him, but shocked to hear that only he and the engineer survived . . . The navigator also must have got out too, but unfortunately his parachute became entangled in a tree. He was found some time later by a local inhabitant, strangled in the shroud lines. What a terrible end, because heaven knows how long he had hung there before he died.'

For two weeks they remained in the hide-out in the Forêt de Morley. Surprisingly, Red, the least burned of the three, was the slowest to heal. But they were getting better, thanks to the treatment from Jean and his father, Raoul.

It was a real source of worry to the three evaders that so many people were visiting the cave, and one night they discussed the problem with Jean. A few days later they had three visitors at the hide-out, two total strangers and one — a local café owner — whom they had already met. One of the strangers was the leader of the local maquis, or so he claimed. Banville:

> 'I could see by the look on Jean's face that he didn't altogether trust this latest visitor, who was rather plump and wore glasses. Accordingly, that was his name to us, "Glasses", from that time on, until we learned his real name. The other chap turned out to be a Jugoslav . . . He was a little chap, and I wasn't struck by him very much.'

They would later discover that 'Glasses' was otherwise Monsieur J. J. Luccioni, a well-to-do wine merchant. He said that he had a safe place for them to hide in if they wanted, but first he had to ask them some searching questions to establish that they were not Gestapo agents in RAF uniform. After Jean and 'Glasses' had jabbered away for a while, the latter declared that he was satisfied that the airmen were genuine, and arranged to collect them around noon the following day.

True to his word, 'Glasses' appeared as promised, and with him were two other men, the Jugoslav again and a stranger. Red recalled that the stranger:

> '. . . was a big guy who was called Colombo. This guy turned out to be a Black Market dealer in meat. Nice company we were getting mixed up in. Each of our two visitors wore two suits of clothes, one over the other. The under suits were for us — just like in the movies! Only when it's real it isn't such good entertainment.
>
> 'We took off our uniforms with regret, and made a present of them all to Jean. He was tickled to death about that.'

A rendezvous was arranged for later that afternoon and, after a final meal with Jean, he led them off through the forest for the last time. After an hour's walk they found 'Glasses' and the other two men, with two vehicles — a Citröen car and Colombo's small charcoal-burning delivery truck. Bidding Jean a sad farewell, the three airmen climbed into the back of the truck, where they were hidden by bags of charcoal piled around them. Red:

> 'There wasn't much room for us what with the charcoal and a spare tyre laying on the floor, but we made ourselves as comfortable as possible. We heard the Serb [sic] and Colombo climb into the front seat and, with a lot of pumping and a good deal of coughing and choking, the engine was started.
>
> 'The truck bumped and rolled out of the woods, and on to the highway . . . We must have driven for about 45 minutes, when Colombo said we were nearing the end of our trip.'

The van pulled up at Luccioni's warehouse next to his house. They were soon tucking into a feast prepared by his wife. Sharing the meal were the Luccionis' daughter and son-in-law, and a woman from the village (Neuville-sur-Ornain). Red:

'I didn't like it one bit, but what could one do about it? They were very good to us. The lady from the village presented us with a carton of Gold Flake cigarettes, and when I expressed astonishment at her having such a brand she explained. It seems that in 1939 and 1940 there had been a British Air Force Squadron* situated nearby, and some of the boys used to stay with her when on leave. Someone had given her the cigarettes a few days before the Squadron was evacuated to England, during the fateful month of June 1940. At that time she vowed that she would keep them, and return them to the first Allied soldier she met when France was liberated. We were deeply touched by this gesture . . .'

All good things must come to an end, and Luccioni gave them the word that they must be on their way; they set off in the same formation as before. There was a small sliding panel in the truck through which Red could see the road running parallel to a railway, over which they shortly crossed:

'Then my eyes nearly popped out of my head. There on a siding were two huge American locomotives, but badly damaged and burned. On enquiry I found that they had been shot up by our fellow airmen.'

Colombo pointed out a large hole in the side of a hill: 'That's where one of your bombs exploded the night you raided Revigny. There are craters all over this area.'

Red guessed that they were near Revigny, and then Colombo told them that that was where they were going to live for a while. Arrangements had already been made with the Chenu brothers that the three men could be brought to their house in Revigny. It was now Saturday 29 July and Banville, Hoyle and Nicholson were the last airmen evaders to arrive there.

★   ★   ★

It is incredible that, with so many hidden in the Chenus' house, the Germans failed to get a hint of what was going on — the Chenu brothers deserved whatever luck went their way. As Denys Teare said:

'We all knew that if any of us was captured alive we would be tortured until we revealed our headquarters, and none of us was foolish enough to say that we would not give way once we were subject to intense pain.'

As the days passed in the confined quarters, tempers became frayed and arguments flared up at the slightest provocation. It was obvious that as the US Third Army fought its way eastwards it was only a matter of time before Revigny was liberated; but even at that late stage the evaders were getting careless:

'Many precautions were being relaxed, conversations were no longer being carried out in a low voice; some of the boys even wandered

* No 1 (Fighter) RAF.

about the house whistling, ignoring the possibility of being overheard by passing pedestrians on the main road which ran along the side of the courtyard wall.'

It was time to clear off. Red Banville summed it up:

'I guess it was the monotony of the life that was making us all jittery. After all, eating half a calf twice per day, and with nothing but water to drink, sleeping in lice-ridden bedclothes and with not even a cake of soap with which to wash ourselves, was enough to put anyone in low spirits.'

The first to leave were Denys Teare and Fred White, after Denys had had a row with Louis Chenu. Red, with his French, was able to mediate:

'I got along with the Frenchmen all right, perhaps because I could talk to them, but there was no love lost between the other English lads and the Frenchmen. I could see trouble brewing, and one day it really flared up. Denys was the one who was most deeply involved. Louis, being the head of the house, and his own gang really started it all. He felt that he should have absolute authority over everyone. Not wishing for any trouble at that time, I didn't argue. But not so Denys and the Australian.
   '"You don't catch me taking orders from any Frenchman," said Denys in French.
   'Naturally, that was enough to get Louis's back up plenty, and naturally all his henchmen were behind him. It was only by my intervention that a real battle was avoided. I took Louis downstairs and made him realise that he couldn't possibly make the English chaps bow to his authority. I also stated that it was high time that the population of the house was reduced.'

Denys wanted them all to go to a house by a lake hidden away in a wood, much safer than in Revigny itself. Louis would not make up his mind, so Denys and Fred set off one day in the middle of August, but with Louis's 'Bonne chance, Denis, mon cher ami' to send them on their way. They walked north, towards Laheycourt, and made contact with a farmer. It was harvest time and the farmer, Camile Louvet, not one to waste such a golden opportunity, was only too pleased to have the help of two more men. So it was that Denys and Fred stayed on at the Ferme de Moulin for about two weeks.

   Then one day they heard that a 'detachment of British paratroops had landed in a forest 30 kilometres away', and though they had become very fond of their friends at the farm, they decided that it was their duty to offer their services and local knowledge to the paratroops. They were taken away in an old charcoal-burning saloon car to Sermaize-les-Bains, on the edge of the Forêt de Trois-Fontaines, having driven past hordes of retreating Germans. After spending the night in Sermaize they carried on to the British camp deep in the forest where they found, not the several hundred paratroopers whom they had been expecting, but Lt D. V. Laws and a handful of men of 'G' Squadron, 2 SAS, engaged in

Operation RUPERT. There were also a dozen or more Allied airmen evading.

The object of RUPERT, as a memorandum from SHAEF directed, was to harass 'enemy communications in the area to the East of the river Marne . . . The initial targets were the railway lines Nancy-Châlons-sur-Marne, and those branching from it, as well as road communications in the area. German repair aerodromes were also indicated as a possible future target.'

It was pointed out that the railways in that area were 'being used extensively by the enemy at present time bringing reinforcements and supplies to the bridgehead area from Germany . . .' and that 'the railway lines which it is proposed to attack are used extensively by the Germans for the transport of munitions and troops . . .'

The first attempt to land 'G' Squadron had met with disaster when, early in the morning of 23 July 1944, 190 Squadron's Mark IV Stirling LJ882 (F/O L. A. A. Kilgour RNZAF) with five crew and nine SAS hit high ground near Graffigny, Haute-Marne. The only survivor, Parachutist R. Boreham, was captured.

It was a fortnight before another party was ready, and on the night of 4/5 August the second RUPERT contingent, eight men in all, led by Lt Laws, had been successfully dropped in a ploughed field near Bailly-le-Franc, some 25 miles to the south-west of Revigny.

When he and Fred moved to Laws's camp, Denys was suffering from malnutrition and could hardly walk. Sores had turned septic and his fingers and wrists were a mass of yellow discharge; large abscesses had broken out all over his body. Fred, too, had contracted scabies, possibly from sharing Denys's bedding for several weeks.

One of the evaders at the camp, Denis Kelly (see Chapter 16), told Denys that he had been treated for a badly sprained ankle by a Doctor Fritsch* who lived not far away in Sermaize-les-Bains. Denys and Fred set off to find him. Having given the slip to a woman who thought they were German deserters, they found shelter in Pargny-sur-Saulx at the house of a Monsieur Adolph, retired foreman of the local brickworks. M Adolph went off to find Doctor Fritsch, and returned with the good news that he would visit them the following day.

Dr Henri Fritsch never arrived. Retreating Germans murdered twelve villagers in Sermaize-les-Bains. The doctor heard the explosions and went to help. Denys and Fred were told that one of the soldiers jumped down from a lorry as it was pulling out of the village, went over to the grey-haired old country doctor who was kneeling down beside one of the dying, pulled out his pistol and shot him through the head.

A few days later units of the US Third Army liberated Pargny-sur-Saulx, and on 2 September 1944 Denys and Fred were sent to the hospital at Bar-le-Duc. Released on 26 September, they were taken to

---

* *Henri Fritsch, born 17 May 1892, was awarded the* Croix de Guerre avec trois citations *and the* Croix de Chevalier de la Légion d'Honneur *for his bravery and conduct during the Great War. In May 1942 he joined the Resistance and spent much of his time assisting Allied airmen on the run to find shelter in the Sermaize area. In January 1944 he joined the* Bureau des Opérations Aériennes *adopting the codename 'Frédéric'. He assisted in several clandestine parachute drops.*

Toul and then to Paris before being flown on to England. For Denys it was an emotional moment:

'Skimming over the Channel in a Dakota I realised how extremely lucky I was. I owed my life to the loyalty, courage and kindness of the dozens of French people who had risked death and torture to protect me; a debt of gratitude which I would never forget.'

★ ★ ★

The day or so after Denys and Fred had headed north for Laheycourt, John Brown, Bill Johnson and Dick Greenwood were preparing for their move to Ligny-en-Barrois, some 20 miles south-east of Revigny. It was M Luccioni who, on or about 16 August, called for the three airmen. John Brown:

'So one morning a lorry arrived at the back garden gate and Bill, myself and Dick were told to get on it. We walked up the garden but as we got near the lorry we saw three German soldiers leaning on it. So we turned and went back to the house again. The lorry was then brought round to the front where we jumped on quickly and off we went . . . On the way we had to keep stopping to allow columns of marching German troops to pass. Our journey came to an end when we stopped by the road-side and were met by a young Frenchman who introduced himself as Peter Ivanoff . . .'

Ivanoff led the three men through woodland for about half a mile until they reached a chalet perched on the top of a hill. Beneath them the ground fell away steeply to the Canal de la Marne au Rhin. The chalet belonged to Ivanoff's parents who ran a chemist shop in the town, about a mile away. They stayed there, supplied with food by the Ivanoffs and by Peter's sister and her husband, until overrun by the Americans on 31 August. It was quite a frightening time for the airmen as they were caught in the cross-fire of the US Third Army tanks and the retreating Germans, busy shelling each other. At about 0900 hours on this last day of the month, Peter arrived to tell them that Ligny had been liberated, and the thankful airmen made their way into the town, where celebrations had already started.

There was a slight panic that evening when a rumour buzzed round that the Germans were on their way back. Barricades were hastily erected in the best French tradition and the airmen, American rifles in hand, stood their turn ready to repulse the foe should the need arise. As dawn broke on 1 September it was clear that the Germans were gone for good; road-blocks were taken down and the flags came out again. On 2 September they were taken back to Revigny, itself liberated a couple of days previously, where they received a warm welcome from Jean and Louis Chenu. John and Bill also found the time to pay a visit to their helpers in Laheycourt — especially to the very pretty Antoinette!

Word reached them that Denys Teare and Fred White were in the hospital at Bar-le-Duc, and they paid them a quick visit. All that now remained was for them to get back to England. With the assistance of American supply lorries from the notorious 'Red Ball Express', they made their way back to Paris, and were accommodated in the Hotel Meurice on the Rue Rivoli. On 9 September they were flown back to England, landing at Northolt barely seven weeks after they had been shot down. Dick Greenwood had managed to get back the previous day.

★   ★   ★

Only Red Banville, Ken Hoyle and John Nicholson remained at the Chenus' house. On 23 August they too were taken to Lt Laws's SAS camp in the Forêt de Trois-Fontaines, but by then Denys Teare and Fred White had already moved to Pargny. It was a busy time for the small SAS party who were having to organise regular supply drops for themselves and for the local maquis, as well as for other SAS being parachuted in at frequent intervals. It was also a time fraught with danger, for the roads in the area were full of enemy convoys moving east.

On 29 August Red, Ken and John, with seven of the SAS party, moved off south through the forest towards St Dizier, stopping when they reached Villiers-en-Lieu, four miles away. They spent the night of 29/30 August in the woods. Next day, 30 August, the Americans attacked the village. Because of the fighting it was not until 2130 hours that night that they were able to make contact with an American patrol of men from a New York regiment. They were escorted to the bivouac area, given a pack of 'C' rations and a shovel and ordered to dig in. The Americans were bedding down for the night: 'This is a combat zone,' a sergeant told them, 'and everyone digs!' So they dug!

They stayed the night with the Americans, and the following day, 31 August, walked the short distance to Hallignicourt, across the main Vitry-le-François to St Dizier road, and a stone's throw from St Dizier airfield. Maquisards took them to Vitry-le-François, where they were handed over once again to the American authorities, who took them to Paris. Ken Hoyle and John Nicholson were flown to Hendon on 4 September and Red Banville followed the next day, the first guests of the Chenu brothers to return to England.

★   ★   ★

All the Chenus' guests returned safely, and all owed a great debt to the many brave French people who had helped them. Jean and Louis Chenu must stand high in the honours list. But there is one poignant reminder that not everyone survived. On 20 September 1944, Harry Kidd's mother wrote to Dallas Banville, Red's wife:

'I hope you will forgive a stranger writing to you. I am the mother of Sgt Harry Kidd who is wireless operator on the same plane as your husband. If you receive any news of him will you please let me know . . . My son had every confidence in your husband and always spoke very highly of him. I feel sure we shall soon have good news and that he is safe and well.'

Harry Hewitt Kidd had been dead for two months.

14

Swiss Stroll

It will be remembered that early on the morning of 13 July 1944 Lancaster LL896 was on fire internally. In the words of the Australian bomb-aimer, F/S Charles Henry Kroschel, 'a parachute escape was necessary'. Floating gently down he saw the Lancaster crash a couple of miles away:

> 'My first experience of falling was when I hit a tree with a thud and was caught in its branches. It took me nearly an hour to get out of the tree and I found my left leg to be fairly badly sprained. I was in the middle of a small wood, and after hiding the Mae West and harness and some of the 'chute, I tried to find a way out. There seemed to be such a noise, but I guess most of it was only in my imagination. When in the open, I walked in an opposite direction to the plane, as I was too far away to be of any assistance after this time. I kept my eyes and ears open to catch any sign of the others, but didn't see or hear a thing.'

As it was about 0215 hours he decided to lie low until dawn:

> 'A hay stack seemed to be the right place to hide and I found a nice one on the outside of the village of Morley, after walking for about three hours across ploughed fields.
>
> 'Early next morning I dried out in the sun and decided to move on in case there were any Germans in the village. The first person I saw was a man riding a push-bike. I stopped him and in my very bad French asked if there were any Germans in the district. He told me that a bus passed by each morning and evening which may carry Germans as passengers, so I decided to risk it and walk along the road for a while.
>
> 'The road ran through a pine plantation and I walked along the grass edge. I heard the sound of horse's hooves on the road and, taking no chances, ducked into the cover of the trees. A few moments later along came a horse with its rider in uniform. He passed by; I came out and continued on my way. More trotting noises, so back into the trees — same person, and I thought that he must be looking for me.

He came back again, this time on the grass. I was caught in the open and could only hope to bluff it out. Luckily he was only a circus performer exercising his horse! Thank goodness for the forthcoming 14th July celebrations.

'After passing through the next village, a couple of farmers, who evidently recognised the uniform, stopped me and after a lot of chatter took me into the middle of their wheat field and hid me there all day. They told me it was dangerous to walk about in uniform and gave me some old overalls and a beret. This was outside the village of Montiers-sur-Saulx.

'That night, when the children had gone to bed, they came out, took me to the farmhouse and gave me some food and wine. We talked about the best thing for me to do, deciding that I was to rest for a few days and they would try to find out about the rest of my crew. The farmer's son was a school teacher and spoke a little English, so with my schoolboy French we could understand each other.'

Charlie was at Grignoncourt farm, run by the Moulun family, where he stayed until 2330 on Saturday 15 July. The young Moulun had ridden off to find out about the rest of the crew and came back with the news that three were dead and three were alive. But the Moulun family would not let him join them because of considerable German activity in the area.

He had to wait patiently in his hide-out, seeing yet unseen: 'Each evening as I lay in the hay-loft I could see the Jerry kites take off to look for our boys.'

As he rested at the farm, Charlie had plenty of time in which to take stock of his situation and, after much thought, he decided to make for Switzerland. 'I thought that if I did get there and could send word back to England, our folks would be relieved of a little worry.'

So, supplied with food and wearing his change of clothes, he left for Switzerland.

He made good progress with the aid of his own escape maps and other basic ones torn from French telephone books. The most frightening aspect of the walk in the darkness was the sudden barking of dogs as he approached farms that he had not spotted. Through Montiers-sur-Saulx to Saudron, on through Germay and Lafauche until, after 18 hours, he reached the little village of Outremécourt where he 'received help from the Mayor'. He had had to move carefully during the daylight hours because of a Fieseler Storch light aircraft which was on the look-out for persons such as himself.

He managed to keep awake by swallowing the benzedrine tablets supplied to him back at Kirmington and which were always issued for the long night trips. There was, however, a side-effect to his marathon walk; the pain in his left leg became so bad that he had to find somewhere to rest. So the Mayor of Outremécourt let him stay the night in an old house that had apparently been empty for some time and was covered in dust. That did not bother him; all he wanted was some hot water in which to bathe his aching feet, to have a wash and then lie down and sleep.

At 0600 hours on Monday 17 July he was given his marching orders. It seemed that the Mayor and his cronies were taking no chances. Even after

a long rest it was still a great effort to walk and he had to stop every hour or
so. As he plodded painfully on he could at least draw comfort from knowing
that he was going in the right direction, thanks to two compasses he had
with him, one hidden in a trouser fly-button and the other sewn into his
lapel. Through Sauville until he reached Martigny-les-Bains, a village which
boasted a large château surrounded by a high stone wall:

'I was walking alongside one wall and on turning the corner saw, not
too far away, a German guard outside the main gate. He was dressed
in black, the colour worn by the SS. I couldn't just stop and turn
around, but luckily there was a small opening in the wall leading to
another entrance about 20 yards before where the guard was standing.
    'I stepped into this and after waiting a couple of minutes came out
and went back the way I had just come. Retracing my steps I headed
across country until clear of the town — a close call!'

A close one indeed. After only 12 hours this time he came to another
farm near Thon-le-Petit, where he was taken in and sheltered:

'This turned out to be with a couple of middle-aged women who had
a few cows and an empty house. One of the women made up a bed
and brought lots of hot water, so I was able to clean up and get some
of the stiffness out of my body. She also brought a bottle full of pure
alcohol to rub into my legs. These were by this time in a bad way.
    'I spent a few days sleeping there and had lots of fresh milk and
food. I needed all this and tucked into any they could spare.'

He stayed at this farm from 1800 hours on Monday 17 July until 0700
hours on Friday 21 July when, having regained his strength, the kind
women put him on the right road for Switzerland. Ever onwards he
went, through Selles, Vauvillers, and Secenans:

'That night I got caught in a rain storm and took shelter under a railway
bridge. After I had been there about an hour I heard voices and knew
they weren't speaking French. I kept still and two German soldiers
armed with automatic rifles walked over the bridge and on down the
railway line. I thought my heart would give me away.'

When the rain stopped he went on his way until he was near Longevelle-
sur-Doubs, where he

'. . . got a bed with some farmers. These men were evidently part of a
Resistance group and later that night [21 July] took me to an isolated
hut where there was a hidden radio; they were expecting a message
from London concerning a parachute drop. It was strange hearing the
BBC coming in with odd messages, all of which had special meanings
to these patriotic bands — "Mary's horse has a new foal"; "Aunt
Mathilda is coming to stay", etc. I had been accepted as genuine and
although no message had come through for them they questioned me
as to the progress of the war and the invasion.

'I was glad of their shelter; unfortunately the bed was full of bugs, fleas or something of that kind, and I got bitten all over. Next day I had to have a wash in a deserted creek to ease the irritation.

'At the end of this day [22 July] I felt in need of a few more days' rest and chose the village curé. He was very kind, letting me shelter with him for a couple of days. The second day I was playing table-tennis with him, but didn't know the score as I couldn't think of all my French numbers. Still, I suppose the exercise was the main thing!'

As if he needed any extra exercise! He left the curé and his hospitality at 0800 hours on Sunday 23 July and walked for most of the day until, near the limit of his endurance, he saw the answer to his prayers:

'Coming down a hill into one village I saw two push-bikes outside a shop and thought "This is my chance to save walking". Tucking my trousers into my socks I made ready to grab one when out of the shop came two German soldiers and pinched my bike. So I walked on. I had got into the habit of counting the posts along the road. These were spaced every 100 metres; I knew exactly how many steps it took between posts. (Even today when doing anything repetitive I find myself counting.)

'Thirst was a problem and I put the plastic water bottle from the escape kit to good use, filling up from streams and village pumps, until I realised that this could give me away, as the Frenchmen only wash in water — they drink wine! Wild strawberries were growing along the way and I picked and ate those without any dire results. Towards the end of the day I approached an elderly man sitting beside the road. When asked for help he just shook his head and pointed up the road.

'Around a bend I came to his village — houses were gutted and smouldering, and the people wandering around in shock. Evidently the Germans had extracted vengeance for something — it was their way of punishing the French people. How wrong they were!'

Near nightfall on Sunday 23 July he reached the outskirts of the village of Pont-de-Roide where he spent the night. At 0530 hours on 24 July, with the distant Swiss Alps beckoning, he started the last stage of his marathon walk:

'I thought that the best way would be to leave the main road and go along a small plateau and try to sneak in through an uninhabited part. Enquiring at every chance I had, I was always told "Just a few kilometres". Eventually I came across a chap picking cherries and when I asked if I was in Switzerland he called to his wife. She could speak English, having worked in London for about ten years. They gave me instructions how to reach the border line, and the old chap even came some of the way with me. He warned me about the German guards and where I would most likely find them.

'It was about ten in the morning and a nice sunny day, and I felt quite excited about getting so far without any serious set-backs. I was just on the last stage of the trip, and about to cross a small valley that was the border line, when I saw two German guards between me and safety.

'I ducked back into the shelter of a wheat field, but not before they had seen me. They started to come towards me, so I thought I would give them a chase for it. I ran around the field in circles, out the other side and headed straight for Switzerland about 400 yards away. I could see the Swiss guards on the roadway watching me.

'The two chasing me came out of the field some distance behind and I saw that I had a chance to make it. Luckily they didn't fire and I was able to get through, but not before I had jumped fences and ditches and climbed through hedges. I raced up to a farm in the first village and asked "Switzerland?". The people said "Yes". Just before I collapsed, I saw the Germans give up the chase, 200 yards behind me.'

From Pont-de-Roide he had passed through Roches-les-Blamont and then, forced north-east up the valley of the river Gland, approached the village of Hérimoncourt. The border lay but 3 miles distant, guarded by Germans with dogs and protected by barbed-wire fences, buried mines and other unpleasant devices. Kroschel's luck, which had been with him for over a week, had not deserted him. He was in Switzerland near the village of Fahy.

It was 1030 hours on Monday 24 July. He had made it!

It is impossible to say precisely how far he had travelled, but it must have been close to 150 miles.

After all the effort of avoiding the German guards, Charlie fell unconscious, which shows how badly affected he had been by the hard walking and lack of proper nourishment:

'When I came round the people told me that I would be safe in Switzerland and gave me some food and drink. The local gendarme started a search of the village to find the person who had crossed the frontier illegally. When he came to the house in which I was sheltering, I walked out and gave myself up. He took me to the local gaol and once again I was treated very well. The village people brought me chocolate, fruit, bottles of wine and cakes. To see me, dirty and with a few days' beard and torn clothes, receiving all these gifts you would wonder what it was all about.

'That afternoon [24 July] the military officials came to take me to their headquarters — this was an old château in Porrentruy [11 kilometres away by road]. I shared a room with two Indian merchant seamen. They had been POWs in a camp near Belfort and had escaped in the confusion after the Americans had bombed their camp in error . . .'*

In the safety and comfort of his Swiss surroundings, Charlie

'. . . was able to look over the town, and at night listen to the music coming from the cafés and watch the lights. It was a change after

---

* On 11 May 1944 52 B-24 bombers from five Bomb Groups of the 2nd Bomb Division, US 8th Air Force, bombed the marshalling yards at Belfort from heights of between 15,500 and 18,000 feet. The USAAF comment at the time was that after the first bombs burst smoke obscured the target area. Some of the 219 x 1,000 lb and 120 x 500 lb bombs fell on the wrong target. Buried in Epinal French National Cemetery, Vosges, are 55 Indians, all of whom died on 11 May 1944. So much for daylight bombing!

the blackout of France and England.

'After a few days here, with regular meals and sleep, I was taken by train to Olten [roughly halfway between Basel and Zurich] and a large reception camp. This was a barbed-wire enclosure in the town square. Here there were Russians, French, Poles, Italians and a few other nationalities, but no British or American. Next day I was joined by a Canadian chap who was an officer in a British Airborne unit and who had escaped from an Italian POW camp. Then came a couple of Americans who had suffered the same fate as myself. It was good to be able to talk to someone in English again.

'We were moved to a quarantine camp at Bad Lostorf, which was part of an hotel taken over by the Swiss Army. We had to spend three weeks there before being allowed to join the others of our own nationality. The two Americans and I shared a room. We had only the clothes we stood up in, so didn't require much space. Our beds were straw mattresses on the floor, but it felt good not to worry about things for a change.

'After a few days I received some money and clothes from the British Legation and was able to enjoy a few extras, such as bread and cheese and a beer in the café.

'My period of quarantine over, I was taken to join the rest of the British Air Force men at Glion-sur-Montreux. Here the British Legation had taken over an hotel about a thousand feet above Lake Geneva overlooking the town of Montreux, and the most beautiful part of Lake Geneva. From my room I could see the French Alps across the lake. We had good accommodation, a room each, good food and marvellous scenery as well as amusement in the town. We were paid five shillings a day — about four and a half francs. This gave us a little to spend and I was able to get along with this. The money came off our pay in England.

'On the whole we had a quiet time until the time came for us to return to England about the end of September. Then we had a few nights of celebration in town. We were taken by train to Geneva and into France to a place called Annecy, and from here we were to be taken back to England by transport aircraft.'

Annecy is a large town in the Haute-Savoie, some 25 miles due south of Geneva, at the north end of the lake of the same name. By the time Kroschel and his colleagues were taken there the Germans had been driven a long way back, nearly but not quite out of France, and the town had been liberated by Lt-Gen Alexander Patch's 7th US Army and Gen Lattre de Tassigny's 1st French Army advancing from the south. By 17 September Allied forces had closed to within six miles of Belfort and were in contact with the Germans fighting stubbornly from prepared positions.

There were old scores to be settled once the Germans had been driven out (the *épuration* as it was known), as Charlie observed:

'People accused of collaborating with the Germans were given a summary trial and then shot. Women whose association with the enemy was of the nature of pleasure had their hair shaved off, and had to run the gauntlet of the town.'

Charlie and the others were soon to be on their way back, but it took longer to get home than expected. The same heavy rain that had been delaying the Allied advance northwards also made the runway at the Annecy airstrip unusable — it was half under water:

'After a few more days we went by truck to Lyons, and went straight to the aerodrome. There were about a dozen Dakotas waiting, and within an hour we were off. It was strange to be flying over country that a few months before we had been bombing. The pilot flew low enough to let us see some of the results of that bombing, particularly around the V-bomb sites. It was just bomb hole after bomb hole and flattened countryside. The last part of the trip across the Channel seemed to take ages. However, we landed at Croydon and were soon in the midst of red tape again.

'The Air Force took over control once more and we spent the night at St John's Wood. This was a centre set up to receive the expected returning POWs. We were questioned about our escape and about any help given whilst on the run. In a medical examination I was given an X-ray of my left knee, but the doctor couldn't find anything seriously wrong. I got some leave and received word that I was to be sent back home to Australia.'

In due course Charlie sailed on the *Queen Elizabeth* (for the second time, having come over on her from the US in the spring of 1943) and spent about six weeks in New York and New England while someone made a decision as to what to do with him. At last he was put on a train to San Francisco where he had to wait another week while a ship arrived to take him and several others back to Australia. A prewar luxury liner took them away and they enjoyed comfortable cabins and good food. But all good things come to an end:

'Even when we were on our way our troubles weren't over, as we landed in New Guinea and had to spend a week there and trans-ship to a dirty old tub to finish the journey.'

Back once more in the bosom of his family, but still in the Air Force, he spent months doing nothing:

'I put in my discharge in April [1945] and was told it would be through in a few weeks. Well, after a couple of months they let us report once a week and we had the rest of the time to ourselves. This went on until I received word that my discharge had come through and I was to report in next day. When I got there they gave me another month's leave to fix up about my future employment . . .'

Charlie Kroschel could have had no idea of what lay in store for him when he enlisted on 22 May 1942. He had completed thirteen operations before being shot down on 13 July 1944, had walked halfway across north-eastern France, been interned in Switzerland and sailed around the world. He had been lucky, but it had needed more than just luck to get back to Melbourne.

15

So Few Survived

Soon after the Revigny-bound Lancasters had crossed the French coast, prowling Luftwaffe night-fighters found them and shot down eleven as they made their way down the long, straight leg to the turning point on the River Aube. From eight there was no survivor; from the other three there were only five.

It is clear from the interrogation reports of the 5 Group crews that just after 0100 hours on 19 July two Lancasters were attacked from below by a fighter, which suggests the use of *schräge musik*, invariably unexpected and usually deadly. *Schräge musik* may well have been the cause of the other losses on this leg, no flak having been reported.

The first victim was JB186 (F/O A. H. J. Begernie, 619 Squadron). The rear gunner was killed in the attack, and the wireless operator's parachute failed to open. The sole survivor was Sgt Borden Gerald Lewis (bomb-aimer). All that is yet known of his subsequent evasion is that he was back in England on 10 September.[*]

The second loss was LM640 (F/O H. J. Wilson, 619 Squadron), and all seven of the crew were killed.

Next down were probably DV304 (F/O H. W. Cooper, 61 Squadron) with, again, no survivors, and LM378 (F/O F. F. Molinas, 619 Squadron) which, hit by a night-fighter near Château-Thierry, exploded in mid-air. Only Sgt James Alexander Nealey (flight engineer) survived:

'I hid my parachute and Mae West in a hedge. I then went to a house in Château-Thierry and asked an old man for help. He took me in and gave me some civilian clothes. He took me by horse and cart to a hotel in Lizy-sur-Ourcq and there a member of the maquis visited me and took my particulars.

---

[*] *He left Halifax, Nova Scotia, on 26 August 1943, on the same ship as fellow Canadian F/S Charles Ratchford (see below). They landed in the UK on 1 September 1943, and went their separate ways. Ratchford was posted to 619 Squadron on 11 May 1944, where Lewis joined him on 3 July 1944. 619 Squadron lost five Lancasters on the 18/19 July Revigny raid. Of the three survivors, two were Lewis and Ratchford.*

'I was later joined there by three American airmen. We stayed there until 23 July when we left for Vaujours dressed as policemen. We stayed there until 8 August; we were then split up and I was taken to a man in the Resistance Group who took me to a house in Livry-Gargan, where I stayed until the Americans liberated the town.'*

* * *

The fifth loss of the night was 619 Squadron's fourth — PB245 (F/O N. W. Donnelley), shot down with no survivors.

As JB318 (57 Squadron) crossed the French coast it was picked up by the searchlights and coned. The pilot, F/L John Alec Bulcraig DFM (won whilst an NCO navigator on 50 Squadron) took evasive action and successfully dodged the blinding beams. But the Lancaster was now out of the bomber stream, flying alone in the hostile night. Not for long.

Suddenly there was a massive explosion in the port wing. There had been no flak, so it could only have been a night-fighter. Young Sgt Len Manning saw nothing from his rear turret before the explosion:

'Immediately flames were streaming past my turret, which stopped working because the hydraulic motors for the turret were operated by the port [inner] engine. I centralised the turret by hand and opened the doors into the fuselage and climbed in. Fred Taylor was already out of his turret and had his 'chute on. He made his way to the rear door, which he had difficulty in opening. He then jumped into the night.

'By this time the fuselage was a mass of flames and molten metal; the plane was in a steep dive. My 'chute, which was stowed on the port side, had started to smoulder. I pulled it from the stowage and struggled to clip it on to my harness; this was made very difficult due to "g". I managed to clip it on to one of the hooks on my harness but not to the second one. With everything burning it was a case of jump now or never. So I leapt through the door.

'I pulled the cord and hoped that the 'chute would open. It did! But I was hanging to one side. I felt something against my face; this proved to be my intercom plug and cord which was attached to my helmet (which I should have removed before jumping). They had become entangled in the shrouds. This probably saved my life as I had something to help take my weight. I looked up and could see something smouldering. I hoped that I would reach the ground before it fell apart.

'On the way down there was a terrific explosion. This was the plane exploding with a full load of bombs as it hit the ground. I landed flat on my back and this winded me. My 'chute started to burn; I quickly smothered the flames and bundled it up. I later pushed it into a hedge and staggered off into the darkness.'

JB318 was the sixth Lancaster shot down, and only the navigator and the two gunners escaped. There could have been little time in which to bale out. The front of the Lancaster was a raging inferno and, as Len

---

* *Livry, some four kilometres from Vaujours, is about 20 kilometres north-east of Paris.*

Manning reported, it was 'completely destroyed by fire'. He himself was badly burned about the face. He had no idea where he was when he landed (rear gunners spent most of the war going backwards) and made his way to a nearby road hoping for some clue as to his whereabouts. He was in fact barely 45 miles from the heart of Paris itself and near the main road from la Ferté-sous-Jouarre to Montmirail. More precisely, he was not far from the village of Bassevelle:

'I staggered on for about 8 miles until I collapsed on the doorstep of a farmhouse. The farmer must have heard my moans, as my face was giving me great pain. He took me in and he and his wife put me to bed. The following morning I was given civilian clothes to replace my battledress and flying boots which were badly burnt and taken to another farm in the village (Sablonnières).

'Here I was put to bed again. To my amazement I was interrogated by a member of the Resistance to ensure that I was not a German spy. This was pretty frightening. Being convinced that I was British I was given a Sten gun which I hid under the bed. Later in the day a doctor arrived to treat my burns. He left some white powder for me to put on the burns. The Germans came looking for me at the farm, but the farmer convinced them that he had not seen me.'

On Sunday 23 July, as the area

'. . . had become dangerous, it was decided to move me on. A member of the Resistance collected me and we travelled on foot across country and through woods to avoid German patrols. At one stage my guide announced that he was lost and would have to go and ask the way at a house. He pushed a Luger pistol into my hand and hid me in the hedge, telling me to shoot if he met trouble at the house. He returned shortly with directions and we continued our journey.

'Eventually we reached a café in the village of la Trétoire which was owned and run by two elderly ladies, Madame Louisette Beaujard and her mother. They made me very welcome, although they spoke no English, and gave me a bedroom in their small hotel across the courtyard. Later I was told that if the Germans came into the village I would have to move out of my room and into the ladies' room over the café. Apparently German officers used the hotel when in the village.

'Two young men were also staying with the ladies. They were on the run from the Germans who wanted them for conscripted labour in Germany. They were Albert Bertin and Jacques Gougnard. Later we were joined by another man, Maurice Leterme. From time to time we were visited by a young lady, Madeleine Faley-Godard, who brought us cigarettes from the Resistance, which were most welcome.'

'I had the run of an orchard behind the hotel, but the café was out of bounds. I was also warned not to be around when the postman arrived as he was suspected of being a collaborator. There were lots of furtive comings and goings by the Resistance.

'One evening a German patrol came into the village and came to the café for a drink. We were having our evening meal in the room behind the café. Madame Beaujard came back to fetch some change and a German followed her into the back room. He stood by the door and looked all around at the four of us. Fortunately, when Madame gave him his change he left the room without a word, much to our relief!

'Some days later we were told that tanks had been seen coming towards the village. I was moved into the ladies' room over the café. The following morning I was roused by the sound of the tanks. Looking down from my window, I saw that the courtyard was full of tanks and Germans were strutting about with machine guns and grenades stuck in their belts. This was another worrying time, but later that day they moved out. This was the last time that I saw Germans.'

Then, at long last, on Sunday 3 September, 'some cheering young members of the Resistance arrived riding a German sidecar that they had taken from the Germans who had retreated. They said that the Americans had arrived outside the village and were setting up a field hospital. My charred battledress had appeared from nowhere, darned and pressed. Someone from Sablonnières must have dug it up! I put it on and the following day I went down to meet the Americans. One of their officers offered me a lift into Paris. He gave me a good supply of coffee and tinned food for my friends.

'That night there was a big party to celebrate the liberation. All the good wines came out of hiding. Next day, after fond farewells, I returned to the American camp and was taken to the Hotel Meurice in Paris where the RAF had set up a reception centre for evaders.'

The luxurious Hotel Meurice in the Rue Rivoli was quite a contrast to a humble café in the country, but it was in such surroundings that RAF evaders were interrogated by IS9 (WEA) before being sent on to England. On 5 September Len was flown back to Hendon:

'I was once again interrogated to make sure that I was not a spy! Next we were taken to Marylebone Hotel where I made my report to Bomber Intelligence [on 6 September]. Telegrams were sent home and I was sent on leave. I arrived home before the telegram. It was quite a shock to my parents to see me standing at the door, having heard nothing from me since I was reported missing.'

He had four weeks' leave and was then sent to Eastchurch re-selection centre. During his enforced stay in France he had lost four stones in weight, and now tipped the scales at a puny six and a half stone. He was put on double rations in an attempt to build him up again. After several medical examinations he was sent on nine months' sick leave, before being discharged from the RAF on medical grounds on 6 May 1945.

As for the other two survivors of JB318, the navigator, F/O E. H. Ruston, escaped safely by parachute but, after a few days on the run heading north-west towards the oncoming Allies, was 'captured early in the morning when foolishly walking on to a well-hidden anti-aircraft site'. He spent the rest of the war at Stalag Luft 1, Barth.

The other survivor was the mid-upper gunner, 30-year-old Sgt Fred John David Taylor, who seems to have had an uneventful evasion. He too landed near Bassevelle, but waited until daylight before going to a farm near the village, where he was taken in and fed. It was arranged that someone would collect him, and later that day 'a sergeant of the Resistance arrived and took me to his house about five kilometres away'. He stayed in the same house until liberated by the Americans at the end of August, when he was sent home via Paris. He left France on 1 September.

★ ★ ★

Another five Lancasters were lost before the bombers changed course north-east to Revigny, some 12 minutes flying time away. Not one of the 35 airmen survived. But the night-fighters continued to take their toll. Six more fell in a short space of time. Only ten of the 42 crew were saved. The first of these (the twelfth of the night) was PB231 (F/O C. Lacy, 49 Squadron). Only the two gunners survived — Sgt W. G. Barlow (mid-upper) and P/O J. C. Wellein (rear). Both were later taken prisoner (see Chapter 18) and sent to Stalag Luft 7.

A few miles from the spot where PB231 crashed lies the village of St Utin. The villagers were already wide-awake when LL969 (F/O S. B. Morcom) roared over their heads in the early morning of 19 July 1944. Marceau Maret, then a young lad of twelve, remembers the tremendous noise of the Lancasters as they headed for Revigny.

LL969 was outward bound at about 8,000 feet when it was hit by a night-fighter, 619 Squadron's fifth loss of the night. The bomber exploded in mid-air, but not before the rear gunner, F/S Charles Ratchford, had baled out. The Lancaster fell into a field close to la Madeleine farm, on the great rolling chalk fields, half a mile or so from St Utin, where roads run arrow-straight in every direction and few hedges and trees break the landscape.

Young Jean Hercot was forbidden to go to the wreck so close to their farm, but his father and uncle rushed out of la Madeleine to see what could be done. When it was light, Jean went to see for himself the ghastly sight, the broken remains of five of the crew — '*désarticulé*', smashed up. A sixth man, F/S Alfred Myres (mid-upper gunner) was dead at his post. Jean noticed that there were five bombs painted on the fuselage, and a swastika too. But where was the seventh man?

Ratchford reported on 30 August 1944:

'I came down safely in a field and made for a hedge at once. There I got rid of my flying suit and hid my 'chute. I then started off SW and walked for 3 hours, mostly in woods and along hedges . . .'

It took the Germans two days to locate the crash, by which time the Canadian was long gone. Before the dead were buried, the Germans stripped the boots and other valuables from the corpses and ordered their immediate burial. The villagers would have none of it, and insisted that the men be given a proper burial. The Germans backed down, and the airmen were laid to rest with due ceremony.

Ratchford was away, across the fields to Jasseines:

'After a while I met two more Frenchmen and spoke to them. One of them spoke English. They were Resistance members. They offered to help me, so I went with them. We all spent the night together in a shack in the woods. Next day they brought me civilian clothes and new boots, and the following evening they took me with another Frenchman to Molins. All were armed.'

At Molins-sur-Aube he spent two days in a barn, the guest of Gaston Jacquot and his daughter, Georgette, before being moved to their house at le Mesnil-Albert, a short way south of the village of Epagne:

'I stayed there for two weeks. The family were very kind to me and I was well taken care of. Ten Germans came through there one day and stopped at the house. I hid in the barn and they did not find me.'

On 12 August, with the Allies at le Mans, he decided to leave le Mesnil-Albert and try to get through to them there. Escorted by Georgette, he cycled to Epagne, where the Mayor advised him to wait for a few days. Whilst there an American evader, Lt Reese, arrived, and in time to witness one of the many minor dramas then being enacted throughout France. The maquis had caught a woman who was allegedly spying for the Germans:

'We guarded her during the night, and in the morning the French took her off to shoot her. She said she was French, but she was a stranger in the region and was quite arrogant and unrepentant about what she had done.'

Then, on 25 August, the Germans began their retreat. They tried to blow up the bridge across the River Aube, between Précy-Notre-Dame and Précy-St Martin, but the maquis were prepared for it and a fight broke out. The French prevailed, but at some price, as the Germans 'shot a lot of people including women and children'.

Two days later the Americans arrived and the Canadian's wait was over. He was picked up by a US Engineer unit and sent back to Third Army HQ. A few more days and he was on his way back to England, reached on 1 September.

* * *

Perched on an escarpment a stone's throw to the east of St Utin is the village of Margerie-Hancourt. A flak battery was positioned nearby and the Lancasters of 5 Group flew right over it. The German gunners were on form that night. They hit LM537 (F/O P. B. Dennett, 630 Squadron). The fuel tanks ignited and flames streamed rearwards, burning the two gunners, Sgt Reg Hilborne (mid-upper) and Sgt J Stones (rear). With his gloves and parachute case burnt away, Reg managed to bale out of the rear door. He counted to ten as instructed (to make certain of clearing the aircraft) before pulling the ring and watching as his slightly charred canopy opened safely above him. It would have been pitch dark, but his descent was illuminated by streams of flak still being pumped up into the sky at LM537 and at other Lancasters on their way to the target. Not surprisingly, Reg was much relieved when he touched down without a bullet hole in him.

Reg had landed in a field near Margerie-Hancourt and was burying his equipment when he heard a whistle. He ignored it as he thought that it was the Germans trying to trap him! The whistler (possibly 'Geordie' Stones) faded into the night. Reg laid up under a hedge for the whole of the next day as he 'was badly burned about the face'. In the end, not caring too much whether he was caught or not, he walked to the nearest railway station which, sure enough, was swarming with Germans. Before they realised who or what he was, a Frenchman grabbed his arm and bundled him into a nearby cottage. The man gave him a drink and a piece of dry bread and motioned to him to stay put whilst he went off somewhere. He had gone to fetch the head of the local maquis, a captain in the FFI.

That same night, Wednesday 19 July, the captain arrived with two bicycles and took him back to his large house where, to his delight, he found his rear gunner, 'Geordie' Stones. The captain's daughter tended to Hilborne's burnt face and hands, and for the next two days and nights the two airmen recuperated at 'les Chênes', home of the Vicomte de la Hamayde.

The flight engineer, Sgt G. A. Alexander, was sheltered by the Vauthier family at St Léger-sous-Margerie and Lucien Riglet, a schoolmaster, in nearby Braux. Lucien managed to hand him over to the maquis, but he was later to be captured by the Germans and sent to Stalag Luft 7 (but see Chapter 18).

The bomb-aimer, F/S Hume Paul Ritchie (RCAF), baled out of LM537 and hid his parachute, harness and Mae West in the foliage at the base of a large tree:

'I then set out walking South in order to get as far from the aircraft as possible. After going for two hours I found some suitable cover and remained in hiding for the whole of the next day.

'About 1730 hours I continued walking until I came to a deserted farmhouse. After observing it for some considerable time to make sure that there were no Germans in the vicinity, I spent the night nearby. The next morning (20 July) I met some French people to whom I declared myself. They sheltered me for the day and provided me with food and clothing. About 2130 hours I set out again, and about an hour later I reached Chavanges. I entered the village and asked the civilians if there were any Germans in the neighbourhood. They told me that there were not. As it was still daylight, I decided it was not a good place to stay for the night, and continued westward, keeping off the main road.'

Chavanges was maybe only three miles as the crow flies from where he had landed. As he headed west across the rolling downland, he was close to la Madeleine farm:

'About 2300 hours I approached another farmhouse, where I was immediately taken inside and given something to eat. I set out again shortly afterwards and continued walking for another three hours. I then lay up in a haystack for the night.

'At dawn [21 July] I entered the village nearby and spoke to some civilians who gave me some food and advice as to which towns to avoid. As I was talking to them firing broke out close by and I left immediately. A short while later, as I was walking along the road, a French civilian came from the direction of the village and passed me on his cycle. Soon after he turned round and went back in the direction from which he had come. My suspicions were immediately aroused, so I left the road and made for a small wood.

'I had no sooner reached it when a German patrol car drew up on the other side. I heard a great deal of shouting and, feeling certain that the wood would be searched, I went into a field and hid in the tall grain. The Germans searched the woods and then began to search the other side of the field. While they were out of sight I was able to make my way unobserved to another wood about half a mile further on.'

A close shave indeed. Ritchie continued westwards as fast as his legs would carry him until, at around 1500 hours, he reached the other side of the downs where there was 'a range of hills with substantial cover, where I lay up for an hour'. He was near the village of Dampierre and as he walked along the road towards it (today the D 48) he saw a girl cycling towards him. He stopped her and told her who he was.

The girl took him home and a 'few minutes later the elder son of the house took my name, number and rank to the Chief of the maquis in the district. He returned late that evening with instructions that I was to remain where I was until further orders. During the six weeks that I was here I received two further messages from the Chief of the maquis telling me to stay where I was.'

It was the Vulquin family in Dampierre to whom Ritchie owed his freedom. Eventually his patience was rewarded when, on 28 August, the Americans arrived and he 'reported to them'. The following day he was sent to Troyes, then on to Bayeux. He was flown back to England on 1 September.

★   ★   ★

At about the same time as LM537 met its end, another Lancaster, ME814 (F/O J. G. Dallen, 207 Squadron), was hit. Early on 19 July, *en route* for Revigny, it was shot down near Margerie-Hancourt, some 30 miles south-west of the target, the 15th loss of the night. F/S Len Aitken, bomb-aimer, was the sole survivor. Like others already mentioned, he lost his flying boots when his parachute opened. Hiding his flying equipment he 'set out walking along a third class road in my stockinged feet. I passed through the town [Margerie-Hancourt] and continued across country for several miles until I arrived at a farm where I was immediately taken inside, given a meal and put to bed.'

The farm, la Cense Neuve, was about a mile to the east of Margerie-Hancourt down a remote track. His host was Georges Humbert. Here he remained for two days, not far from Reg Hilborne and 'Geordie' Stones.

On Friday the 21st, Hilborne and Stones were collected by the maquis and, after they had been joined by Aitken from la Cense Neuve, they were 'taken by car to some woods near Lévigny' where, at the camp, they met the other evaders. Len Aitken and Reg Hilborne decided to leave Lévigny on the night of 30/31 July and head for Switzerland. 'Geordie' Stones stayed with the other evaders at Lévigny. They rested at a farm the following day (31 July), but their suspicions were aroused that the farmer and his family might be sympathetic to the Germans, and so wasted no time in leaving. Soon after, they had a very close encounter near Bar-sur-Aube when they were spotted by an enemy patrol and nearly arrested.

Wiser for the experience, they spent the next three days travelling east through the dense woods. After nearly two weeks in France they surprisingly still had the food from their escape kits, but, once the contents had been devoured, they had no option but to seek help elsewhere. They found it at the Ferme de Moslains, home of the Esmard family, halfway between Lignol-le-Château and Bar-sur-Aube, and within spitting distance of Route Nationale 19 which was being heavily used by the Germans.

On 5 August Marcel Esmard escorted the airmen south-east through the great forest of Clairvaux to another farm, les Vieilles Forges, near the village of Montheries, which they reached that same evening. There they stayed for eight days, sheltered by the Demarson family. On 14 August Pierre Demarson took the two men by bicycle and lorry to Captain Hibbert's SAS camp (see Chapter 10).

*　*　*

The 16th and 17th losses on the night of 18/19 July were ME833 (F/O L. J. Wood, 9 Squadron) and DV312 (F/O W. J. Long, 50 Squadron). The accounts of their fate may be found in Chapters 18 and 10 respectively.

The 18th victim was Lancaster ME796 (F/O G. E. Maxwell, 630 Squadron). Hit by a night-fighter and blazing furiously, it was heading straight for the village of Villers-le-Sec, half a dozen miles west of Revigny. Three men baled out.

Before he left his position, F/S Stan Hawken (wireless operator) looked round the bulkhead. The navigator was making no effort to move. Stan waved goodbye and thought that John Bush nodded in reply, but could not be sure. Was he dead? There was no time to find out. Detonating the H2S set, he grabbed his parachute and headed for the rear door. The two gunners, Sgt Albert De Bruin (mid-upper) and F/S W. Leary (rear), were trying to get it open. Frantic activity by the light of a feeble torch followed before they succeeded. A terrifying sight greeted them, with flames from the blazing fuel tanks streaming back towards them, a sight that was to give Stan nightmares for a long time to come.

De Bruin was in the correct position to jump, hands on either side of the doorway, but seemed unable to bring himself to take the one vital step. With every passing second the Lancaster was more likely to explode in a fiery ball. It was no time to be polite. Stan kneed Albert vigorously in the bottom, propelling him into space, and dived out after him through the flames. Floating gently down he saw Albert's parachute below. Paddy Leary followed them down.

* * *

Awoken by the roar of aero engines, the villagers of Villers-le-Sec and neighbouring Alliancelles, despite the curfew, watched the drama unfold above them. They watched in awe as a stricken bomber came nearer, and lower. According to the Mayor of Villers-le-Sec, those aboard had plenty of time in which to abandon the doomed aircraft. But he swore on his oath that, had they jumped when they had the chance, the aircraft would have crashed out of control on to the houses below. There would undoubtedly have been many casualties.

The low-flying Lancaster was easily held in the beams of several searchlights, and presented a simple target to the German flak gunners. Fortunately for the villagers of Villers-le-Sec, the pilot (F/O Gordon Maxwell) kept ME796 flying until it was over the open ground between them and Alliancelles, where F/S W. E. Griffiths released the bombs. At that moment, a shell from a flak gun blew a wing off. The burning remains crashed uncontrollably on to an open piece of land known as 'la Malouette' between the two villages.

The horrified witnesses rushed to the burning wreckage to help however they could. It was to no avail. In any case, German troops had already thrown a cordon around the aircraft. The silent throng watched helplessly as flames devoured the remains of 'S-Sugar'.

So impressed by the courage of these unknown airmen were the villagers of Villers-le-Sec that they resolved that the least that they could do would be to give the men a decent burial. The stony-hearted Germans from the Kommandantur at nearby Sermaize-les-Bains were in no hurry to do any favours for either the quick or the dead. It was a further two days before the Mayor obtained permission to hold a burial service, on the strict understanding that the gathering was not to be used for any other purpose. One of the German officers callously told the Mayor that there was no point in holding the service anyway as the bodies were only fit for the crows.

The French, however, were determined and, despite the Germans' orders, they came from all over the area to show their gratitude. They brought wreaths and bunches of wild flowers gathered from the fields and hedgerows, and they packed into the church of Villers-le-Sec. A short memorial service was held and the four were laid to rest — Maxwell, Bush, Griffiths and Howie. And when the service was over the graves were covered with their floral tributes, a gesture not only of defiance but of respect.

16

Massacre at Robert-Espagne

It was a few minutes before 0200 hours on 19 July when Albert De Bruin jumped from Lancaster ME796. As he floated down in the moonlight he saw a silvery strip of water below* and had to manipulate his parachute lines to ensure a dry landing. Then, to his horror, he spotted some high-tension wires right in his path. At the very last moment a light breeze blew him away from the deadly obstruction, and he landed close to a wood between Sermaize-les-Bains and Cheminon, barely five miles south-west of Revigny. Stan Hawken and Paddy Leary had both landed nearby. They would all three meet again a few weeks later. In the meantime Albert spent three days and nights wandering in the woods, never quite plucking up enough courage to knock on the door of some isolated farmhouse.

He was forced to live off his escape-kit rations. It was only a matter of time before they ran out, and he was left with no choice but to approach a farmer for food and help. At the first farm he tried he was given a couple of eggs and a glass of beer, but the farmer's wife, scared of German reprisals, begged him to leave as soon as he had finished his meal. It was not a difficult decision for him to have to make — his life against those of the farmer and his family. He went on his way, south-east, towards the Swiss border.

Now, deep in the heart of the Forêt de Trois-Fontaines to the south of Revigny, he came upon another isolated farm. Dogs barked furiously. Two men came out of the farmhouse and saw him standing there, frightened and confused. It was a difficult situation for the two men as well as for Albert, as it was not unknown for the Germans to infiltrate their own men, dressed as RAF or American aircrew, into the escape lines. But as they looked at Albert the two men realised that the fear in his eyes was genuine and that he just didn't look like a German. They took him inside, where he produced the small phrase-book issued to all aircrew and spoke three sentences in French: 'J'ai faim.' 'Pouvez-

---

* *Judging by the spot where he landed this could probably have been either the River Saulx or the Canal de la Marne au Rhin. The Ornain river is also near.*

vous me cacher?' 'Où est la frontière Suisse?'

There was no mistake — he had to be English! So Albert De Bruin was introduced to the people who were to feed and shelter him at the peril of their lives and of those of their families for several weeks to come — Adrien Gillet and his wife, their son-in-law, Marcel Bernier, and his wife and children.

It was lunch-time when Albert had arrived at 'la Neuve Grange'. Food was soon provided. The Gillets and the Berniers watched him silently as he ate. Then tears began rolling down his cheeks. All the tension of the past few days came flooding to the surface. He was being cared for; he was safe. The emotion was too much for him and, unable to eat, he pushed his plate away.

There was still the problem that neither could understand the other. It was agreed that Marcel should get help from Constant Ponsard in St Dizier, seven miles away. Ponsard, however, was unable to do much to help personally because several months previously he had been arrested by the Germans. Although released for lack of evidence, he was under constant surveillance; in addition, it was somewhat difficult for him to give open assistance as his house, in rue Thiers, happened to be directly opposite the German Feldgendarmerie — the police station!

Nevertheless, he promised to do what he could and telephoned Monsieur Schmit. Schmit agreed to go over to the house in rue Thiers where he was introduced to Marcel Bernier, who explained the problem. They knew that Monsieur Schmit had spent several years in London as a chef and that he could speak English fluently, so would he help? Unhesitatingly he agreed, and scribbled a note in English for Marcel to give to Albert.

Next morning, accompanied by his beautiful daughter so as to allay any suspicion, Schmit went to the farm. Again, the emotion of the moment proved too much for Albert who once more found himself in tears. Regaining his composure, he asked Schmit whether they could get him to Switzerland. No, it was too far away. 'Impossible,' said Schmit, and that was that.

Albert, however, was truly worried that if he stayed too long at la Neuve Grange he would eventually be discovered by the Germans, and he knew that they would not hesitate to shoot all those who had helped him — men, women or children, it made no difference to them. He was eventually persuaded to stay at the farm by the 'Jedburgh' Captain Jacques Taschereau (see Chapter 10).

He stayed there until 10 August, continually worried that his presence would be discovered. At the farm, however, there was a crude but effective early warning system that gave them some protection from a snap raid. La Neuve Grange, about one and a half miles from the village of Trois-Fontaines, did not have the luxury of 'mains electricity' — its only power source was the telephone. Now it so happened that the post-mistress at Trois-Fontaines was none other than Nelly Bernier — Marcel's sister! From the post-office she could see the German barracks at the ancient Abbaye de Trois-Fontaines; and it was the easiest thing in the world to ring through to la Neuve Grange to alert them whenever a German patrol was heading in their direction. Albert once spent a quarter of an hour suffocating under a straw mattress as a result of one of Nelly's warnings.

But the telephone had another use. There was no wireless at la Neuve Grange, so when the BBC news was broadcast Nelly switched on her set, telephoned through to the farm and held the mouthpiece against her wireless!

In the end, all his pleadings to be moved bore fruit, and on 10 August it was arranged that Albert would be moved to Robert-Espagne, five miles away in the valley of the River Saulx. As a precaution M Schmit advised him that when he got there he should, for everyone's safety, pretend to be deaf and dumb. The man who came to collect him, Jean Mickaeli, leader of a small maquis group in the Bar-le-Duc area, had only one bicycle; Albert had a rough ride on the cross-bar.

Mickaeli dropped him off at the house of Monsieur Lamoureaux and went himself to get further advice from Mademoiselle Suzanne Marson who, as well as being a member of the Resistance herself, was post-mistress of the village. Mickaeli asked her whether she could trust anyone in Robert-Espagne to shelter an English airman. She went at once to see Monsieur and Madame Evrard.

They agreed immediately, and in no time at all Albert found himself welcomed into the house of a very brave French couple, for whom the hideous drama that was to unfold 19 days later would have tragic consequences.

On 20 August Albert was taken to meet Stan Hawken and Paddy Leary and they tried to get him to stay. He spent the night with them but in the morning decided to return to Robert-Espagne. He set off into the forest, but was soon lost. Some maquisards found him and took him to Monsieur Marchal's farm near Robert-Espagne. Albert was in a quandary. He knew the golden rule was never to mention any names to anyone whom you neither knew nor trusted. And so, when a certain Monsieur Valero arrived, he said not a word. Valero therefore decided that Albert would stay with him, and there Albert remained until Jean Mickaeli tracked him down on the morning of 29 August, and took him back to the Evrards at Robert-Espagne.

At around 0900 hours on the same day, several lorry-loads of SS troops set up their headquarters in a large house at nearby Pont-sur-Saulx. Most Frenchmen were out at work on their farms, but a Lieutenant Fritsch ordered them to be rounded up. With this done, he announced that he had orders to shoot all males aged between 15 and 60. For the rest of the morning the Germans indulged themselves in an orgy of looting.

Around mid-day lunch was being prepared in most households. Suddenly a company of German soldiers, automatic weapons at the ready, roared into Robert-Espagne and made straight for the post-office, where the post-mistress, Suzanne Marson, was busily making Allied flags ready for the day of liberation. The Germans demanded the keys to the telephone exchange, but Suzanne refused to hand them over. The soldiers went outside into the road, turned and threw two hand-grenades into the post-office.

The sound of the explosions echoed around the village. Honoré Evrard and Monsieur Mariez went to see what had happened. M Mariez was immediately arrested, but Honoré managed to slip home. Breathlessly he urged everyone to finish eating as he had a feeling that things would soon start to get hot. Also staying with the Evrards, besides Albert, were Jean Mickaeli and a deserter from the Revigny Gendarmerie, Levrault.

There was a loud bang on the door. Germans! Honoré went to answer it, knowing that he had to stall them long enough for his guests to disappear, and for his wife to clear the three extra places from the table. Quickly the 'lodgers' went down into the cellar, its trap-door hidden carefully by a carpet.

Madame Evrard never saw her husband alive again.

At about 1330 hours a lorry with some 15 Germans aboard pulled up at the Tabary's farm. They found the family hiding in a cellar. One of the Germans stood guard as others put the buildings to the torch. Paul Bon, ignoring the danger to himself, rushed out of the cellar to save the animals trapped in the burning pens, and was scythed down by a burst of automatic fire, fair and square in his back. M Tabary and a friend, Pierre Fraîche, had been out in the fields when the Germans arrived and tried to find refuge by the nearby river, but they were spotted by two Germans on a motor-cycle combination. Madame Tabary also never saw her husband alive again.

Now the soldiers went from house to house putting them to the torch. Great plumes of smoke stained the sky.

The Frenchmen who had been rounded up earlier watched as another lorry arrived with an officer and some 20 heavily-armed soldiers. The officer stood up on the lorry and barked out his orders. The 49 prisoners of all ages were marched off to the station, where they were lined up into three ranks, their backs to the embankment. Three heavy machine-guns were then set up — one in front and one at each end.

Some of the Frenchmen had not had time to eat, and their wives arrived with food. The German guards turned them away. One of the guards offered his cigarettes. Young Paul Tanguy took one and asked: 'Is this a last cigarette for the condemned?'

He did not need an answer.

Madame Daimé, wife of the level-crossing keeper, looking out of her house, could see her husband, Daniel, and one of her sons, Raymond, standing no more than 40 yards away. They seemed quite calm and resigned to their fate. Madame Daimé and the rest of her family watched with tears streaming down their faces. In another house nearby Madame Paumier, too, was taking her last look at her husband and her son.

Suddenly the officer gave the signal. The three machine-guns opened fire in unison. Three long bursts echoed the length and breadth of the village. Under the deluge of flying bullets the Frenchmen were ripped to pieces. It was soon over. Anyone still alive was finished off with a shot from a pistol. Their foul crime accomplished, the Germans forced the villagers to look at the carnage. They then set fire to any house so far untouched, and joined their pals in the château at nearby Pont-sur-Saulx.

Madame Evrard, meanwhile, fearful not only for her husband's life, was worried for the three men trapped in the cellar. It had been impossible for her to let them out until evening because, by ill chance, a German had been standing in front of the house. Flames from neighbouring houses were spreading; smoke was already pouring into the house. One more look out of the front door — the sentry had gone! Quickly opening the trap-door, she released the men, and led them to the bottom of the garden, where they remained hidden amongst tobacco plants until nightfall.

Robert-Espagne continued to burn, and some time in the night Albert De Bruin crept to the bank of the River Saulx and hid in the rushes. There he stayed until the following day when armoured units of the US Third Army reached the village. He got a ride on one of their tanks, but it was heading east! He went forward with the unit as far as Dieuze, to the east of Nancy, before he decided that it was his duty to return as soon as possible to England. He hitched a lift on a supply lorry heading back for Paris, and was sent to Laval for the usual preliminary interrogation. On 9 September he was flown back to England.

* * *

The question remains: why were 49 men murdered that afternoon of 29 August 1944? Robert-Espagne was not the only village in the Saulx valley to suffer. Couvonges, barely two miles to the north, was also put to the torch and 26 were murdered there. Two of the dead, Pierre-René Petitprêtre, aged 78, and Théophile Vignon, 88, were too weak to walk to the place of execution. They were burned alive in their houses.

Their names appear with 24 others on the simple memorial in Couvonges:

'EN SOUVENIR des Martyrs de Couvonges massacrés par les Allemands en retraite le 29 Août 1944.'

Two other nearby villages, Mognéville and Beurey-sur-Saulx, also suffered atrocities — six men murdered at the former and three at the latter.

It was reported that the officer at Robert-Espagne had said that one officer and three men had been killed near the village and that the village and others nearby were going to pay the penalty for the outrage. Some sources attribute the ambush of the German officer and three men to the SAS who, as seen, were certainly active in the area.

It is clear from the SAS report on Operation RUPERT that one day at the end of August 1944 they ambushed a German staff car. As the report states, briefly:

'Capt Walters, Cpl Smith, Pcts Chambers and Henderson, ambushed a German staff car on the St Dizier-Chancenay road at T 963102. Both occupants were killed when the car overturned. Pct Chambers was wounded.

'At this time the SS battalion in Troisfontaines killed all the civilians they could find and then withdrew, firing villages on the way.'

And on 27 August the 120-strong maquis 'de la Fontaine Saint Jean' attacked a German column on the road to St Dizier, taking one prisoner and killing three others. They lost one killed and one wounded themselves. This, too, could have been the incident that sparked off the massacres.

Attached to this maquis from 1 September to 19 September were two English officers, Major Bodington and Captain Peters! An American, Lieutenant Robert Cormier, had also been with the maquis since 25 August.

The Germans possibly were provoked by the many maquis attacks, and the Saulx valley massacres were their way of venting their collective spleen. Retreating, they would not have worried about the killings. But there was no valid military reason for the massacres. Surely it was no more than one last chance to give the French a lesson they would never forget, and one last opportunity to deal with the villages they believed, rightly or wrongly, to be sheltering partisans?

Three years later Albert went back to the area to thank the many brave French people who had given him shelter — the Gillets and the Berniers at la Neuve Grange; M. Schmit of St.Dizier; Suzanne Marson, now a government official in Bar-le-Duc; Constant Ponsard; and Madame Evrard who, having lost everything in Robert-Espagne, had moved to Bresse in the Vosges.

He brought with him a letter from the Dagenham branch (his home town) of the Royal Air Force Association, addressed to the Mayor and the People of St Dizier, dated 23 July 1947. It would be fitting to quote an extract from it:

'We cannot speak highly enough of the great spirit and heroism which was found throughout the entire German occupation, and we are proud to have, through one of our members, proof of the magnificent work that was done so well and so valiantly . . .'

* * *

Having baled out of ME796, Stan Hawken collided with a tree and was knocked out. A while later he regained consciousness. He was flat on his back, staring up at his parachute in the tree. He could not have been out for very long because he heard the drone of Merlin engines as the last Lancasters made their way home. He hacked his parachute down from the branches, buried it and his Mae West in the bushes and decided to get away from the scene of the crash as quickly as possible. Realising from the position of the North Star and the sound of the raid that he was south and west of Revigny, he headed south along a gravel track through the woods. It was a bright, starlit night and he had no difficulty finding his way.

When dawn broke he discovered that he was near a village (later identified as Cheminon) and stayed in the woods until evening (19 July). At about 2200 hours, when darkness was falling, he headed south-east until 0700 hours on 20 July, when he came to an isolated farm. He stayed in the woods until satisfied that its only occupants were an elderly woman and a young boy. Towards evening he plucked up courage and knocked on the door. The boy and the woman, who appeared terrified, answered. It was only through the lad's pleading that Stan was allowed in.

After a struggle to understand each other the boy went to fetch help. He returned with a Frenchman who asked Stan to identify himself. The man in turn told him that his name was Jean Vidal, and he would be back later. Around midnight Jean and another man, Alfred Lallemont, appeared and told the woman that Stan would be hidden in the forest. This was a necessary precaution as it was believed that she was pro-Nazi; the less she knew the better.

In fact, Jean Vidal took Stan back to his house in St Vrain, where he stayed for a month:

> 'There I met his wife, Margot, and I was shown his three daughters, Jacqueline (ten years old), Denise (six) and Michelle (four) who were asleep in one of the two bedrooms of their quite small house. Even though they had known me for such a short while and I was such a risk to these people, their eagerness to help me already had me feeling like a valued friend, and a most welcome guest in their house. What an incredible piece of luck it was for me to meet such people.'

Then the Vidals told him that the boy who had helped him was Marcel Cassagne and that the elderly woman was Madame Roberts, his grandmother. Suspicions that she was pro-Nazi proved well founded when she denounced Margot after she had tried to get a piece of Stan's Lancaster as a souvenir. Margot told the Germans that she wanted the souvenir to remember the great deeds of the Luftwaffe! They believed her and let her go free!

Stan was confined to his tiny room, measuring nine by six feet, during daylight but emerged into the living room at night to eat and chat to his hosts. He was anxious to discover whether anything was known of the rest of his crew. It was Doctor Henri Fritsch who told him that there were some dead in the wreck of the Lancaster, but Paddy Leary was with Monsieur Adolphe Bertrand and his wife in Bois-du-Roi about four miles from St Vrain.

After baling out, Paddy was spotted by Monsieur Blaisot, who was out fishing. The Frenchman at once consulted M Bertrand who returned with a change of clothes for Paddy and then took him back to his home in Bois-du-Roi. Dr Fritsch was duly contacted.

The Vidals suggested that Paddy should come and stay at their house. Paddy agreed to the transfer and on the evening of 26 July cycled over to St Vrain with Pierre Blanchard, Margot's brother-in-law. According to Stan Hawken, despite having readily agreed to the move, Paddy found it difficult to fit in to his new surroundings, and seemed to be unable to appreciate the sacrifices that were being made on his (and Stan's) behalf.

On 29 July Jean told Stan that he would be flown back to England on 1 August. Paddy would be included only if one of the five scheduled passengers failed to show up. On the appointed night Stan, Paddy and Jean set off to rendezvous with a guide who would take them to the makeshift airstrip. Their hopes were dashed when the guide failed to arrive, and there was nothing to do but return to St Vrain. Their disappointment was only increased when they later heard that the aircraft had indeed landed and had picked up only two people. The intended guide had been arrested by the Gestapo.

On 20 August the Germans arrived in force in St Vrain and began what seemed to be a house-to-house search. Although only looking for billets for the troops, it was impossible for Stan and Paddy to remain in the village. They left hurriedly in broad daylight, taking their few possessions with them. Jean led the way. Stan:

> 'All was going well until we turned a corner. There, to our horror, were 50 or 60 German soldiers, lounging on the side of the road. The sight of them gave me quite a shock . . . 'Everything went well and we walked past the soldiers without attracting their attention. It was a great relief when we rounded the corner and were out of sight.'

It was a narrow squeak, not only for the two airmen who, if captured, might well have suffered no more than a rough beating, but also for the Vidal family who would have been shot without mercy. Stan and Paddy were again taken to the Bertrands' house in Bois-du-Roi. Jean told them to stay there until he had had a chance to discover what was going on in the village. Jean and Margot returned that evening with the news that they would not be able to go back to St Vrain as the Germans seemed likely to remain there for some time. Stan thanked the Vidals for all that they had done for him, although Paddy was somewhat less forthcoming in his appreciation.[*]

On 24 August Stan and Paddy were taken to Laws's SAS camp in the Forêt de Trois-Fontaines, where they met more evaders — four of the crew of R5485, three USAAF First Lieutenants (Bernoski, McCurdy and Rhiner) and Red Banville, John Nicholson and Ken Hoyle, who had just arrived from Revigny. Laws had arranged accommodation for the evaders at la Neuve Grange farm. 'Mac' McCurdy, a fighter-pilot, and Jack Rhiner, a B-17 pilot, had both been shot down on a daylight raid to Cologne some months earlier; Bernoski had damaged an ankle and was not too mobile.

The SAS were not in France to act as nursemaids to a bunch of evaders. So, at 0730 hours on 25 August, Laws radioed to England: '16 RAF here. Send Dakota to landing ground registered by Marechal [sic] of Eclan. Send earliest possible date of pick-up.'

But the US Third Army was speeding ever nearer, and at 1930 hours on 27 August he sent a second message: 'Have sent RAF men south of Marne to await Allied advance. Do not think plane of much use now.'

The Marne was several miles away to the south (it flows through St Dizier) and beyond the edge of the forest where the men were hiding. The SAS had by now given up their shepherding role and the camp broke up. A few of the evaders remained billeted on la Neuve Grange farm.

Stan Hawken joined up with a gang of ruffians whose behaviour was so outrageous that they could scarcely be called maquisards. They had no qualms in taking what they needed, by force if necessary. Stan disapproved of their methods:

---

[*] *According to Stan in his book* Missing Presumed Dead *(Hill of Content Publishing, 1989).*

'Next day there was another event that confirmed my future with the gang was on very shaky ground. Late in the afternoon, four or five of the gang brought two French girls into the camp. The girls looked as if they were in their late teens or early twenties and they were absolutely petrified.'

The girls had good reason to be, for they knew that their 'crime', consorting with the Germans, was regarded as a serious offence. Justice was of a very summary nature, and Stan was deeply shocked when he realised that the gang were actually going to 'try' the two girls. He asked their leader, Henri, if he had correctly understood the verdict. He had — they were to die:

'The two girls, who by this time had become piteously hysterical, were taken away by the same men who had brought them in. A few minutes later a burst of machine-gun fire was heard. I presumed that the worst had happened . . .'

Soon after this distressing incident Stan bumped into Mac and Jack when all three were looking for food, and they decided to stay together, away from the brigands. Paddy Leary remained with the SAS. They never saw him again.

Laws and his SAS party, possibly with Paddy Leary, had moved off and left Stan Hawken and his pals based on la Neuve Grange, waiting for the arrival of the advancing Americans. Then, on 2 September, hiding in the bushes near the road to Cheminon with Jack Rhiner, Stan was 'amazed to see in the distance, a patrol of American jeeps and light tanks'. It was the advance guard of XII Corps, men of the 25th Light Cavalry. The spearhead was moving on, and Stan and Jack decided to go with them. He remembered Jean Vidal telling him that Albert De Bruin had been hidden at Robert-Espagne. They made a brief halt there, and Stan asked if anyone knew the whereabouts of an 'aviateur Anglais'.

He was told to go to a spot just outside the village. He might find him there:

'I hadn't understood their meaning about going to that particular place so, when I arrived, I wasn't prepared for the horrible spectacle with which I was confronted. There were bodies of approximately 50 men . . . It was carnage of the worst kind, a sight which I have never forgotten.'

He then had the ghastly job of searching every corpse to see whether Albert was one of them, and was greatly relieved not to find his body. Stan gave details of the killings to an American officer, and word soon spread amongst them: 'It was a grim-faced crew who drove out of that village that afternoon . . .'

Stan woke up in the early hours of one morning with a premonition that all was not well. He decided that they had gone far enough with the hospitable American officer, so made their excuses and hurriedly left westwards. Within a couple of hours of their leaving, the Germans put in a strong counter-attack against the Americans and caused many casualties. Weeks later, on his way home aboard the *Queen Mary*, Stan met the same American officer, who told him how lucky he and Jack had been.

Stan and Jack hitched a ride to Paris, where they parted, Stan being directed to the Hotel Meurice for interrogation by 'British Intelligence'. After a little sight-seeing with a fellow Australian, Stan caught a plane from Paris to Hendon on 7 September, and the following day was given the treatment by IS9(W) and ORS Bomber Command.

The days dragged by until at long last, on 13 November 1944, he sailed for Australia. But it was to be two months before his train pulled into Spencer Street Station, Melbourne, on the evening of 19 January 1945. The next day he caught the train for Pyramid Hill and home, his war finished.

★ ★ ★

One of the three Lancasters shot down at or near Revigny on 18/19 July was R5485 (F/O T. E. W. Davis, 467 Squadron), the 21st victim of the night. It was on its way home when attacked by a night-fighter a few miles west of Revigny, and blew up into two sections. The pilot was strangled by his intercom leads after baling out and fell by the side of the road from Pargny-sur-Saulx to Heiltz-le-Maurupt. The rear gunner was killed in the attack. The others survived, one of them by the skin of his teeth.

F/O Frank Haddlesey DFC, mid-upper gunner, found himself trapped in the rear section, and only with great difficulty managed to extricate himself from his turret. He jumped out and pulled the rip cord. His parachute opened, and he knew he was safe. But something was wrong with his right leg. He reached down. It had been severed just above the knee. He reckoned that he must have hit the tailplane as he baled out.

Frank had been wounded before, on the Düsseldorf raid on 3/4 November 1943, when his Lancaster had been attacked by an Me210. Hit by three bullets in his right shoulder, he also suffered shrapnel wounds to the face but, despite his serious injuries, shot down their attacker and then helped the rear gunner, also wounded, out of his turret. He made no mention of this to his skipper until they had returned to base, whereupon he was awarded the DFC. He spent the next two months in the RAF Hospital at Rauceby, and was not passed fit for operations again until 31 May 1944.

Now his thoughts turned to the imminent landing and to jagged bones being driven up into his body. With great presence of mind he inflated his Mae West which, as he had hoped, cushioned his fall as he hit the ground. He applied a rough tourniquet to his leg and found shelter in some trees, where he spent what was left of the night.

At daybreak he crawled to a farmhouse. A doctor was summoned, but there was little he could do as the Germans had taken most of his surgical equipment. There was no alternative but to hand him over to the Germans, who packed him off to the Fatherland by hospital train. He spent most of the journey sitting in a carriage full of wounded Germans, sleeping with his head on the shoulder of a German sergeant. All were dressed in regulation hospital garb — white with blue vertical stripes — and as Frank could speak a little German he was treated as one of them, until they realised that he was not!

The stump of his right leg later became gangrenous. Fortunately, Reichsmarchall Hermann Göring himself visited the hospital. On learning of Frank's problem he insisted that he be given the best possible treatment. Happily, this was a success. Not many Allied airmen can claim that Göring saved their life!

In February 1945 he was repatriated via Switzerland and Marseille, sailing to New York on the Swedish-American Line ship *Gripsholm**. He arrived in Toronto on 23 February.

★ ★ ★

R5485's navigator, F/O Mark William Edgerley, landed near Heiltz-le-Maurupt, a few miles WSW of Revigny. He buried his bits and pieces and set off along the bank of the River Ornain, away from Revigny. The following day, 20 July, he met a Frenchman who agreed to help him and took him back to his house in nearby Jussecourt-Minecourt, where he stayed for the next four weeks. On 19 August he was taken to la Neuve Grange in the Forêt de Trois-Fontaines, where he met the SAS and the other evaders. He stayed thereabouts until the Americans arrived on 1 September. He was in Paris the following day. Records are silent as to his movements thereafter but, unusually, he seems to have escaped being formally interviewed on his return to England.

The wireless operator, F/S Denis Vaughan Kelly, managed to land

'. . . in a field near some woods not far from the village of Pargny-sur-Saulx. I hid my parachute and Mae West under some scrub and crawled to the woods, as I had broken my ankle. I slept in the woods until daylight. I crawled for about three miles and was eventually picked up by a Frenchman, who took me to his house, where I received food and shelter until 26 July.'

He had been found by a lock-keeper and a *garde-champêtre*† who knew of a trustworthy doctor in nearby Sermaize-les-Bains — Dr Fritsch! He was unable to treat Kelly's ankle and on 26 July a maquis guide took him to Châlons-sur-Marne for proper attention. He returned to Sermaize on 2 August. With the Germans retreating, it was too risky for Kelly to stay there any longer, and on 18 August he was moved to the camp in Trois-Fontaines forest. He, along with the others in the neighbourhood, were liberated on 1 September by the 2nd Cavalry, 4th Armored Division, US Third Army.

F/S Lawrence William McGowen, bomb-aimer, landed in a field near Jussecourt-Minecourt and, having hidden his 'parachute and Mae West

---

* *The* Gripsholm *and her sister ship the* Drottningholm *were on charter to the International Red Cross for the repatriation of wounded prisoners-of-war. Painted on the ships' sides in very large letters was the word DIPLOMAT.*

† *Literally a 'rural policeman'.*

in some bushes . . . started to walk in the direction of Paris'. He got as far as Ponthion, close to the Canal de la Marne au Rhin, a distance of some three miles, when he 'contacted a member of the FFI who took me to his camp at Sermaize-les-Bains where I remained for about one month'.

On 18 August McGowen met an 'SAS paratrooper' who said 'he would try and arrange for an aircraft to take me back to England. This fell through, so I decided to walk to the Allied lines.' However, on 20 August he made contact with members of his crew 'who were staying with the maquis in Forêt de Trois-Fontaines', and he returned with them. Perhaps he returned with Kelly after the liberation, for both reached England on 6 September.

Sgt W. F. Marshall, flight engineer, landed safely and hid for three days in the woods before being 'found by the FFI' on 22 July. For five weeks he stayed with Eugene Blanchard in Jussecourt-Minecourt, but his stay there ended on 26 August when he too was told that an aircraft would be arriving to take him back to England. It was a vain hope, of course, and so he 'stayed at another farm near Cheminon (name and address unknown) for approximately six days'.

The rest of the time he spent with the maquis in the woods, except for one day when he met the SAS and his fellow evaders. It was now 30 August and, with the Americans so close, Marshall set off alone to St Dizier to find them. He walked through the German lines without a problem, and was in Paris on 2 September. As with Edgerley, the trail runs cold at Paris! But at least he was safe.

17

The Final Losses

Heading more or less westwards after bombing Revigny, Lancaster LM117 (630 Squadron) was barely 25 miles into the homeward journey when a burst of flak ripped into it. The aircraft caught fire and was soon out of control. It crashed near Togny-aux-Boeufs, 10 miles south-east of Châlons-sur-Marne and close to a busy railway line which threaded its way beside the rivers Marne and Guenelle. The crew baled out but one was killed, so it is said, by a German. It was the Germans' practice to post guards at intervals along the railways, and it is presumed that one of them saw the ghostly form of a parachutist coming towards him and fired, with fatal consequences.

Another of the crew reportedly landed on the roof of the school and escaped to the west at high speed across the fields. Of the six survivors, three were taken prisoner and three evaded.

The bomb-aimer, F/S Ernest Couchman, spent a quiet evasion at the home of Georges Adnet and his wife at 31 rue de Plain, Courtisols.*

The mid-upper gunner, Sgt D. A. Grant, landed near Mairy-sur-Marne. He was helped to dispose of his parachute and other equipment, and advised to leave the area as quickly as possible as there were several German garrisons close by. He found his way to Cernon where he was assisted by Monsieur H. Camille. From there he was taken a few miles across the downs to the Laurent family in the rue de Fontaine, Dommartin-Lettrée, where he remained 'until the Americans came through on the morning of 29 August 1944'.

The pilot, F/O Bruce William Brittain, landed safely in a field just north of Aulnay-l'Aître (eight miles north of Vitry-le-François), and walked all night, thinking that he was travelling due west. In fact he was describing a half-circle. At daybreak he laid low in some bracken, where he remained until dusk. He made contact with a farmer who took him back to his house on the outskirts of St Amand-sur-Fion, only two miles south-east of Aulnay-l'Aître!

---

* Also there was Sgt Joseph Orbin, navigator of Lancaster ND531, 460 Squadron, lost on Mailly-le-Camp, 3/4 May 1944.

Fed, and with a new overcoat, he set off westward on 20 July, and walked until evening when he reached Montépreux, some 20 miles distant, where another farmer told him to go to a house just outside the village. On the morning of 21 July he was taken to a second farm where he remained for the rest of the day, before being taken to yet a third farm, where he stayed until the morning of 22 July. Here he met two other evaders.

⋆   ⋆   ⋆

After an uneventful journey to the target, bombs dropped, JB473 (F/O R. M. Deacon, 49 Squadron) was cruising homeward when the mid-upper remarked that he could see two crews baling out (possibly LM117 and PD210). He had no difficulty seeing them in the clear moonlight, and was about to suggest to the pilot that he might like to do a bit of 'corkscrewing' when there was a terrific bang — just as LM117 had done, JB473 had strayed over a concentration of flak guns. The rear gunner reported flames streaming past his turret from the starboard wing and, as the Lancaster filled with smoke, the pilot ordered the crew to bale out.

A prowling night-fighter saw the stricken aircraft and closed in to finish it off. Soon after 0200 hours on 19 July, JB473 crashed a short way north of Vassimont. Men from the village, ignoring the curfew, rushed to the burning wreck. They found only the Canadian mid-upper gunner, P/O A. J. Rammage, amidst the debris. He was quickly taken back to the village. All, however, was in vain, and it was the sad duty of the Abbé Duchesne to lay him to rest.

Cannon shells smashed into the nose where Sgt J. A. Diley (wireless operator) was feverishly trying to attach his harness. Luckily he was not wounded, but it may have been this attack that prevented the mid-upper gunner from baling out. John Diley was probably the last to bale out. He had made his way to the forward escape hatch and was about to leave when the explosion from the night-fighter's attack blew the nose open. John was out through the gap in a flash and landed in a tree near Vassimont, with nothing more than a bruised shoulder and slight cuts about the head.

The blazing Lancaster crashed not far away in a clearing. Sure that it would attract unwelcome attention, John hid his parachute as quickly as possible. In his confused state he had been worried about the noise he was making as he tugged his silken umbrella clear of the branches! Then machine-gun fire! He made off into the trees as fast as his legs would carry him, before it dawned on him that the gunfire was the Lancaster's ammunition being set off by the heat!

He hid in a nearby wood until daylight before moving off through the trees. Some while later he found himself back at the wreckage of JB473, now guarded by the Germans. He ducked back into the wood, where he stayed for the night. Next day, 20 July, having cut off the tops of his boots to make them look like shoes, he headed south away from Vassimont, and after an hour or so met three Frenchmen. He explained as best he could that he was very thirsty, but not hungry as he had been tucking into his escape-kit rations. One of the Frenchmen told him to stay there and he would be back later.

It was well into the afternoon before he returned, with a very large horse pulling an equally massive cart. He had also brought a bottle of champagne, six hard-boiled eggs and some bread. Not wishing to give offence, John drank some 'bubbly' and managed a couple of the eggs. The farmer told him to climb on to the cart, and off they went.

It was a hot day. John took off his RAF tunic top and shirt and sat there, vest bared to the world, but still wearing his RAF trousers and boots. Clopping peacefully along a quiet track, in good spirits thanks to the champagne, they came to one of the main German east-west arteries (the RN4), along which convoys were flowing in both directions. Nearing the junction John saw to his horror that not only was a large convoy passing at that very moment but, worse, a large German *feldgendarme* was on point-duty, who signalled the farmer to stop and wait! After what seemed an eternity they were allowed to proceed straight across, through a pair of massive iron gates on huge stone pillars into the courtyard of la Maltournée farm, home of the Mageski family.[*]

Already at la Maltournée was F/S Allan Russell Harpell (bomb-aimer), who had landed some way to the south-east of Vassimont, near a wood. He too had waited until the sun was up before setting off westwards. During the afternoon of 19 July he met a farmer who had given him food and then taken him to la Maltournée.

John was offered a drink of clear liquid. A warning from Allan proved timely as the *eau de vie* burned the back of his throat. Madame Mageski produced another glass of the spirit — in it was a finger, which they were told was from their dead comrade — the French were preserving the gruesome digit! The young son of the family, thrilled at having the airmen to stay, showed them his souvenir — JB473's camera cover complete with holes.

Too dangerous for the airmen to sleep in the farm itself, their beds were made up in the hay-loft, their lavatory the adjacent field. The two men had no complaints on that score; anyway, it was safer out there!

The following evening (21 July) Brittain arrived. Next morning the three evaders were escorted by five members of the FFI to their camp in a wood just over a mile north-east of Ecury-le-Repos where, to their delight, John and Allan found their rear gunner, F/S Donald Wilson.

He too had baled out near Vassimont (probably north-east, near the N77 Troyes to Châlons-sur-Marne main road) and had landed in a clearing in the middle of the woods. He hid in the trees until first light, taking the opportunity to remove all identification badges and insignia from his battle dress:

'I was unhurt, and at daybreak commenced walking westwards by means of the sun and the small compass from my aids-box. Throughout the day of 19 July I made my way, at all times in the forest, resting periodically; and at night I slept there, having encountered no one all day.'

[*] *Here another Mailly-le-Camp evader, Sgt H. S. Chappell, mid-upper gunner of Lancaster LL787, 9 Squadron, had earlier been sheltered.*

He set off again on 20 July heading in the same direction until, at around
1700 hours, he emerged from the forest and saw the village of Lenharrée.
He had now gone almost 40 hours without water and had been eating
only what was in his escape kit. Despite his hunger and thirst, he decided
to see who was there first, and watched patiently from the shelter of the
trees. He soon fell asleep, not waking until early the following morning,
21 July.

Throwing caution to the wind, he decided to go into the village anyway,
and was making his way towards the nearest house when suddenly the
door opened and a soldier emerged. The unsuspecting German failed
to notice him and Don beat a hasty retreat into the woods. The sound
of a motor-bike shattered the stillness of the morning as the German
roared off into the distance. Deciding that it was too risky to enter the
village, he walked round it.

Resting for a few hours he resumed his travels in a north-westerly
direction, along the Lenharrée to Normée road (now the D18):

'I kept to the highway, and after about 15 minutes I met a
Frenchman on a bicycle who stopped and spoke to me. I still had on
my flying boots, which this man evidently recognised. He turned
out to be a member of the FFI. He questioned me and learned that
I had crashed in a Lancaster. He told me that they were looking for
the crew, as they knew that they were free and in that area. He
instructed me to hide in the forest which bordered the road until
2100 hours, when he would bring me food, clothes and possibly a
bicycle.'

True to his word, the maquisard returned at the appointed hour with
all three things. They pedalled off together in the same direction in which
Wilson had originally been heading, passing through the villages of
Normée and Ecury-le-Repos, before turning off the road into a wood
and down a ravine leading to a tented camp. It was now late evening on
21 July. The following morning, Brittain, Harpell and Diley arrived; but
one further evader was still to come.

Sgt Harold Sharp (flight engineer, JB473) baled out and landed in a tree
without injury. He left his parachute firmly snared in the branches and
walked west for about half an hour, to put some distance between the
tell-tale canopy and himself. He lay down in the undergrowth until
sunrise, in all probability not too far from Wilson, who had also reached
Lenharrée that same day (19 July) having followed foresters' haulage
tracks through the woods. It was 2130 hours and, while Wilson spent
the night in the woods, Sharp found a barn on the outskirts of the village
and stayed there for the night. Bright and early on 20 July he walked to
Normée, where he met a farmer who took him home and gave him food
and drink.

Refreshed after his lunch, he set off north-west across country, parallel
to a road, but not actually on it. This was a wise precaution for, just as
he approached Ecury-le-Repos, several lorries loaded with Germans
passed on their way back to Normée. It was a near thing and he hid in
the fields until it was dark, when he headed in the opposite direction —

south! He walked through some woods for a while and then grabbed a little sleep.

At dawn on 21 July he continued southward until he reached the main Fère-Champenoise to Châlons-sur-Marne road, now the D5, then a German priority East-West route. To his horror he found, as had John Diley, an endless stream of German troops moving in both directions. There was nothing for it but to go to ground again.

He kept to the woods for two more days, until the morning of Sunday 23 July, when he returned to the same road. This time there was a gap in the traffic and at last he was able to cross. But as he did so he was seen. A man was pedalling furiously towards him. The cyclist, who to his great relief turned out to be French, told him to stay where he was, leaving as quickly as he had come.

He soon returned with some civvies, into which Sharp at once changed, and motioned to Sharp to get on the back of the bicycle. They pedalled off until they came to a wood about a quarter of a mile south of Ecury-le-Repos, where they waited for an hour or so. Eventually two other men arrived on bicycles, with a third one for Sharp. From there it was a short ride to the camp where Wilson, Brittain, Diley and Harpell were already in residence.

The camp was only a hundred yards or so from a road used heavily by the Germans, so it was a great relief to the evaders to be told that they would be staying there for only five days before being moved to Paris. In the event they stayed there for nearly two weeks! After the first week the maquis leader told the men that they could send telegrams to England to say that they were alive and well. Wilson:

'We were asked many details, such as our squadron number and its location, and in fact such items that we were instructed in our briefing not to divulge to anyone. The leader stated [that] these questions must be answered, and after some deliberation and hesitation the five, although considering it somewhat strange, believed in the Frenchman and supplied the information. In each case a message was to be sent to the squadron concerned, and then on to the next-of-kin, indicating that the airman was safe. I never heard of any of these messages being delivered.'

Perhaps the messages were never sent because, soon after the chief's visit, the maquisards stepped up their sabotage, to the obvious annoyance of the Germans, never ones to allow such behaviour to go unpunished for long.

The time came for the camp to be moved and the five airmen were taken to a house in Semoine, ten miles south (and only five miles west of Mailly-le-Camp). The owner of the house was a stocking manufacturer — John Diley was a popular man when he returned home to Manchester with several pairs of nylons!

They stayed at the new camp for four days, on the fourth night rejoining six of the maquisards from the first camp at a temporary location. The following day, 4 August, they helped set up another camp between Fère-Champenoise and Semoine. It took the Germans about a week to find this one, most likely having been given a tip-off by an informant for, on 12 August, a small but heavily armed force of six German officers and 15 men was seen making its way purposefully in the direction of the camp.

The sentries sounded the alarm in time and everyone managed to get clear. Wilson:

'We, after much running and evading and crossing of German-patrolled highways, were, by the aid of FFI guides, installed in another temporary camp for the night. The next day, 13 August, we marched through the woods for 4 kms and aided in setting up what was called another permanent camp. Here all our French companions remained until 21 August when all but one set out on anti-German activities.'

They were now near the village of Salon, five miles south-west of Semoine.

The one Frenchman who was left with the airmen was clearly not of a warlike bent for, according to Don Wilson, he 'seemed to be always setting out for a walk with a book under his arm'. Nevertheless, he made all the necessary provisions for running the camp and, most importantly, for keeping the men supplied with food, which was largely brought by two men from one of the neighbouring villages. Though not apparently themselves active members of the Resistance, these two were quite prepared to help in whatever way they could.

One day they brought their horses with them, as the Germans were scouring the countryside for every conceivable means of transport. They also brought news bulletins, and early on the afternoon of Sunday 27 August came the wonderful news that American soldiers were actually in Salon.

Wasting no time, the airmen went to the village and made themselves known. After a night's celebration, an American major took all five of them in his jeep to the front line, which was just east of Fère-Champenoise. They went to the town itself where a 'liberation party was held', and met a liaison officer from Montgomery's HQ, who noted their particulars and ordered them to stay where they were until further notice. The joys of being back in the armed forces again!

It was during these happy days that the four crew of JB473 paid a sad visit to Vassimont. They found their mid-upper gunner's grave marked by a simple wooden cross. Abbé Duchesne told them that the French had originally erected a more elaborate cross with Rammage's name carved on it, but the Germans had ordered it to be replaced with a plain wooden one bearing only the word 'Canadian'. The abbé also handed over Rammage's identification tags.

Three days later, on 31 August, they were told to report to the Town Hall, and were driven to the maquis HQ at Epernay. The following day they travelled to Paris in a truck driven by the FFI. Some were billeted at the hotel Pullman Windsor.

John Diley stayed at the luxurious Hotel George V. He heard of a Dakota that was going back to England and, on 3 September, managed to get a place aboard it. The other four — Harpell, Sharp, Wilson and

Brittain — flew back the next day to Hendon, Monday 4 September.

★ ★ ★

F/O Roy Deacon, pilot of JB473, baled out without any problem but broke a leg badly when he hit a tree on landing. He was found by the French and taken to a house in Vassimont, but there was nothing that they could do for him. On 20 July, with no other choice, they handed the luckless pilot over to the German authorities, who took him to the Military Hospital at Châlons-sur-Marne for proper attention. On 1 August he was transferred to the hospital attached to the POW camp at Châlons-sur-Marne.

Four weeks later, on 28 August, with the Americans knocking at the gates of the city, the German guards and hospital staff evacuated themselves, leaving their wounded patients behind. Accompanied by an English soldier, Lieutenant Donald Heselton Pasfield, 14 Field Squadron, Royal Engineers, attached to the Guards Armoured Division, Deacon 'walked' out of the camp. Pasfield had been wounded and captured on 1 August at St Martin-des-Besaces, south-west of Caen, after the 8 Corps attack on 30 July.

Deacon and Pasfield found their way to the Americans and were handed over to the Red Cross. Sent in stages to Orléans, they were flown back on Saturday 2 September in a B-24 to Horsham St Faith airfield near Norwich.*

★ ★ ★

Sgt Bill Fortune, navigator of JB473, certainly lived up to his name that morning of 19 July when, in pitch darkness, he parachuted on to a path no more than six feet wide, plumb in the middle of a large spruce wood. Floating down he saw the Lancaster burning brightly on the ground as its flares and ammunition ignited. He was not particularly religious, but the first thing he did was to kneel and give thanks, which surprised him! He hid his parachute and left the area as quickly as possible. His snap decision was to walk to Normandy. Quickly glancing at *Polaris*, he set off into the night.

He headed north-west, descending by a narrow path into nearby Vassimont, making no attempt to hide. There was no sign of life and he carried on walking as bold as you like through the village, and did the same at the next village, Lenharrée. He then struck off across the fields:

'It was a beautiful night, clear sky and warm. I could identify *Polaris* easily and just continued to walk for part of the night. I then entered a cornfield; it had already been cut and the stooks were stacked. So I made myself comfortable on one of these and went to sleep.

'As soon as it was light I awoke; I continued walking, keeping to the edges of fields or walking through woods. I came to an open field under cultivation and saw a farmworker and his wife working in the

---

* *The B-24 was possibly from the 458th Bomb Group, VIII Bomber Command USAAF, which had been ferrying fuel across to France for the thirsty vehicles of the US First and Third Armies.*

middle of the field. I thought this a good opportunity to make a contact and crossed the field to join them. In schoolboy French I got them to understand that I was RAF and asked if there were any Germans in the neighbourhood. I had my silk map and the Frenchman pointed to Sézanne and roughly indicated where I was. He wanted me to go home with him but his wife was very frightened and I thought in the interest of family peace to carry on walking. They made me a present of their breakfast, including a bottle of wine, for which I was very grateful.'

He carried on walking for the rest of the day, and after another night sleeping in the rough found himself next morning (20 July) on the outskirts of the village of Bannes. His stomach told him it was time to eat, and he scrounged a couple of small turnips for breakfast. He had already eaten the chocolate and some of the malted milk tablets from his escape-kit. Confronting him was an enormous field, but he walked across it anyway and came to the hamlet of le Mesnil-Broussy, tucked away in a clump of trees. By now very tired, he decided to get some rest, and an adjacent cornfield, uncut this time, would be his bed.

After only half an hour or so a Spaniel sniffed him out and began barking, followed shortly by its curious owner, Gilbert Lachasse. It was in his field that Bill was trying to sleep. Not that Gilbert minded one little bit, but he questioned the stranger closely, examining his flying-boots and clothing, before accepting that he was genuine RAF. He took Bill back to his farm, a couple of hundred yards away, and told him to hide in the loft of one of the barns. With Bill stowed away, Gilbert removed the ladder!

Gilbert explained to him, after his nap, that he had been seen by Suzanne, one of his three sisters, who had been out minding their cattle. In early 1940 there had been seven members of the family — Gilbert, his three sisters (Suzanne, Rolande and Andrée) a brother, Elphège, who at the time was a prisoner-of-war in Germany, and their parents; the latter had been tragically killed by strafing Luftwaffe fighters later that year.

Bill stayed with the family until the Americans arrived at the beginning of September. In the meantime he had been put in touch with Andrée Derouineau of Epernay, who supplied him with a forged identity card — just in case. Before the 'liberation', the maquisards 'swept' the surrounding countryside for any Germans who were left behind, and Bill was only too willing to lend a hand.

The 'sweeps' continued after he had gone home, and on one of them the Frenchmen 'ran into a German unit hiding behind a hedge. As the French descended towards them, the Germans opened up with a machine-gun.' Gilbert Lachasse was killed. A monument was erected in memory of a hero of France on Mont Août, a few hundred yards south of Broussy-le-Grand, Marne.

When Bill gave himself up to the Americans they took no chances and put him on a lorry together with some 20 German prisoners-of-war. He was taken to the POW cage at Sézanne, where there were so many prisoners that the Americans could not 'process' Bill quickly. So for a while he found himself behind barbed-wire, alone with a thousand of the enemy!

The Intelligence officers were soon satisfied and, together with three other American airforce evaders who had been in hiding in the area, he was taken by jeep to Paris, 70 miles away. After calling at the USAAF HQ he was driven to the RAF HQ which had only recently been taken over — Nazi flags were still hanging on the walls! He was interrogated again, by IS9(W), and next morning was flown to Arromanches. He was given passage in an LCT ('landing craft — tank') and spent eight very seasick hours being ferried to Dover.

Back in London he was given a medical, clean clothes, new kit and three weeks' leave. From his home at Stockton-on-Tees, he was posted to the ghastly holding unit at Brackla, near Nairn in Scotland, officially an Aircrew Allocation Centre. To his surprise he met John Diley and Harry Sharp there, but managed to see them for only a few hours as they were leaving the very next day. They never saw each other again.

In 1946, IS9 Awards Bureau in Paris asked the Air Ministry for news of Bill, on behalf of his helpers in France. On 22 March 1946 Department AI 1(a) P/W sent an 'Urgent' postagram to the Air Force records office in Gloucester: 'Will you please supply latest posting and rank of 1369450, Sgt W. Fortune.'

Though the mills of God grind slowly . . . He was probably languishing somewhere in Scotland, or attending the Staff Navigation Course at RAF Shawbury in Shropshire, from whence he was posted, as a navigation instructor, to Bishops Court: '. . . the last place on earth, back where I started!'

And his first students there were Free French!

* * *

It was mid-day on a hot summer's day and Pierre Lahanque, the village baker at Marson, a small village some six miles south-east of Châlons-sur-Marne, was about to sit down to a well-earned meal when the bell rang. He found a woman in a state of considerable agitation. She explained that she had found a wounded man near a calvary on a ridge off the road from Châlons. Could he help?

Indeed he could, despite serious doubts that it was a Gestapo trick. Nevertheless, he arranged to meet the woman near the calvary. They would go independently. Filling his pockets with water, sugar and a first-aid kit, he grabbed his bicycle (stolen from the SS!) and set off. When the woman arrived, she pointed into the trees. A wounded man who had been leaning against the trunk of a fir tree was trying to get up. Pierre motioned him to stay where he was. There was no mistaking the uniform of an Allied airman, nor that he was wounded. Pierre indicated to the woman that it was best for her to leave and, turning to the airman, told him that he would take him back to his house, but not in broad daylight and in uniform.

Pierre asked what had happened and the airman explained that they had been attacked by a night-fighter, possibly an FW190, that had taken them by surprise. It was all over in a few seconds. The fuel tanks exploded and that was the end of Lancaster PD210. Only he, the wireless operator, was blown clear. He added that the rest of the crew were dead. Pierre asked him how he could be sure of this, and the man replied that as he floated down, the sky lit up by the blazing Lancaster, he could see no other parachute. He was alone.

His name was John Chapple, and he came from London.

Pierre told John that he would return after dark to collect him. He went home and told his wife what had happened, then set off to look for the remains of the Lancaster and its crew, just in case. Searching high and low he came upon the tail section sitting there 'like an enormous toy', riddled with cannon holes.

Then he found the first body.

It was lying in a pool of blood, the blue-grey uniform now predominantly red. The dead man's partially deployed parachute was beside him. As Pierre spread it out, he could see that it had been so badly burned that it could have been of no use. He continued looking for the rest of the aircraft and then saw it, close to an elm tree, broken and burnt like a half-smoked cigar. An engine had scythed a path through the long grass, its propellers sticking into the earth. The huge wheels were some way away. There was no sign of anyone in the fuselage.

Widening his search with each circuit of the wreck, he found a second body. The dead man was lying on his back, his eyes staring unseeing at the sky. Then a third corpse, horribly broken, a light breeze ruffling red hair. Pierre read the word 'Canada' on the upper arm. The fourth and fifth men were soon located, close together. But of the sixth body there was no sign. Pierre determined to find the man who might, perhaps, be wounded and hiding in the woods. The light was fading fast. First he had to find John Chapple again.

John was unconscious, and with difficulty Pierre got him to his feet and helped him back to his house in Marson. His uniform was removed and his wounds dressed as well as possible; John had a graze across his forehead and a dislocated right leg. He was also grief stricken at the loss of his comrades, and was in a state of shock and refused to speak. He spurned, too, the offer of food and drink. Pierre understood, and let him be.

Six days later they went to the site of the crash, and searched desperately for the missing man. The other bodies had long since been removed and buried. It was a blazing hot day and they stopped for a rest. A shout echoed across the fields. Germans! Pierre told John to act deaf and dumb. Two men in uniform were coming towards them. There was no escape. The men got closer. Thank God! The 'Germans' were French workmen in their blue overalls!

The men had discovered a body in an oat field. The four of them walked back to the body which, sure enough, was that of the missing airman. He had fallen like a stone, without his parachute, his oxygen mask still across his mouth. Pierre told the two workmen to contact the mayor of St Germain to arrange for the burial. As they went their separate ways, John told Pierre that they had just found his pilot, Ross McNaughton.

Life went on. John remained at the bakery at Marson, where there were occasional moments of high tension, the Germans being wont to call at any time demanding food and drink. Once two soldiers entered the bakery without knocking. They were looking for lodgings but, despite Pierre's assurance that there were but two rooms (one for him and his wife and the other for their two young children), they insisted on searching the premises. Outside they saw a ladder leading to a loft and demanded to know what was up there. Pierre's heart began to pound, but he blurted out that it was only the store for the grain. The Germans wanted to have a look anyway. Now Pierre was in trouble, for in the store was John's bed, and John was in it. Pierre thought about grabbing the *feldwebel's* pistol and shooting them, but decided that it was too risky. They burst into the room, and there in the far corner was the bed. Beside it was a French-English dictionary, with brightly embossed gold letters on the cover. One of the men pulled the blanket off the bed and stepped back, pointing. Pierre had to think fast:

'He's my worker, do you understand? He's very tired. Makes the bread at night, then sleeps a little, like that.'

'Yes, yes,' replied the soldier. 'Understood.'

Pierre's heart returned to its natural position and they filed out, the dictionary unnoticed. Back in the house, the soldiers demanded champagne and Pierre decided that this was the right moment to produce a bottle. The soldiers consumed the contents and left.

Pierre tried to get John sent home, but an influential member of the Resistance told him that it was too risky. Days passed. American bombers often flew overhead, to remind them that there was a war on.

Then, on 27 August, the sound for which they had been waiting so long — the distant rumble and thunder of American armour. Free at last, but before he could go home John was asked to attend mass at the church at St Germain-la-Ville, where his six comrades were buried. The curate, Monsieur Vinot, summoned everyone from the area to be present to honour the young men who had given their lives for Liberty. The church was packed to overflowing when the curate suddenly announced John's presence amongst them.

It was a highly emotional moment. Everyone tried to shake John's hand, to give thanks for the supreme sacrifice made on their behalf. Speeches were made and, when it was all over, the people filed past the six graves barely visible beneath a mass of flowers. There was many a tear-stained cheek that day. Goodbyes were said and John went home.

18

For You the War Is Over!

The ominous clicking of the 'Fishpond' tail-warning device was the first indication to the crew of ME833 that they were being stalked by a night-fighter. Immediately F/O Les Wood flung the heavy Lancaster, bombs still aboard, into a 'corkscrew'. The Luftwaffe pilot was no novice and the grim chase lasted for several minutes. Thinking that he had at last shaken off the determined German, a very tired Les ordered the bombs to be dropped, though they were still short of Revigny. This done, he asked the navigator, F/S Norman Oates, for a course back to base.

Norman calculated that they could pick up the track home from Revigny a few miles to the north. Hardly had he passed the new course to his pilot when the end came. An unseen night-fighter (perhaps their first assailant) crept up from behind and below and blasted the Lancaster. Soon ME833 was in flames.

Norman vividly remembers metal turnings appearing on his navigation table as the cannon shells ripped through the thin metal sides of the Lancaster. He had a clear view forward and could see that the nose escape hatch had been released, and caught a glimpse of the bomb-aimer leaving. He wasted no time in diving out after him. Presumably the figure he could vaguely see in the darkness below was the bomb-aimer.

Safely on his way down, he watched ME833 stream earthwards in a fiery ball and crash in a great explosion. Then suddenly he was down. Amazingly he had not felt a thing. One moment he was swaying gently under the canopy, the next he was standing upright on the ground. He looked up and saw his parachute caught in the branches of a tree, yet he had not received the slightest cut or scratch and had had no indication that he was falling through trees. But there he was, on the ground alive and well. A tug on the parachute lines brought it to earth.

What happened to the bomb-aimer is not known, but, having undoubtedly baled out, he did not survive the landing and was buried at Châtelraould-St Louvent. The other five, unable to escape from the tumbling Lancaster, were buried at Somsois, some five miles to the south of Châtelraould.

Realising that he was in the middle of a wood, Norman decided to stay there until daylight:

'I buried the parachute and using the escape equipment in my uniform, the compass and the map, I set out to walk in the direction of the Swiss border.

'Keeping inside the woods I was able to cover quite a good distance. When I came to a road I crossed with great care and used it to estimate where I was. I made use of my emergency rations and drank water from a river, but made sure I used an anti-bacterial tablet. At mid-day I slept for a short while in a sunny clearing.

'My rations ran out later in the day and I realised I would never reach Switzerland without help. From the edge of the woods I watched a farmer working in a field. He was very poorly dressed so I decided to risk revealing myself. I stepped out into the open and called his attention to me. He carefully looked round in all directions before approaching me. I indicated my uniform and said 'RAF'. He walked away following the edge of the wood and indicated me to follow.

'He took me to a very run-down farmhouse where his wife gave me bread, meat and some very rough red wine. (A letter I received from the Air Ministry dated 17th June 1947 told me that it was a M Gerard of les Grandes Noues, par Somsois (Marne), who sheltered me that night, 19th July 1944.)

'I was shown to a bedroom where I quickly fell asleep. In the middle of the night [19/20 July] I was wakened to find there was a man I had not seen before in the house. He indicated by sign language that I was to follow him. We walked for two or three hours and finally arrived at what I can only describe as a château — certainly it was a very large building.

'I was introduced to a man who was obviously of some consequence. I remember the panelled room and, curiously, a very luxurious toilet which seemed to have no base inside — open to the outside in some way! I was given a meal, part of which was a jar of cherries.'

He had inevitably stumbled upon the Resistance, and the following day (20 July) an old lorry arrived at the house (les Chênes, home of the Vicomte de la Hamayde) with three or four men in it, all wearing workmen's clothing. It was explained that it was not possible for him to travel openly in his RAF uniform, and he was asked to change into a set of working clothes:

'I did as I was told because I considered the maquis a quasi-military organisation and I must carry out their orders.'

He was driven east for some 15 miles until, deep in Mathons forest, they came to a stone cottage, 'des Gaudes', headquarters of the maquis 'Garnier' led by Georges Debert. As we have already seen (Chapter 10), there was evidence that this man consorted with the Nazis; he was without doubt a 'bad egg'. After the war a French officer, Captain Raymond Krugell, testified that he had been asked by the Gendarmerie 'for a report on the burning of Marizien Farm . . . The persons named are Georges Debert and Roland Truchy. Debert was actually employed by the SNCF at Etrepy (Marne).'

Krugell, though unable to comment on this incident, added that he himself had been given command of two maquis — the 'Mauguet' and the 'Garnier' — and that at that time Georges Debert was leader of the maquis 'Garnier' in the Sauvage-Magny area. On 14 July 1944 Captain Jacques Taschereau found Debert's wallet, and in it were a membership card of the LVF* and a Gestapo identity card, with photograph, both in the name of Georges Debert. These documents were shown to Captain Krugell by Taschereau, who had closely questioned Debert and who stated with certainty that Debert was, or had been, a member of the LVF and of the Gestapo.

Krugell continued his testimony:

'Throughout 1944 I heard it said that Debert committed several acts of robbery in the Chavanges and Wassy area. I was told that it was to a certain Bertin, a café owner in Wassy but by no means a collaborator, that Debert used to take his merchandise.

'On 5 September 1944, when I was a Commander in the Army at Bar-sur-Aube, I learned the following information:
  – Debert had been in hiding in Bailly-aux-Forges, passing himself off as an American Lieutenant.
  – He attacked M Renard at his dairy at Laneuville.
  – He burned a car on the way out of Laneuville.
  – He stole 2,000 francs, wine and other alcohol from Madame Muret in Laneuville.'

The maquis 'Garnier', small by any standards, never amounted to more than 40 poorly-armed men. Formed in the spring of 1944 under Debert, they were originally located to the west of Mathons, in the woods near Bailly-aux-Forges. Debert's criminal activities did not go unnoticed by the authorities, and he was obliged to strike camp and seek pastures new. It was to this second camp that Norman Oates was taken and to which, in due course, P/O J. C. Wellein and five other RAF evaders would also be brought. It has not been possible to establish who the five were, but they might have been Sgt G. A. Alexander, F/S S. R. Ashton, Sgt W. G. Barlow, F/S E. H. Wells and F/L K. Stevens. Norman Oates recalled that they arrived at 'des Gaudes' separately.

Debert and his men were poorly armed, desperate for any gun on which they could lay their hands. One day they brought in some badly damaged machine-guns which had been removed from a crashed German aircraft at Arrembécourt by Georges Humbert. Together with one of his six companions (Norman recollects that he was an air-gunner from Liverpool) they took the bent guns 'to the nearest farmhouse and, using the tools we found there, managed to put together one working gun which we tested and handed back'.

---

* *Légion des Volontaires Français, French military collaborationists who fought on the Russian front in German uniform.*

John Wellein, a Canadian, understood French the best of them and acted as interpreter, though communication overall proved very difficult. But he understood enough one day to know that there was danger in the offing. At around 1800 hours on 7 August the maquisards were warned of possible action against them by a strong force of Germans. Debert doubled the guard, but the night passed peacefully and, when day broke, patrols on the edge of the woods saw nothing unusual. The next day, 9 August, was also quiet — the quiet before the storm.

At around 0100 hours on the morning of 10 August an unusual noise disturbed the sleep of the villagers of Mathons — it was only Debert returning to camp with a lorry. One of its rear tyres had burst and was coming off, and the metal rim of the wheel was making an infernal noise on the road. The inhabitants of Mathons would get little sleep for the remainder of that night.

It was common knowledge amongst the French locally that there was a group of maquisards hiding in the forest and inevitably word reached the Germans. A gendarme from Wassy had originally informed Debert of the impending attack, but he did not know the time and date even though the Germans had been preparing for it since 7 August. He discovered the vital details too late. Barely one hour after Debert had clanked through the streets of Mathons, other vehicles were heard approaching, and so many could mean only one thing. The attack had started.

The alarm was raised by one of the sentries rushing into the camp with the news that the Germans were on their way in large numbers, estimated at between 1,200 and 1,500. As usual, the German force was made up of men from many different units. It was some two hours later that the attack began. The Germans came in two columns. The first, from St Dizier to the north-west, sealed off all the exits from Mathons itself and deployed around the northern edge of the forest. The second column arrived along the track from the hamlet of la Folie, away to the south-east of Mathons, and went around the forest from the south, completing the circle.

Debert had already recalled the sentries and split the maquis into two parties — one under his command with several men all armed, the other led by his second-in-command, 23-year old forester Gabriel Sanrey. Sanrey's group was 22 men strong, and included the seven RAF evaders. Debert and his small party headed south and, managing to slip through the German cordon, apparently reached the vicinity of Brachay without loss.

The Sanrey party at first headed north and were about to break out of the woods when a burst of machine-gun fire forced them to return to the undergrowth. No one had been hit, but the Germans now knew where they were. The net was closing. Sanrey, in his green forester's uniform, hoped to fool the Germans into thinking that they were wood-cutters and decided to try to regain the cottage to the south. The plan was soon agreed but only Sanrey, three Frenchmen and the seven RAF airmen set off into the forest. The rest of the group hid in the woods. One of Sanrey's group later recorded what happened:

'We were part of the Sanrey group; we were going to cross the road to Brachay with him when bursts of machine-gun fire stopped us, forcing us to return to the middle of the wood. Although shaken, Sanrey, with his three comrades, determined to get to the hut. We were unaware that they had actually left us.

'There were 11 of us, spread around a large oak tree and well hidden under a carpet of leaves. Suddenly we heard footsteps treading on dead twigs . . . flat on our stomachs, pressed into the ground, holding our breath, we listened to our beating hearts . . . A German was coming towards us . . . 50 metres away. He was advancing cautiously, his gun ready to fire. We were done for. I looked at my watch — ten past eight. I'll always remember that. But about 100 metres away one of his comrades shouted to him: "Look out! British airmen!"

'Our Boche immediately half-turned towards his pal and both of them ran to the edge of the wood. We had had a lucky escape.'*

Norman Oates remembers being told to follow Sanrey as he tried to lead them to safety:

'We were quickly clear of everyone else and following a system where the Frenchman went forward on his own, then called out to us to follow. We did this repeatedly until, even in the very poor light, we realised we had walked into an ambush. We were confronted by a line of Germans in camouflage uniforms. The Frenchman [Sanrey] was standing there with his hands up.'

Norman was next to the Liverpudlian who carefully reached down into his sock and produced a .303 bullet. He let it slip to the ground and the pair of them, as surreptitiously as possible, buried it in the earth with their heels. It was a moment of high tension. When the shouting had died down and everyone appeared to be calmer, Norman, who was the only one of the seven airman in mufti, stepped forward and announced that he was 'RAF'. The Germans were not interested, and he was tied up, hands behind the back, together with the other six airmen, Sanrey and the three maquisards.

They were bundled into a lorry and driven away to the farm 'des Bons-Hommes'. Norman:

'As we travelled along one of the roads surrounding the wood I was aware of a field between us and the wood and in it were a lot of hayricks. Behind every hayrick was an armed soldier. There were a number of different uniforms, so I got the impression that the Germans had used every available man in this operation against the local maquis.'

Meanwhile, the 11 maquisards stayed in their leafy hiding place until evening, long after the Germans had left. Only when everything seemed quiet did they dare to leave the forest, and make for Wassy. From enquiries that they then made it transpired that Sanrey and his three companions were missing; no one knew what had happened to them.

* *Translated from Volume II* La Résistance en Haute-Marne *(Dominique Gueniot, Langres, 1983).*

Gendarmes from Joinville (six miles to the east) joined in the search, high and low, for the missing men. It was three days later that the unmistakeable stench of rotting flesh led the searchers to the mutilated corpses of the four men in the woods by a track running from Mathons to Brachay. The bodies were riddled with bullets, an ignominious end for young Sanrey; for Maurice Launois, 26; for Serge Kervaire and René Jakubas both 17.

Back at the farm the RAF evaders, still for the most part in uniform, were spared the fate of Sanrey and his three companions. Norman was singled out from the other six, possibly because he was in plain clothes:

'I was then separated from the rest of the aircrew and put in the front seat of a van. I was in quite a lot of pain by then because my hands had been tied so tightly that the circulation had been cut off. After an hour or two I was taken out of the van and made to sit down on the grass next to the others. Half an hour later or so an officer arrived, our hands were untied and we were put into a lorry. As we were being driven away I saw the farmer's wife and others being driven away in another lorry.'

Georges Douillot and his wife who lived at 'des Bons-Hommes' on the eastern edge of the forest had been supplying the maquisards (and the seven RAF evaders) with provisions, and the Germans strongly suspected them of so doing. It is possible that the Germans had forced the information from a youth who was known to have been arrested that same morning. A lorry driver had earlier witnessed a young man being savagely beaten near the Douillots' farm.

At around 0900 hours on 10 August the Germans sealed off 'des Bons-Hommes'. A man calling to collect milk from the farm was stopped from going there, but he saw the 11 men under guard sitting by the side of the road — Gilbert Sanrey, the three French maquisards, and the seven RAF prisoners.

A German officer interrogated the Douillots, and accused them of supplying the maquis with food. Although this was perfectly true, they both denied it vehemently and to every question put to them simply replied that they knew nothing. What else could they do? They well knew that by admitting the truth they would have signed their own death warrants. The Germans were not fooled by the stone-walling and took them away for further questioning.

Before leaving, the Germans ransacked the farm, took everything from it that was of any use and then burned it to the ground. They made the Douillots watch while they did it.

Their son, Bernard, aged 10, and daughter Yvette, together with her husband, René Leblanc, a wounded maquisard, and a farm labourer had escaped from the farm to the Leblanc's house at Nomécourt, a short way to the north. The next day, 11 August, young Bernard Douillot and his sister, anxious for news of their parents, returned to the farm to find out what had happened. Several others had already gathered at the farm, gazing at the smouldering ruins. Suddenly a company of Germans emerged from the woods, and they were in an ugly mood. Everyone ran for cover and Bernard ran too, towards a beehive.

He did not make it.

A burst of machine-gun fire hit him in the legs and scythed him down. The Nazis fired wantonly again. No doubt when it was all over they cared nothing for the dead 10-year-old French boy. A few days later Georges Douillot and his wife were released from prison. In 1945 a memorial was erected to the memory of those who were so casually murdered. A quiet service is held each year in remembrance.

★ ★ ★

The seven RAF men spent their first night in captivity (10/11 August) in Chaumont prison. For their supper they were given round loaves of black bread which, to their fussy palates, proved inedible. In six months time they would be very grateful for bread in whatever condition. Languishing in new and unfamiliar surroundings, Norman was still suffering from the painful effects of having had his hands so tightly bound. They had swollen to such an extent that none of the bones in his fingers was visible. By the morning, though, the pain had eased and the swelling had subsided considerably.

On 11 August the seven aircrew were bundled aboard a lorry and driven off towards Germany. Norman Oates:

'The next night was spent in a wooden hut where we were fed a large bowl of very good broth. The next day was our last in the lorry for we arrived at the aircrew interrogation centre at Frankfurt, where I was put into solitary confinement.'

They had arrived at the notorious Dulag Luft at Oberursel near Frankfurt, where they would be subjected to all the considerable interrogation skills of the Luftwaffe's Intelligence corps. Very few airmen by this stage of the war fell for the trick of completing the bogus Red Cross form. So the Germans tried another plan, as Norman remembers:

'I received the "nice guy — nasty guy" treatment. One interrogator would shout and bully and the next would apologise for the uncouth behaviour of his colleague. The quiet one showed me photographs of "Gee" and "H2S" equipment and of some I didn't recognise. It was during this time that my legs began to tremble under the desk. The interrogator repeatedly suggested that as I was not wearing RAF uniform they had no way of knowing that I was who I claimed to be; and I can only assume that it was beginning to get through to me that I was still in great danger.'

In the end the Germans grew tired of playing their games, probably because they knew that they already knew everything that Norman could tell them:

'After three days I was taken from my cell for the last time. The other six aircrew I was captured with and myself were now members of a large group of aircrew *en route* to prison camps. We filed past an area manned by Red Cross officials who gave us each a suitcase and a number of personal items such as soap, toothbrush, towel, etc. I think it must have been at this time that I was given a new RAF battledress, trousers and shirt.

'We were loaded on to a train of cattle wagons and we set off on our journey to the POW camp — Stalag Luft VII, Bankau. The only memory I have of the journey was of one incident. The train stopped and the Germans boiled cauldrons of water. We supplied the coffee and we all had a hot drink. I shall never forget the taste and smell of that coffee! But also to be out of the cattle wagon, and to have an uninterrupted view over the fields to the distant horizon. I think we were two days and one night on the train.

'My next memory is of being marched into a large compound surrounded by a high double-wire fence and watch towers; but even more surprising was the realisation that the "dog-kennels" were for us to live in!'

The 'dog-kennels' that greeted the new arrivals were, in fact, small wooden huts sleeping six men. The camp had only been opened on 6 June 1944 and was lacking in many of the comforts that could be found in older camps. Bankau would not provide decent accommodation for four months from its opening, and during this period there was no electric light for the 'kriegies' and a very poor water supply — one pump for 800 men!

When the camp was opened the Germans had asked for a British *vertrauensmann* ('man of confidence'), and on 21 June 1944 W/O Richard A. Greene RCAF was appointed on his arrival from Stalag VIIA (Moosburg). Greene was asked by the Germans to supply volunteer labour to help in the construction of the new compound, but the request was turned down and Greene made it quite clear to his fellow 'kriegies' that their services were definitely not to be offered. If the Germans wanted to build the new compound, then they could bloody well do it themselves!

Eventually, on 13 October 1944, the prisoners moved into their new and better quarters. There was now a cookhouse, an adequate water supply (with the luxury of occasional hot showers) and electricity. The theatre/recreational hut would come later.

The camp was built to the usual square pattern surrounded by a 16-foot-high fence liberally covered in barbed wire. The top 4 feet of the fence sloped inwards, to prevent people crawling over the top! There were also nine wooden towers placed at regular intervals around the perimeter, each of which contained a guard, a searchlight and a machine-gun. Several feet inside the perimeter fence was a single wire nailed to posts about 18 inches off the ground, the 'trip wire'. Any prisoner caught crossing it was liable to be shot, as the Germans were to prove. Within the square were the prisoners' huts, some 20 in all including sundry utility buildings — theatre, showers, toilets.

In charge of security at Bankau was Major Peschel, formerly of Stalag Luft III, who, according to a report written by Greene, was 67 inches tall, weighed 135 pounds and was of a slight build, had grey thinning hair, blue eyes and a sallow complexion. In Greene's own words it was considered that most of the camp's problems could be laid at his door.

Some servicemen who suddenly found themselves thrust into a POW camp had great difficulty in adjusting to their new surroundings. Most made it with the help of fellow 'kriegies'. But some did not, as Norman Oates observed:

'One day I stopped in my tracks unbelievingly as I saw one of our chaps step over the boundary wire (we had been told that we would be shot if we did so), walk across the grass and start to climb the wire fence. A guard on one of the watch towers shot him. We were very angry and felt it was quite unnecessary, as the poor fellow had quite lost touch with reality.'

There was to be a second shooting, on 27 December 1944, as Russell Margerison, another Bankau 'kriegie', recalled:

'By chance the sirens wailed one day an hour before "soup up" at lunchtime. To avoid a long wait behind a queue, should we not be quick off the mark for our soup, we all crowded at our respective doors waiting to dash across the compound as soon as permissible. A distant "all clear" was heard, probably from Kreuzburg, but the camp siren remained silent. Unfortunately one anxious Canadian burst from his barrack, carrying his tin. Calm as you please, a guard carefully knelt on one knee, levelled his rifle and needlessly shot him in full view of everyone. He appeared to stop his run in mid-pace, hung there for an instant, then collapsed on the ground, where he rolled over two or three times. With the camp siren now blaring we arrived at his side as he gasped his last words. "Get that bastard for me."'

Life in a prison camp, however boring and monotonous, had its rare, brighter moments. 'Goon-baiting' became a popular pastime with some 'kriegies', who derived much pleasure from tormenting the German guards. John Ackroyd, 192 Squadron, recalls with glee the following episode:

'Luft 7 was a camp for NCOs and an NCO was not compelled to work . . . Well, as it happened in our room we had three RAF Regiment men, LACs by rank, taken prisoner in the invasion in the south of France. Being RAF they were sent to Luft 7. Now the Germans suddenly realised they could put these men to work, so they were detailed to form a working party.

'It was decided that three out of the whole camp working did not seem fair. We had three volunteers who were not mad but could act that way. On the morning for the work to begin, the three NCOs were there at the main gate. The work that they were set to do was the erection of two of the hen huts that we had lived in in the old compound in a small compound in front of the main gate. They set to work levelling the site, digging holes and then filling them up with soil dug from other holes.

'This went on for some time until the German guards got a bit fed up and told them to get on with the erection of the huts, and just where they had to be! So the floor was laid, one wall was lifted and the guards were asked to hold it in position while the end was lifted. Instead of lifting the end the lads went over to the wire near the gate and started talking to all who were looking on. It turned out to be quite a circus.

'After a while the end was put in position, with guards holding them together while the bolts were found . . . They never were found . . .!'

The camp's theatre was completed in November, and gave much enjoyment. The first production was a play, 'Rookery Nook'. The second effort was a musical revue, 'Leo Mackie's Hepcats', which included a snake charmer and 'a continuity comedian in the style of Tommy Trinder'. It was, as Russell Margerison remembers,

'. . . held on two consecutive nights so as to enable the whole camp to see it, along with the senior German officers. Apart from a sketch entitled "The Rape of the Lighthouse Keeper's Daughter", which was disgusting, the show swung along at a fast pace, being thoroughly enjoyed by all.

'The star of the show, a youngster impersonating a female singer, was nothing short of brilliant.

'After the first performance the Germans banned the singing of "God Save the King", which brought an immediate response from Pete Thomson [an Australian officer, the camp's leader].

'"Right chaps," he announced from the stage at the conclusion of the second performance. "Open all windows and doors. I want you to sing like you've never sung before. Two choruses of 'Land of Hope and Glory'." Never did men respond so willingly. The hall and surrounding countryside echoed and re-echoed with the stirring music, sung as loud as each individual could sing, by youths from no fewer than seven countries. It was a particularly moving spectacle.'

Whilst such entertainment brought rare moments of sheer delight, the greater part of each waking day was spent thinking about food, or rather the lack of it. By late summer 1944 the German transport system was perilously close to breaking point, though it was not until 1945 that it was reduced to chaos. The end result was that Red Cross parcels destined for Bankau were taking longer to reach the camp than was desirable, and prisoners there were forced willy-nilly to eat what was given to them by their captors. The diet was very poor, insufficient indeed for healthy young airmen, and it was freely admitted by many prisoners that they only survived the war because of the added calories provided by the Red Cross. Their parcels were quite literally the difference between life and death. Many lives were saved by that wonderful organisation.

A typical American Red Cross parcel consisted of one 12 oz tin of Spam; one 12 oz tin of corned beef; one 6 oz tin of milk liver paté; one 6 oz tin of salmon; one 16 oz tin of Oleo margarine; one 6 oz tin of jam or orange juice; one 16 oz tin of dried milk (Klim); one 16 oz packet of raisins or prunes; one 8 oz packet of Kraft cheese; one 8 oz packet of biscuits; one 8 oz bag of sugar; one 4 oz tin of coffee; two 8 oz bars of D Bar chocolate; one tin-opener; and 100 cigarettes.

Contrast this feast with what greeted Norman Oates and his companions on arrival at Bankau:

'Food was a daily bowl of boiled "grass" and a small ration of boiled potatoes. I heard that the "grass" was shredded sugar-beet tops. At first I could not eat it, but after a few days I was so hungry I managed.'

Christmas 1944 brought little cheer, as Don Gray, 50 Squadron, wrote in his diary:

'In December a further intake created overcrowded conditions, ten to a room designed for eight. Food suddenly in short supply. Very poor Xmas fare. Another stage show "Bob Burns and his Orchestra" failed to reach the standard of the previous shows. A film projector had now arrived and we did see a few old Hollywood movies.'

It is important, in view of what lay ahead, not to forget the poor diet that each prisoner suffered for months. When in January 1945 they were compelled at bayonet point to leave Bankau, they would struggle to stay alive.

19

The Long, Cold Walk

Bankau is today in Poland, some 40 miles east of Wroclaw (formerly Breslau), and in January 1945 was nearer to the advancing Russians than to the Allies. On 12 January 1945 Marshal Ivan Stepanovitch Koniev's 1st Ukrainian Army Group broke out of the Baranov bridgehead west of Sandomierz on a wide front and headed for Kielce, 150 miles east of Bankau.

The Russians were supported by a prodigious concentration of artillery, and after two days' bitter fighting had pushed a wedge forward some 25 miles deep and 40 wide. This was achieved in the face of 1,500 German tanks, many of which were often immobilised due to a chronic shortage of fuel.*

Kielce itself fell on 15 January 1945. Koniev was transferred north to command the 1st Belorussian Army Group which had broken through the German defences south of Warsaw and, after three days' fighting, had penetrated on a 75-mile front to a depth of 40 miles. On 17 January Warsaw fell without serious opposition. The Germans' eastern front was now opposed by eight Russian army groups, from the 1st Baltic in the north to the 3rd Ukrainian in the far south.

At approximately 1100 hours on the day Warsaw fell the prisoners in Stalag Luft 7 were told that they had one hour in which to pack up all their belongings and be ready to march out of the camp. At the same time, Oberfeldwebel Frank told them that for every man who fell out of the column when they were on the march, five would be shot. In the event, the march was postponed until 19 January, which at least gave the prisoners the opportunity to evacuate 68 sick men to the civilian camp at nearby Kreuzberg. It was believed that these men were later removed to Stalag 344, Lamsdorf.

Each man was issued with sufficient rations for two and a half days' marching. There was no transport for the 1,565 prisoners, nor for the German guards, when the march began at the ungodly hour of 0330

---

* *Albert Speer, Reichsminister for Armaments and War Production, attributed this to the Allies' bombing of 'oil' targets.*

hours. The weather was extremely cold (sub-zero temperatures were the norm rather than the exception) with frequent snow-storms. Norman Oates had found the camp library a rich source of learning and, before leaving, had managed to grab a couple of textbooks on mathematics and economics which he stuffed into his pack.

Into the freezing early morning of 19 January they all marched, German and prisoner alike.

As the first day's march wore on, the extra weight of the text books proved too much for Norman and away they went. At last, having covered 17½ miles via Kreuzberg and Konstadt, they arrived at the village of Winterfeld where the only accommodation was several small barns and a school. Norman was one of many who spent the first night in the schoolhouse, lying on the floorboards of the unheated building. For most in the barns it was impossible to lie down, so densely were they packed. And for them sleep proved elusive as the freezing wind whipped through the cracks, bringing snow with it.

Norman was woken some time between 0400 and 0500 hours on 20 January and 'had the utmost difficulty in getting off the floor I was so stiff . . . However, once on the road the stiffness vanished and I never suffered from it again.' With much shouting and crashing about the German guards managed to rouse the prisoners and after a breakfast of thin, watery soup, which at least had the merit of being hot, the column was under way once more. It was just 0500 hours. The next stage of the journey was only 7½ miles, but took 5½ hours to cover!

This time their accommodation was a disused brick factory. Captain D. C. Howatson RAMC, the camp's medical officer, and Pete Thomson, Camp Leader, made a joint report when it was all over. They noted:

'Here for the first time we were provided with two field kitchens with which to cook for 1,550 men. Each field kitchen was actually capable of cooking sufficient food for 200 men.'

Norman remembers the brickyard, but has no recollection that he ever received any food:

'All I can remember was wandering aimlessly round the brickyard trying to find somewhere to rest. I did think of how to protect myself from the intense cold of Silesia in January. I took my towel, folded it, and stitched halfway down the two sides. I took off my battledress, put the towel over my head and along my shoulders, put my battledress back on over the top and then I opened up my forage cap and jammed it on over the towel! At least my face and head had some protection!'

There was precious little cover from the harsh elements, but mercifully the snow had temporarily stopped. And soup and coffee were available. The long rest, though, was welcome, but like all good things it came to an end after some 11 hours, and at 2000 hours the Germans ordered the prisoners to take to the road. Thomson and Howatson 'protested against further marching until the men were adequately fed and rested'.

However, the Germans were in no mood for arguing and their officer told them 'that it was an order and must be complied with'.

Along with the two field kitchens, the Germans also produced transport for the sick — one horse, one cart! It was laughable, but better than nothing. Off into the freezing night the sorry prisoners trudged, with temperatures falling to minus 13 degrees centigrade! Within three miles the cart was full of sick, and from then onwards it became a case, as men collapsed by the side of the road, of picking each man up and forcing him to continue on foot. Russell Margerison:

'The night march turned out to be the worst and the longest so far. Whilst it mercifully did not snow there was no escaping the strong bitter winds that continually howled and whistled through the ranks. The moon, along with the starlit sky, made the white frost, which soon formed on greatcoats and forage caps, glisten like tinsel. Hundreds of luminous bodies, crouched low, trying harder and harder to shrink into the confines of their coats, struggled and stumbled through the deep snow, hour after tiring hour.'

What the prisoners did not know was that it was imperative that they reached a certain bridge over the Oder river by early next morning — German sappers had orders to blow it up later that morning. It was a punishing 20 miles to the river, and only the prisoners' doggedness saw them through. They had to go a further five miles before they were allowed to stop, at Schönfeld. It was 0900 hours, 21 January. Once again, accommodation reached heights of luxury — cowsheds and barns — but at least the men were out of the chill wind. Norman managed to brew up some coffee using handfuls of straw but, being a non-smoker, had difficulty in getting a light. Food was handed out to go with the coffee, roughly 100 grams of biscuits per man!

Howatson/Thomson report:

'At 3 am orders were given by the Germans to prepare to march off at once. It was dark and there was some delay in getting men out from their sleeping quarters because they could not find their baggage. The German guards thereupon marched into the quarters and discharged their firearms.'

There was no arguing with guns, and they had the desired effect. Norman was shaken awake by his Liverpudlian friend:

'It was daylight and he showed me a mug of broth and told me to go and get some. I walked out and saw the field kitchen standing unattended in the middle of the farmyard, so I walked over and helped myself to a mugful, returned to my friend, and we sat side by side drinking the soup.'

Finally, at around 0500 hours on 22 January, off they went again. But not all of them — 23 sick men were given transport to the SS hospital at Lossen. They were liberated by the Russians on 4 February, who sent them to Oppeln. From there they walked to Gleiwitz and reached Odessa at the end of the same month.

A further 31 sick men were evacuated to, it was thought, Lamsdorf camp.

Pitiful sights greeted the equally pitiful column of prisoners, for heading in the same direction as themselves were countless others all bent on escaping the Russians. Not all were civilians. Russell Margerison:

'Seeing a blue greatcoat by the roadside, spread out on a backcloth of white, we moved over to investigate for there was something different about this one. It was an old German Luftwaffe officer, face buried in the snow, his hat lying forlornly by his side. He was quite, quite dead . . .

"Leave him lads, nothing you can do." It was Father Berry's voice, our chaplain, who had joined us just prior to the march.'

They staggered 21 miles to Jenkwitz where, once more, they were housed in barns. Howatson/Thomson:

'Here we were issued with a total of 114 kgs of fat, 46 tins of meat, barley, peas and three-quarters of a pig. Soup was issued, the ration being about a quarter of a litre per man. No bread was issued.'

There was to be little respite for the cold, very tired and very weak prisoners. Away to the north-east, Marshal Konstantin Rokossovskii and his 2nd Belorussian Army Group had captured Tannenberg the previous day, and East Prussia was lying at his mercy. Marshal Gregory Konstantinovitch Zhukov and the 1st Belorussians were continuing to threaten the north, heading directly for Berlin. Silesia was no place for prisoners of war, and Hitler had ordered that to prevent their falling into Allied hands they were to be moved to central Germany. Whilst not exactly in a state of panic, the German guards were anxiously looking over their shoulders. There was, then, a certain urgency about the march.

The starting time from Jenkwitz was 0600 hours on 23 January and the prisoners managed $12^{1}/_{2}$ miles to Wanzen, where they were able to rest for 36 hours. The humble barn was to provide their shelter as ever, but no one complained on that score. A further 31 men who were too sick to carry on were transferred to Sagan.

Food was still uppermost in the prisoners' minds, but it was very scarce, and the Germans provided nothing until the following day, 24 January, when 400 loaves of bread were issued. Norman Oates:

'Word was passed into the barn for us to queue outside for food. It was dark, and this may be partly the reason why my next memory is of lying on my back on warm, soft straw. When I moved I was offered a mug of something hot, which I drank and then I laid down again. Later I was asked how I felt and I said I was OK, so I was told to rejoin the others. I had fainted in the queue and had been carried into the cowshed where the camp doctor was looking after the sick.'

The wonder is that so many men, although in shocking health, managed to keep going for so long on such meagre rations and in such freezing weather. But they were magnificently cared for by Captain Howatson who worked prodigiously on their behalf whilst walking the same roads as the others.

On 25 January the horrendous march was under way once more. Another early start, at 0400 hours, heralded a long walk of 19 miles to Kiedersdorf. Nothing untoward occurred. The diarists could find no bad event to write about. Even the Germans themselves seem to have got over their panic, although on this very day Koniev's 1st Ukrainians took Gleiwitz, 100 miles to the south-east of Breslau. But, more alarmingly, they also captured Ostrov in Polish Silesia, only 50 miles north-east of Breslau.

Friday 26 January was another rest day and it gave the Germans time to collect 600 loaves of bread, which were to last for two days and somehow feed 1,500 men. The next day the refugee prisoners were off again, but only 12 miles to Pfaffendorff, which they reached at night.

After only a brief rest during the cold night they were roused at some ungodly hour on this Sunday, 28 January, and by 0500 hours were *en route* for Standorf, another jaunt of 13 miles. It was worth the effort for at journey's end there was food, and what a feast it was — 24 cartons of knackerbrot, 150 kilograms of margarine and 50 kilograms of sugar! More men had succumbed to the rigours of the forced march, and 22 were evacuated via Scheidnitz to Sagan. Perhaps these men were lucky, for they would miss the nightmare that was just around the corner.

Before they moved on again, there was a further food distribution — 104 kilograms of meat, one sack of salt, 25 kilograms of coffee and 100 kilograms of barley. It was dark at 1800 hours on Monday 29 January when the prisoners were cajoled to their feet and ordered on to the road. Not even the promise of transport for all the men at Peterwitz, 14 miles distant, was enough to prepare them for what lay ahead as they stepped out into the freezing night. Russell Margerison:

'From the outset a blizzard raged, the like of which we had not experienced. Huge snow flakes whipped across the countryside parallel to the ground in such quantity as to give the effect of a solid white, impenetrable sheet, continuously speeding across our path. On numerous occasions it was a sheer impossibility to see another person. My boots froze solid on my feet, whilst the whole of my right-hand side held inches of snow which, if shaken off, was replaced in seconds . . .'

The snow was so deep off the road that one could barely see above it. Escape would have been easy, but no one could have survived in it for long. Norman remembers that awful march: 'Looking back I don't know how I survived that night.'

His mind and body were slowly but surely reaching the point of no return, where the decision had to be made whether to go on living or to give up. Norman, as they all did, held on, though he remembered little of the next few days:

'The dreadful conditions and lack of food had, no doubt, begun to take their toll on my mind as well as my body. These curious blanks in my memory interest me, as those episodes I describe are quite clear. I have, for instance, a picture in my mind of walking down a street in a large town, and in one of the pauses which a long column of men endures we were harangued by a German woman from the pavement while other citizens ignored us.'

He recalls another incident, date and place forgotten, that occurred as they stumbled along in the dark:

'A whisper went round that there were vegetables stacked under soil in the fields beside us. Dozens of us scrambled through the hedge. I managed to unearth a turnip which I stuffed inside my battledress, then I hurried back to the column. As I walked along in the dark, I rubbed as much of the dirt as I could off the turnip and then, gnawing at it, I managed to eat the whole turnip.'

Hunger can reduce a man to a wild animal. Russell Margerison saw a grim example:

'Only once during the march did a civilian offer us anything at all. A frail old lady came to the door of her outlying little cottage and, noting our state, disappeared, only to return with the familiar long large brown loaf tucked under her arm and a carving knife with which she began to saw off a thick slice. That was as far as she got. Youths shot across the road like a swarm of bees, brushing aside the startled guards. The old lady was knocked flying as the vultures pulled, tugged and tore at the bread. The column just kept on walking. Even the Germans did not stop to see what condition she was in. For the first time in my life I felt ashamed to be British. We were starving, yes, but this was too much.'

The awful march ended when the 14 miles to Peterwitz were covered at 0400 hours on 30 January. All were utterly exhausted. Here the survivors were joined by 30 prisoners from Stalag 344 who had been left without guards. They arrived at the right time, for yet again the Germans were to hand out more food — 296 loaves of bread, 50 kilograms of oats and 35½ kilograms of margarine. It is not difficult to calculate how much each of the 1,500 men received.

At Peterwitz the tired men were able to rest for the remainder of 30 January and for the whole of the next day. More food appeared — 300 kilograms of nourishing oats, 50 kilos of coffee and 40 kilos of margarine.

But life went on — just. The promise of transport from Peterwitz was broken on 31 January when the Germans announced that none was available and they would have to continue on foot. The prisoners were furious and the strongest possible protests were made, including the threat not to move one more step, regardless of the consequences. But the Germans held all the trump cards. Russell Margerison:

'The appointed time for moving on drew near, and every available German, armed with rifle, sub-machine gun or revolver, appeared. They were determined to stir us into activity and the nearest group came in for the guttural rantings and ravings at which the Germans were expert, but no one moved. On orders from their officers, some 20 guards stood in a line with rifles levelled at the POWs whilst others physically pulled the men to their feet. Having got each man standing, the guards followed the same procedure with the next group, but the first batch of men, with considered deliberation, sat down again.

'At this the Germans went completely berserk and the lot of them, including the officers, joined in the mêlée. Bodies rolled over the place till once again the first batch were on their feet. But the second lot had sat down. The deafening, frightening, crack-crack of rifle fire reverberated around the timber yard as bullets whistled and ricocheted over our heads. Still no one moved, and whilst I was inwardly scared the episode helped to restore some of my lost faith, for we stubbornly sat it out.'

The Germans gave up. The prisoners had won against all the odds, although had the guards been SS one suspects that the result would have been much, much different. Later that day the Germans promised faithfully that a train would be waiting for the prisoners at Goldberg, 12½ miles away.

From Peterwitz on Thursday 1 February a short trek of only 7½ miles to Prausnitz was the order of the day. Food, still in insufficient quantities, was being issued now quite regularly and on arrival at Prausnitz the prisoners were given 580 loaves and 37½ kilos of margarine.

They remained at Prausnitz until 5 February. No food was given out on 2 February, but the next day the issue was 112½ kilos of margarine, 250 loaves, 100 kilos of sugar, 200 kilos of flour and 150 kilos of barley. Yet more food appeared the day after that — 150 loaves.

As the prisoners sat around in the farm, Koniev's and Zhukov's armies were engaged in fierce fighting around the river Oder and its tributaries. The upper Oder was in flood and unfrozen; the Germans had blown all the bridges across it and were manning its banks in force. At the beginning of February Koniev's 1st Ukrainians attacked and, after three days of intense struggle, had forced a bridgehead 12 miles deep and 50 wide to the south-east of Breslau, and another to the north-west of that city 35 miles deep and 100 wide. To the north Zhukov's 1st Belorussians continued their advance towards the lower Oder and, by 29 January, had crossed the German frontier into Pomerania, Brandenburg and West Prussia. By 7 February they had reached Frankfort-on-Oder and Küstrin. They were now only 60 miles from Berlin.

Back at Prausnitz on the evening of 4 February, safe from the Russians, the German commandant, Oberleutnant Behr, arrived at the farm and read out an order from the German High Command 'to the effect that five men were to be released and would be liberated at the first opportunity. The purpose of this we were unable to understand.'

On 5 February 1945 the last stage of the hellish march got under way, but not before there had been another food issue — 500 loaves, 96 kilos of margarine and 530 tins of meat. The five miles to Goldberg were soon accomplished and, wonder of wonders, the prisoners were taken to the marshalling yards and put on a train as promised, 55 men to each cattle truck.

Before being consigned to his truck, Norman Oates remembers:

'A train crossing a few lines of rail for some reason caught my eye and attracted my interest. I walked across and looked into the open door of a cattle truck and found it full of bunks holding German wounded. I climbed into the truck, took a packet of cigarettes out of my battledress — the last I had — and showed them to the nearest soldier so that he could understand and slipped them under his pillow. I then realised our guards were shouting so I hurried back to where our men were milling about.'

Norman was a non-smoker and cigarettes were worth their weight in gold as barter. Despite all the suffering that he had suffered over the past few days, he recognised in that wounded enemy soldier somebody worse off than himself. What he would endure on the train journey, and afterwards, would test his compassion to the limit.

The prisoners had arrived at Goldberg in a weakened and debilitated state. Dysentery reared its ugly head, but history does not record its type, amoebic or bacillary. Bacillary differs from amoebic in that the period of incubation is much shorter, generally one to three days, its onset is more acute, with fever that may persist for several days or more, and it is extremely contagious. Furthermore, it is epidemic in character with a higher death-rate than amoebic.

The breeding conditions for the spread of the disease were ideal, men crammed into cattle trucks with no proper sanitation and no water. They were to remain in these filthy, stinking trucks for three days and two nights. The prisoners complained bitterly, but to no avail. Quite frequently the train was stationary, but even then the men were not let out. Russell Margerison:

'Lying down was impossible, so we arranged that half should sit and half should stand, and changed about periodically. Like stricken animals we stood or sat in the soon stinking truck. To keep up morale we spoke of food and its preparation, we spoke of home and its comforts, we spoke of restaurants, cafés and 'Smokey Joe's' and the pies the old ladies used to make for us at Blyton. We had become stupidly obsessed with the subject.

'By this time many of the boys had contracted dysentery, which entailed constantly holding one individual after another up to the open grills, which served as windows, with the results of their efforts mainly running down the inside walls and down the backs of lads unable to move out of the way. The results were anything but funny.

'An occasional man would collapse but our shouting and banging to draw attention to our plight, when at a stop, were completely ignored.

'The nightmare journey amongst that filth ended 50 kilometres from

Berlin and we tumbled out of those wagons just in time. Much longer and I, along with hundreds of others, would never have made it.

'Never have I been so physically weak, never so desperately hungry, never so thin and never so bitter and angry.'

He was not exaggerating. The journey ended on 7 February 1945. According to records 1,493 prisoners completed the march and every one of them was suffering from severe malnutrition. Surprisingly, there were only 69 cases of dysentery; 20 of frostbite; 23 of sceptic feet; 40 of diarrhoea; eight of bronchitis; 25 of muscular rheumatism; and 150 were so weak that they were unable to attend outdoor parades. It could have been worse. Norman Oates:

'The journey was a nightmare — no food, no water, no room to sit down. With ever more men going down with dysentery the total lack of toilet facilities amounted to three days of hell.'

But they had arrived at another prison camp, Stammlager IIIA Luckenwalde (25 miles south of Berlin), which was to be their home until liberated by the Russians. The strong kept going, but Norman was not amongst them:

'On arrival at Luckenwalde I finally collapsed with dysentery. For the next few days, if I'd had the mental ability left to evaluate my chances of survival, I'd have estimated them as zero. I can remember crawling time and time again to the toilets, too weak to walk, and sitting propped up by a wall outside a building, past caring, hearing two Australian voices complaining about the Germans and saying they had a lot to answer for. I received no help of any kind. But I survived!'

He hung on while nature took its course. Not all made it. On 14 February 1945 Don Gray recorded: 'One lad died from illness. Conditions poor and morale low.'

Conditions indeed were still far from ideal in the camp, flotsam and jetsam from all over Europe concentrated within its barbed-wire walls. French prisoners appeared to dominate proceedings, being the most numerous and having been there longest. They did little to help the new arrivals.

The plight of the sick was brought to the notice of the International Red Cross when they made one of their periodic visits to the camp. As a result, at the end of their second week at Luckenwalde the ex-Bankau prisoners (and the others too) each received one whole Red Cross food parcel. Despite the extra food the prisoners remained very hungry, but the scales were now tipped in favour of life.

The weeks rolled by. The war news was exciting; it was a race between the Allies from the west and the Russians from the east as to who would get to them first. By the end of March 1945 Zhukov had cleared the east bank of the Oder and together with Rokossovskii (2nd Belorussians) had annihilated the Germans in Pomerania. Rokossovskii, on Zhukov's right, was clearing up resistance in the Danzig area; Koniev, on Zhukov's left, had reached the river Neisse on a broad front. The Allies in the west had forced their way across the Rhine over the bridge at Remagen, and had surrounded a large German force in the Ruhr.

On 13 April 1945 a Canadian lad at Luckenwalde was shot dead trying to escape, and his companion was badly wounded.

The next Russian onslaught did not begin until 16 April. There had been delays in bringing up reinforcements and Koniev had been further frustrated by fierce German resistance in Breslau, which finally fell to the 1st Ukrainians on 7 May after an 82-day siege. There was no doubt now that the Russians would reach Luckenwalde first when, after three days' bitter fighting, Zhukov's and Koniev's armies crossed the Oder-Neisse river line. It was 19 April and, when the wind blew in the right direction, the prisoners could clearly hear the sound of battle away to the east.

Zhukov pushed round to the north of Berlin whilst Koniev, who had appeared to be heading due west to the south of the capital, suddenly swung north and entered Berlin's suburbs from the south on 22 April.

The German guards at Luckenwalde were clearly aware of the imminent arrival of the Russians, as Norman Oates remembers:

'One morning I was awoken by a commotion and heard men saying that the Germans appeared to be leaving. I went out of the hut in time to see them all lined up outside one of the gates and, as I watched, they marched off down the road and soon disappeared from sight. The POWs milled around and talked about what to make of this.'

It was true. The Germans had gone, and as the vast camp came to life men stood gaping at the empty watch-towers. There was not a single guard anywhere. Norman Oates:

'We were now free of the Germans but soon we were to be aware that we were now under the control of the Russians. Some time later we were told that we were to assemble in the central square of the camp where we were addressed by the senior RAF officer from the adjoining quadrant which was occupied by commissioned RAF aircrew POWs. He told us that since the Germans had gone he had taken command and his first order was that we were confined to camp. That afternoon I wandered over to the officers' quadrant and was amazed to find myself face-to-face with my childhood class-mate.'

Norman had last met this man, a flight engineer, at No 5 LFS over a year before!

It was in fact the following day, Sunday 22 April, that the Russians arrived at the camp. The first to appear came in a jeep-type vehicle. There was, however, the small matter of dealing with an SS-manned anti-tank gun, whose crew of three had bravely remained. When the Russians arrived the SS promptly surrendered. A Russian officer dismounted from his vehicle and ordered the SS to kneel. Then 'as casually as one might butter a slice of bread the officer grasped the hair of one and promptly shot him in the head. Polishing off the other two in similar fashion he studiously climbed back into the vehicle which disappeared whence it came as quickly as it had appeared.'

A few hours later Norman Oates

'. . . heard a rumbling sound which grew in volume. From the east came Russian tanks bursting out of the surrounding forest, heading straight for the camp. One or two of them drove straight through the main gate and down the central roadway which divided the four quadrants of the camp. The Russians were standing up in their tanks, shouting and cheering, and appeared to be inviting us to join them. They did not stop, however, but ploughed straight through the camp and out of the far side, disappearing into the forest again, knocking down anything in their way, such as the gates.'

After this extraordinary display there followed a more sedate Russian convoy which included an armoured car surmounted not by a machine-gun but by a newsreel camera, its operator blithely filming away as the happy, cheering prisoners waved back to the grinning tank commanders. The Russian propagandists were not about to waste such a golden opportunity!

Momentary euphoria soon gave way to a realisation that they, the prisoners, were still prisoners, not of the Germans any longer but of the Russians. The incident with the SS soldiers gave them an idea of the kind of troops with whom they were now dealing. It clearly would not pay to trifle with them. The Russians for their part were not about to let the prisoners go, notwithstanding that they were allies.

The Russians were not too interested in feeding large numbers of prisoners whilst there were still Nazis to kill. Food for the prisoners was at first scarce but, after they had been allowed to forage in the nearby countryside and towns, things improved. They got even better when one of the foraging parties found thousands of American Red Cross parcels in a deserted train in Luckenwalde sidings. The parcels were soon safely within the camp and one distributed to every British and American prisoner. The French got one between four, in recognition of their earlier behaviour.

Negotiations were all the while in hand for the release of the prisoners. The Russians were in no hurry and, as was their wont, made the process as difficult as they could. At long last, on 5 May 1945, the inmates' hopes were raised when the Americans arrived, promising that a large convoy of trucks was on its way. The prisoners waited and waited, and no convoy came. Then, on Sunday 6 May, a notice in the camp announced the arrival of the convoy later that day. No one really believed it — they had been let down so many times before.

But then, unbelievably, the promised trucks appeared. It was time to go home.

The Russian commandant, however, had other ideas. First, he had not received any orders to allow the Americans to take away his prisoners, and second, the prisoners were to be repatriated in the Russians' own time via Russia! This was too much for some of the prisoners who slipped out of the camp that night and made their own way home. Norman Oates:

'Eventually arrangements were made to the satisfaction of the Russians and the Americans, and our journey home began. The first part of our journey was by Russian lorries, which stopped when they reached a certain point at a river. This river seemed to be the border between the Russian and American armies at the time — it may have been the Elbe. We were told by the Russians to walk over the bridge and on the far side we were greeted by the Americans who put us on to lorries and drove us to an American air base. There we were showered, deloused and given new clothes. I still remember my first meal — not only the strangeness of pineapple served with meat, but the white bread tasted like angel cake. Our taste buds had adapted to the food we had been eating for so long. It didn't take long to re-adapt!

'From there we were flown to England where we were de-briefed, given new uniforms, money and travel passes, and sent home on indefinite leave.'

So, ten months late, the last men shot down on those fateful raids to Revigny in July 1944 returned to England. The war in Europe was over. But for Norman Oates, in the cold winters of 1946 and 1947, the pain returned to his fingers to remind him of those dreadful days in France and Germany.

Epilogue

'In 1947 my wife and I went to France to find out exactly where my unfortunate crew members were buried. During my visit to see the Mayor, he informed me that after the parachutes had opened the aircraft was attacked by a fighter. To my knowledge, after my pilot Gordon Maxwell had ordered us to abandon the blazing aircraft, I expected all the crew to leave at once.

'I have to this day thoughts of them and wonder why they did not leave by the exit under the nose. Had I known that fighter attack was to take place I would have stayed by my guns irrespective of anything else, even to dying with them. Death among such angels as those who were my dearest friends would have indeed been a great honour — any such sting would have been a suffering of love for my fellow men whose names, I am sure, are written in that wonderful Book of Gold.'

Albert Ernest De Bruin (630 Squadron)

★ ★ ★

18 July 1944

'I've learned today that one of my best pals, Bobby Younger from Newcastle, was shot down. Frank [Stebbing DFM] and I both feel sick at the news because the three of us trained together and were great pals.'

Fred Whitfield DFM (9 Squadron)
Sgt R. D. B. Younger was lost on the third Revigny raid in
Lancaster DV374 (463 Squadron).

★ ★ ★

January 1990

'. . . It is 45 years ago, and life has moved on, and although I have answers to the many questions you ask, I would really like to let it all lie sleeping.'

Anon (letter to Author)

Appendix I

The Organisational Structure of No 1 Group as at 1800 hours, 13 July 1944

Air Officer Commanding		AVM E. A. B. Rice CB CBE MC
No 11 BASE		A/Cdre G. G. Banting CBE
RAF HEMSWELL		G/C G. F. Macpherson AFC
No 1 LFS		W/C F. S. Powley DFC AFC[1]
RAF Ingham		W/C J. J. Bennett DFC and Bar
1687 BDTF		
and 1481 (B)GF		S/L H. A. England DFC
RAF Lindholme		G/C L. W. Dickens DFC AFC
1656 HCU		W/C R. T. Sturgess DFC
No 12 BASE		A/Cdre A. M. Wray DSO MC DFC AFC
RAF BINBROOK		G/C H. I. Edwards VC DSO DFC
460 Squadron	20/4	W/C H. D. Marsh
SDF	7/0	S/L H. F. Breakspear DSO DFC[2]
RAF Grimsby		G/C I. B. Newbigging
100 Squadron	21/0	W/C R. V. L. Pattison DFC
RAF Kelstern		G/C R. H. Donkin OBE
625 Squadron	20/1	W/C D. D. Haig DFC and Bar

No 13 BASE		A/Cdre F. R. D. Swain OBE AFC
RAF ELSHAM WOLDS		G/C W. C. Sheen DSO
103 Squadron	20/0	W/C J. R. St John DFC
576 Squadron	20/0	W/C B. D. Sellick DSO DFC and Bar
RAF Kirmington		G/C G. P. H. Carter
166 Squadron	29/1	W/C D. A. Garner DSO
RAF N Killingholme		G/C R. V. McIntyre DFC
550 Squadron	19/0	W/C P. E. G. G. Connolly[3]
No 14 BASE		A/Cdre R. S. Blucke DSO AFC
RAF LUDFORD MAGNA		G/C P. J. R. King[4]
101 Squadron	24/9	W/C R. I. Alexander
RAF Faldingworth		G/C N. C. Ogilvie-Forbes
300 Squadron	21/5	W/C T. Pozyczka
RAF Wickenby		G/C P. Haynes
12 Squadron	17/1	W/C J. D. Nelson
626 Squadron	18/2	W/C G. F. Rodney AFC

Notes:

The columns of figures shows the Daily State of each squadron's operational Lancaster aircraft. The first number is that available for operations, the second those unserviceable. Nos 460, 166 and 101 Squadrons were 3-flight squadrons with an establishment of 30 Lancasters; the others were 2-flight and 20 aircraft strong.

Stations shown in capitals were Base stations. The others were sub-stations or 'satellites' of the Bases. 11 Base was non-operational, its stations being used for training purposes.

[1] W/C Powley returned to operations as CO of 153 Squadron when it reformed on 15 October 1944. He failed to return from a mining operation to the Kattegat on the night of 4/5 April 1945.

[2] S/L Breakspear, though nominally CO of the SDF, was screened from operational flying duties on 5 July 1944.

[3] W/C Connolly was killed on the second Revigny raid. His successor, W/C A. F. M. Sisley, was killed on 31 August 1944.

[4] G/C King was the former TFU station CO at Hurn and Defford.

Appendix II

The Organisational Structure of No 5 Group as at 1800 hours, 18 July 1944

Air Officer Commanding		AVM The Hon Sir Ralph Cochrane KBE CB AFC

No 51 BASE		A/Cdre E. I. Bussell
RAF SWINDERBY		G/C R. Coats
1660 HCU		W/C J. N. Derbyshire DFC
RAF Wigsley		G/C R. E. Vintras
1654 HCU		W/C R. Kingsford-Smith DFC
RAF Winthorpe		G/C J. H. Woodin
1661 HCU		W/C B. R. W. Hallows DFC
No 52 BASE		A/Cdre S. L. G. Pope DFC AFC
RAF SCAMPTON		G/C J. W. F. Merer
1690 BDTU		S/L J. L. Munro DSO DFC
Aircrew School		W/C P. Burnett DSO DFC
RAF Dunholme Lodge		G/C E. S. Butler OBE
44 Squadron	17/2	W/C F. W. Thompson
619 Squadron	20/1	W/C J. R. Maling AFC[1]
RAF Fiskerton		G/C C. T. Weir
49 Squadron	19/2	W/C L. E. Botting
1514 BATF		S/L W. A. L. Johnson[2]

No 53 BASE		A/Cdre A. Hesketh CBE DFC
RAF WADDINGTON		G/C D. W. F. Bonham-Carter CB DFC
463 Squadron	18/3	W/C W. A. Forbes
467 Squadron	20/2	W/C W. L. Brill DSO DFC and Bar[3]
RAF Bardney		G/C C. C. McMullen AFC[4]
9 Squadron	16/5	W/C J. M. Bazin DFC[5]
RAF Skellingthorpe		G/C J. N. Jefferson
50 Squadron	19/1	W/C R. T. Frogley
61 Squadron	18/0	W/C A. W. Doubleday DSO DFC[3]

No 54 BASE		A/Cdre A. C. H. Sharp ADC
RAF CONINGSBY		G/C A. C. Evans Evans DFC[6]
83 Squadron	18/1	G/C L. C. Deane DSO DFC
97 Squadron	19/2	W/C A. W. Heward DFC AFC
RAF Metheringham		G/C W. N. McKechnie GC[7]
106 Squadron	19/2	W/C E. K. Piercy
RAF Woodhall Spa		G/C M. G. Philpott
617 Squadron	24/4	W/C J. B. Tait DSO DFC
627 Squadron	14/2	W/C G. W. Curry DFC and Bar[8]

No 55 BASE		A/Cdre H. N. Thornton MBE
RAF EAST KIRKBY		G/C R. T. Taaffe OBE
57 Squadron	20/1	W/C H. Y. Humphreys DFC
630 Squadron	17/3	W/C L. M. Blome-Jones DFC[9]
RAF Spilsby		G/C S. H. V. Harris
207 Squadron	12/8	W/C J. Grey

Notes:

The columns of figures shows the Daily State of each squadron's aircraft (all Lancasters bar those of 627 Squadron equipped with Mosquitoes). The first number is those available for operations, the second those unserviceable. The total of operational Lancasters was 276, and of Mosquitoes 14. There were 37 unserviceable Lancasters and 2 Mosquitoes. Establishment strength of each Lancaster squadron was 20.

Stations shown in capitals were Base stations. The others were sub-stations or 'satellites' of the Bases. 51 Base was non-operational, its stations being used for training purposes.

[1] Maling went missing on the night of 25/26 July 1944 (in Lancaster ND935 'K', on a raid on Stuttgart).

[2] Johnson was awarded the AFC in the 1945 New Year Honours List. 1514 BATF was finally closed on 9 January 1945 having been in operation since 21 September 1941. During that period 20,439 hours were flown with only one fatal accident.

[3] Brill and Doubleday were both farmers from Wagga, Australia, prior to the war. They joined up together in 1940. Their promotions were simultaneous and each won the DSO and DFC. Brill later added a bar to his DFC and on 12 May 1944 was posted to command 467 Squadron from 463. He died in 1964.

[4] McMullen replaced Group Captain N. C. Pleasance (who was lost on the 22/23 March 1944 attack on Frankfurt in LM430 'B', 9 Squadron, piloted by F/O Manning).

[5] Bazin was CO of 9 Squadron from 15/6/44 to 18/5/45. He was awarded the DSO in September 1945. Remarkably, he flew with 607 (Fighter) Squadron during the Battle of Britain.

[6] Evans Evans was killed when Lancaster NE165 was shot down on 21/22 February 1945, raiding the Mittelland Canal.

[7] McKechnie went missing whilst piloting a 106 Squadron Lancaster on the 29/30 August 1944 raid to Königsberg.

[8] Curry, ex-Flight Commander on 57 Squadron and experienced heavy-bomber pilot, was posted to 627 from 1660 HCU on 3 June 1944 for a third tour of operations.

[9] Blome-Jones was posted to 630 Squadron on 12 July 1944, having previously been a Flight Commander on 207 Squadron. The previous CO, W/C W. I. Deas DSO DFC and Bar, was killed on his 69th operation on 7/8 July 1944 to St Leu d'Esserent.

Appendix III

Losses on the Revigny Raids in Probable Order of Loss

Notes:

Nationality: AUS = Australian; BEL = Belgian; CAN = Canadian; EIR = Irish; NZ = New Zealander; USA = American. The others were British.

Position (in crew): B = bomb-aimer; F = flight engineer; M = mid-upper gunner; N = navigator; P = pilot; R = rear gunner; W = wireless operator.

The letters in brackets after the place of burial indicate the French *départements* in which the cemeteries are located, as follows: Ai = Aisne; Au = Aube; H-M = Haute-Marne; Ma = Marne; Me = Meuse; M-M = Meurthe-et-Moselle; Oi = Oise; S-M = Seine-et-Marne.

Name/initials/ rank	Nation- ality	Position	

FIRST RAID, 12/13 JULY 1944

1PA999 — 103 Squadron

Bull F. W., F/S		R	Greenwood was the only
Faulkner A. J., F/O	CAN	N	survivor. He evaded and was
Greenwood R. E., F/S		B	back in the UK on 8/9/44. The
Harrison J. A., P/O		P	others were buried at Véel (Me).
Howles H. H., Sgt		F	
Mitchinson J. M., Sgt		W	
Whelan L. P., Sgt	EIR	M	

2LL796 — 550 Squadron

Boocock W., F/O	NZ	P	All killed. Buried at Fains-les-
Dagless L. E., Sgt		W	Sources (Me). The bodies were
Eckhold M. C., F/O	NZ	N	later re-interred at Perreuse
Mudford A. J. W., F/S	AUS	B	Château Franco-British
Muir M., Sgt		N	cemetery, Signy-Signets (S-M),
Setchfield T., Sgt		R	date unknown.
Sutherland G. T., Sgt		F	

3ME674 — 103 Squadron

Bancroft W. S., F/S		R	All killed. Buried at Couvonges
Gaythorpe K., Sgt		B	(Me).
Eastham J. S., Sgt		F	
Kilgour J., Sgt		M	
Olsen G. O., F/S	CAN	N	
Phillips C. R., F/O		P	
Rhodes J., Sgt		W	

4ND993 — 103 Squadron

Abbott P. J., F/O		P	All killed. Buried at Montiers-
Clayton V. N., Sgt		N	sur-Saulx (Me).
Gleeson A. G., P/O		F	
Kewn P. R., Sgt		R	
Labern S. F., Sgt		W	
Miller G., Sgt		M	
Morrison A. J., F/O	CAN	B	

5PD202 — 166 Squadron

Davey D. J., F/S	AUS	W	All killed. Buried at Prez-sur-
Lawrie J. B., Sgt		F	Marne (H-M).
Muir D. W., F/O		M	
Relton A., Sgt		R	
Welchman E. J., F/O		P	
Wood M. G., Sgt		B	
Worrall L. J., Sgt		M	

6JB644 — 166 Squadron

Broad S. P., F/O		B	Broad and Summers were the
Chalk J. T. E., Sgt	CAN	R	only survivors. They both
Collins F. J., Sgt		M	evaded and were back in the UK
Ellerker L. H., F/O		N	on 28/8/44. The others were
McLaren J., P/O		P	buried at Chevillon (H-M).
Paton D. F., Sgt		W	
Summers E., Sgt		F	

7LL896 — 166 Squadron

Banville R. T., F/O	CAN	P	Julier, Kidd and Watkins killed.
Hoyle K., Sgt		M	Buried at Montiers-sur-Saulx
Julier E. W., F/S		N	(Me). The others evaded. Hoyle
Kidd H. H., Sgt		W	and Nicholson were back in the
Kroschel C. H., F/S	AUS	B	UK on 4/9/44, Banville on
Nicholson J. H., Sgt		F	5/9/44, and Kroschel reached
Watkins W., Sgt		R	Switzerland on 24/7/44.

8LM647 — 550 Squadron

Baker A. D., Sgt	F	All killed. Buried at Vignory
Davies J. E. H., F/O	P	(H-M).
Davies N. A., F/O	W	
Donoghue D. A., Sgt	R	
MacKenzie D. B., Sgt	N	
Pyke C. M., Sgt	B	
Taylor G., Sgt	M	

9LM388 — 166 Squadron

Ashton E., Sgt		R	Ashton and Scott killed. Buried
Gibbons D. C., P/O		P	at Vitry-le-Croisé (Au). The
Lewis L. A., Sgt		F	others evaded. Walsh was back
Millett T. F., F/S		N	in the UK on 25/8/44, Gibbons
Rose C. T., F/S		B	on 6/9/44, Lewis and Rose on
Scott R. F., F/S		W	7/9/44 and Millett on 8/9/44.
Walsh M. R., Sgt	CAN	M	

10ND859 — 576 Squadron

Glenny C. J., P/O	CAN	M	Glenny and Keeler were the only
Greig W. H. M., Sgt		F	survivors. They were taken
Hart C., P/O		P	prisoner and sent to Stalag Luft
Jones C. L., Sgt		B	3 and Stalag 357 respectively.
Keeler P. H., F/S		R	The others were buried at Giey-
McHugh J. F., Sgt		N	sur-Aujon (H-M).
Mitchell E., Sgt		W	

SECOND RAID, 14/15 July 1944

1LL837 — 550 Squadron

Connolly P. E. G. G., W/C	P	All killed. Buried at Bussy-la-
Fuller K. W. L., F/L	R	Côte (Me).
Kermack J. T., Sgt	W	
Naunton J. D., Sgt	N	
Nunns N., F/O	B	
Penton J. R., Sgt	F	
Watson C. J., Sgt	M	

2PA984 — 156 Squadron

Coker H., F/O		N	Only Davies and Stevens
Davies G. G., S/L		P	survived. They were both taken
Debrock F. C. G., F/O	BEL	F	prisoner. Davies went to Stalag
Holbrook F., F/O		N	Luft 1. It is not known to which
Lockwood F. J., F/O		M	POW camp Stevens was sent.
Platana D. D., F/O	CAN	R	The others were buried at
Robinson H. G. M., F/L	AUS	W	Ancerville (Me). Debrock's body
Stevens K., F/L		B	was not found until March
			1945. It was returned to
			Belgium in August 1950.

3ME755 — 460 Squadron

Allan A., Sgt		F	Only Raftery and Wade survived.
Dickerson K. L. T., F/S	AUS	B	They evaded and were back in
Jeffries F., F/S		N	the UK on 13/9/44 and 6/9/44
Kilsby H. S., Sgt		R	respectively. The others were
Raftery B. F., F/S	AUS	W	buried at Chevillon (H-M).
Vaughan W. A. H. P/O	AUS	P	
Wade D., Sgt		M	

4NE136 — 103 Squadron

Armstrong F. T., Sgt		M	All killed. Buried at Biencourt-
Brooke K. A., F/S		W	sur-Orge (Me).
Farnham F., P/O		R	
Mitchell G. C., F/S		B	
Ogden C. H., P/O		P	
Pratlett O. J., W/O	CAN	N	
Thomason E., Sgt		F	

5ME773 — 103 Squadron

Anthony H. R., P/O		P	Only Taylor survived. He was
Birkbeck H. D., Sgt		N	taken prisoner and sent to Stalag
Beard E., Sgt		F	Luft 7. The others were buried
Maughan N. H., Sgt		B	at Magny-Fouchard (Au).
Richards J. A., Sgt		W	
Taylor W. H., F/S		M	
Wass W., Sgt		R	

6ND994 — 576 Squadron

Beattie W. W., Sgt		W	All killed. Buried at Loches-sur-
Koslowski S. J., F/S	CAN	N	Ource (Au).
Linklater R. E., F/O	CAN	P	
MacIntosh D. M., F/O	CAN	B	
McCollum W. J., F/S	CAN	R	
Pringle J. W. G., Sgt		F	
Sims G. R., F/S	CAN	M	

7ND621 — 166 Squadron

Dutton W., Sgt		F	All killed. Buried at Lusigny-sur-
Jones P. G., F/S		W	Barse (Au).
Llewellyn W. G., F/O		R	
Martin S., P/O		P	
McClure J. E., W/O	CAN	N	
Omoe F. M., F/S	CAN	M	
Rodgers A. O., F/O	NZ	P	
Wood L. G., F/S		B	

THIRD RAID, 18/19 JULY 1944

1 JB186 — 619 Squadron

Begernie A. H. J., F/O		P	Only Lewis survived. He evaded
Birks W. S. A., F/S	CAN	N	and was back in the UK on
Bright F. C., Sgt		F	10/9/44. The others were buried
Geddes J., Sgt	CAN	M	at Auger-St Vincent (Oi).
Hinett W. F., Sgt		R	
Lewis B. G., Sgt	CAN	B	
Marper A., Sgt		W	

2 LM640 — 619 Squadron

Britten A. G., F/O	CAN	N	All killed. Britten and Wilson
Garbutt J. A., F/S	CAN	R	have no known grave. The
Logan R., F/O		W	others were buried at Villers-St
Mara J. F., F/S	CAN	M	Genest (Oi).
Morrison E. L., F/O	CAN	B	
Mullen T., Sgt		F	
Wilson H. J., F/O	CAN	P	

3 DV304 — 61 Squadron

Blane J. H., F/S		M	All killed. Buried at Marcilly
Cooper H. W., F/O		P	(S-M).
Davey G. A., F/O		R	
Hardy T. E., Sgt		F	
Little B. S., F/O		N	
McLaughlin C., P/O	CAN	B	
Merrifield K. F., Sgt		W	
Thompson J. B., F/O		P	

4 LM378 — 619 Squadron

Cox R. B., Sgt		M	Only Nealey survived. He
Curtis A. E., Sgt		W	evaded and was back in the UK
Habergham A. W., F/S		N	on 1/9/44. The others were
Loosli M., Sgt		R	buried at Montreuil-aux-Lions
Molinas F. F., F/O	AUS	P	(Ai).
Morgan L., F/S		B	
Nealey J. A., Sgt		F	

5 PB245 — 619 Squadron

Donnelley N. W., F/O	NZ	P	All killed. Buried at Ussy-sur-
Frogley T. F., Sgt		R	Marne (S-M).
Grant D. I., F/O	NZ	B	
Harwood R. T. W., P/O		W	
Johnson J. K., P/O	CAN	N	
Ling S. W., Sgt		F	
Tate J. F. R., W/O		M	

6JB318 — 57 Squadron

Bulcraig J. A., F/L		P	Ruston was taken prisoner and
Gale N. L. E., F/S		F	sent to Stalag Luft 1. Manning
Loughlin T., Sgt		W	and Taylor evaded and were
Manning L. E. S., Sgt		R	back in the UK on 5/9/44 and
Robson E. C., F/O		B	1/9/44 respectively. The others
Ruston E. H., F/O		N	were killed. Buried at Bassevelle
Taylor F. J. D., Sgt		M	(S-M).

7PB236 — 630 Squadron

Adams K., Sgt		N	All killed. Buried at Neuvy
Barker N., Sgt		R	(Ma).
Moffatt D. D., Sgt		F	
Nelson K., F/S		B	
Rae J., Sgt		M	
Sargent A. J., F/O		P	
Withers D., Sgt		W	

8ME681 — 207 Squadron

Fennell L. R., F/O	CAN	B	All killed. Buried at Margny
Findlay J. A., Sgt		W	(Ma).
Holt A. E. S., F/S		N	
Lappin R. G., Sgt		F	
Longman F. D. P., Sgt		M	
Paine K., Sgt		R	
Weekes N. L., F/O		P	

9ND684 — 49 Squadron

Appleyard W. D.,F/O	AUS	P	All killed. Buried at Granges-sur-
Blumfield D. W., F/S		N	Aube (Ma).
Matheson A. M., P/O	CAN	M	
Jameson G. W., F/S		B	
Perry G. J., F/S		W	
Turner H. E., F/S		F	
Viollet R. F. H., P/O		R	

10DV374 — 463 Squadron

Chapman H. G., F/O		W	All killed. Buried at Droupt-Ste
Hamoniaux G. E., Sgt		F	Marie (Au).
Hymas C., Sgt		N	
Ind R. V., Sgt		M	
Simonds M. J., F/S	EIR	B	
Worthington J. R., F/O	AUS	P	
Younger R. D. B., Sgt		R	

11JB178 — 49 Squadron

Ansell A. A., Sgt		M	All killed. Buried at Herbisse
Davison C., F/S		W	(Au).
Green W. R., F/L	NZ	P	
Hands G. E. D., Sgt		R	
Hollard M. C., P/O	NZ	B	
Neal H. R., F/S		N	
Seymour F. S., Sgt		F	

12PB231 — 49 Squadron

Barlow W. G., Sgt		M	Barlow and Wellein were the
Gallagher V., F/S		B	only survivors. Both taken
Holmes L. B., W/O	AUS	N	prisoner, they were sent to Stalag
Lacy C., F/O		P	Luft 7. The others were buried
Ryan D. J., F/S	AUS	W	at St Ouen-Domprot (Ma).
Shingles I., Sgt		F	
Wellein J. C., P/O	CAN	R	

13LL969 — 619 Squadron

Lebatt W. H. G., F/S		B	Ratchford was the sole survivor.
Mackintosh J. E., Sgt		F	He evaded and was back in the
Morcom S. B., F/O		P	UK on 30/8/44. The others were
Myres A., F/S		M	buried at St Utin (Ma).
Ratchford C. E., F/S	CAN	R	
Thomas W. J., F/S		W	
Whitehurst S., F/S		N	

14LM537 — 630 Squadron

Alexander G. A., Sgt		F	Dennett, Jarman and Jerwood
Dennett P. B., F/O	AUS	P	killed. Buried at Chassericourt
Hilborne R. A., Sgt		M	(Au). Alexander was taken
Jarman W. J., Sgt		W	prisoner and sent to Stalag Luft
Jerwood C. R., F/S		N	7. Hilborne, Ritchie and Stones
Ritchie H. P., Sgt	CAN	B	evaded and were back in the UK
Stones J., Sgt		R	on 7/9/44, 1/9/44 and 6/9/44
			respectively.

15ME814 — 207 Squadron

Aitken L., F/S		B	Aitken was the sole survivor. He
Dallen J. G., F/O		P	evaded and was back in the UK
Shaw W., Sgt		F	on 7/9/44. Dallen has no known
Smith F. B., Sgt		M	grave. Wensley was buried at
Wensley D., Sgt		R	Lignon (Ma), the rest at
Williamson A. J., P/O	CAN	N	Margerie-Hancourt (Ma).
Woodward B., Sgt		W	

16ME833 — 9 Squadron

Gordon T. M., Sgt		F	Oates was the sole survivor. He
Hannah N., Sgt		M	was taken prisoner and sent to
Lutwyche L. R., F/S		B	Stalag Luft 7. Lutwyche was
Mumford D. G., Sgt		W	buried at Châtelraould (Ma), the
Oates N. F., F/S		N	others at Somsois (Ma).
Shuster J. E., P/O	CAN	R	
Wood L. J., F/O		P	

17DV312 — 50 Squadron

Desautels R. V., F/O	CAN	B	Desautels was the sole survivor.
Latham W. H., Sgt		F	He evaded and was back in the
Long W. J., F/O	USA	P	UK on 28/8/44. The others were
Lunnin T. H., P/O	CAN	R	buried at Robert-Magny (H-M).
Maltais F. G., P/O	CAN	M	
Thomas R. E., Sgt		N	
Whiteley M., Sgt		W	

18ME796 — 630 Squadron

Bush J. F., F/O	AUS	N	De Bruin, Hawken and Leary
De Bruin A. E., Sgt		M	were the only survivors. They
Griffiths W. E., F/S		B	evaded and were back in the UK
Hawken S. A., F/S	AUS	W	on 9/9/44, 7/9/44 and the middle
Howie J. N., Sgt		F	of 9/44 respectively. The others
Leary W., F/S	EIR	R	were buried at Villers-le-Sec
Maxwell G. E., F/O	AUS	P	(Ma).

19LM551 — 463 Squadron

Boydell J. C. B., F/S	AUS	M	All killed. Buried originally at
Fripp A. W. G., F/S	AUS	W	Revigny (Me), the bodies were
Gifford B. H., F/O	AUS	P	removed to Choloy cemetery
Newell H., Sgt		F	(M-M) in June 1954.
Pearce P. J., F/S	AUS	R	
Shipway R. G., W/O	AUS	N	
Spencer F. G., F/S	AUS	B	

20PB234 — 467 Squadron

Beharrie D., F/O	AUS	P	Beharrie, Rogers and Schott
Brown J. T., Sgt		B	killed. Buried at Brabant-le-Roi
Brownhall E. E., Sgt		N	(Me). Brown, Johnson and
Johnson W. G., Sgt		F	White evaded and were back in
Rogers F. R., F/S	AUS	M	the UK on 9/9/44, 9/9/44 and
Schott K. J., F/S	AUS	W	late 9/44 respectively. Brownhall
White F. K., F/S	AUS	R	was wounded, taken prisoner
			and sent to Stalag Luft 7.

21R5485 — 467 Squadron

Allen C. F., F/S	AUS	R	Allen and Davis killed. Buried
Davis T. E. W., F/O	AUS	P	at Pargny-sur-Saulx (Ma) and
Edgerley M. W., F/O	AUS	N	Heiltz-le-Maurupt (Ma)
Haddlesey E. F., F/O	CAN	M	respectively. Haddlesey was
Kelly D. V., F/S	AUS	W	badly wounded, taken prisoner
Marshall W. F., Sgt	AUS	F	and repatriated to Canada in
McGowen L. W., Sgt	AUS	B	2/45. Edgerley, Kelly, Marshall
			and McGowen evaded and were
			back in the UK on 3/9/44,
			6/9/44, 3/9/44 and 6/9/44
			respectively.

22LM117 — 630 Squadron

Ashton S. R., F/S		N	Only Beckhouse killed. He was
Beckhouse G. E., F/S	AUS	W	buried at Togny-aux-Boeufs
Brittain B. W., F/O	AUS	P	(Ma). Brittain, Couchman and
Couchman E., F/S		B	Grant evaded and were back in
Gannon R. F., Sgt		F	the UK on 4/9/44, 1/9/44 and
Grant D. A., Sgt	CAN	M	2/9/44 respectively. Ashton and
Wells E. H., F/S		R	Wells were taken prisoner and
			sent to Stalag Luft 7. Gannon
			was also taken prisoner, but his
			POW camp is not known.

23PD210 — 207 Squadron

Chapple J. K., Sgt		W	Chapple was the sole survivor.
Edmunds H. F., P/O	CAN	R	He evaded and was back in the
Hague J., F/S		N	UK early in 9/44. The others
Higgins C., Sgt		M	were buried at St Germain-la-
McNaughton W. R., F/O		P	Ville (Ma).
Supkovitch A., Sgt		F	
Tibbs R., F/O		B	

24JB473 — 49 Squadron

Deacon R. M., F/O	CAN	P	Rammage was killed and buried
Diley J. A., Sgt		W	at Vassimont (Ma). Deacon was
Fortune W., Sgt		N	wounded, taken prisoner and
Harpell A. R., F/S	CAN	B	liberated from Châlons-sur-
Rammage A. J., P/O	CAN	M	Marne hospital on 28/8/44. The
Sharp H., Sgt		F	others evaded. Diley, Harpell
Wilson D., Sgt	CAN	R	and Sharp were back in the UK
			on 3/9/44, Wilson on 4/9/44 and
			Fortune in early 9/44.

Appendix IV

The Milice

The Allied landings on 6 June 1944 finally persuaded many Frenchmen that it was the right time to desert their post. Many had already joined the *Résistance* when, in the autumn of 1942, the Vichy government, under pressure from Berlin, introduced *Service du Travail Obligatoire* (STO), the forced deportation of Frenchmen for work in Germany. Understandably, many young Frenchmen preferred to live as outlaws rather than go to Germany. STO had been forced on Vichy when an earlier voluntary system, the *relève* (it promised the return of one POW in exchange for three workers), failed to produce sufficient volunteers. As men drifted off to join the maquis, so the Vichy government determined to combat the growing menace.

The Prime Minister of Vichy, Pierre Laval, was put on trial after the war for, amongst other alleged crimes, his part in authorising the removal of Frenchmen from France to Germany:

'On 22 June [1942] he revealed his hand once more when he appealed to the French workers to go to Germany on the pretext that this would free agricultural workers from the concentration camps in Germany to France, according to a promise of Hitler, for which he was publicly thanked by Laval . . .

'Despite his appeals, volunteers for work in Germany were not forthcoming and Laval was obliged to resort to force. First in order came a law governing the use of industrial man-power . . . Next came a law preventing employers from enlisting workers without a formal authorisation of the Government . . . Then came the law making work obligatory, which was a cover for a virtual conscription and veritable slave markets for workers to be delivered to the Reich with all the consequent measures such as refusals of food cards, organised man-hunts and the whole series of measures which were recommended to the Prefects in a stream of instructions.'

In his 'Unpublished Diary', written in Fresnes prison while awaiting his trial — and his death on 15 October 1945 — Laval tried to excuse his actions, saying that he 'struggled to obtain better terms but it was impossible and I decided that the return of 50,000 Frenchmen was better than nothing at all . . . I was convinced that no better terms could be obtained at that time.'

Fritz Sauckel, Gauleiter of Paris, continued to put pressure on the Vichy government to force its own countrymen to go to Germany to work. When the Allies landed in North Africa in early November 1942, the Germans immediately marched into the Vichy-controlled 'Occupied Zone', and the pretence that France had its own government came to an end. Sauckel continued to go through the motions of asking Laval to round up the required number of workers and likewise Laval pretended to be stubbornly refusing German demands.

Rather than do the dirty work themselves, the Germans allowed the French to do it for them:

'In January 1943, to meet the threat posed by the formation of the Maquis and the widespread opposition to the STO, Vichy created the Milice, a special repressive force composed largely of the dregs of society, but including as well some misguided patriots and even a few youths who would do anything to avoid work in Germany. The Milice was headed by Joseph Darnand, a fanatical anticommunist and superpatriotic former war hero. As Secretary-General for the Maintenance of Order after December 1943, he became the chief police officer for Vichy. Under his enthusiastic leadership, the Milice showed no scruples in its pursuit of the resisters. The flimsiest suspicion warranted torture or execution for anyone suspected of aiding the Maquis. In its cruelty the Milice rivalled the Gestapo.'

In August 1943 Darnand was given the rank of SS Sturmbannführer (equivalent to a major in the British Army). He was sentenced to death by the Haute Cour de Justice and duly executed on 10 October 1945. One of the French 'underground' newspapers, *Le Franc-Tireur*, in its 5 February 1944 edition, exhorted its readers to shoot the miliciens wherever and whenever found:

'Joseph Darnand and all members of the Milice, decreed public enemies and traitors to the Nation, are put outside the law. From today every milicien must be thought of as a mad dog and treated as such . . . Shoot the Milice!'

Appendix V

Escape Kit

Every man who flew on operations carried with him a small tin packed with certain aids essential for survival in a German-occupied country. For this he had to thank an eccentric genius called Clayton Hutton.

Hutton relates that one day in the summer of 1940, Wing Commander Basil Embry burst into his office, having just returned from France where he had crashed on 27 May 1940 after his 107 Squadron Blenheim was shot down by flak. He got back to England on 2 August 1940, and wrote of his harrowing two months of escaping:

> 'I have often been asked what was my immediate reaction on finding myself swinging down into enemy-occupied France. I felt a great relief at having extricated myself from my doomed aeroplane, and I did not realise that the ordeal through which I had passed was only the overture to things to come. Had I been trained, equipped and more mentally prepared for the test, I might have acted differently immediately on landing from the way I actually did.'*

It was this lack of training and equipment that spurred Embry to visit Hutton. Christopher Clayton Hutton, known by all as 'Clutty', was officially an Intelligence Officer with MI9 and his job 'was to invent, design and adapt aids to evasion and escape . . . His enthusiasm was as unlimited as his ingenuity, or his capacity for getting into trouble with the staid authorities of service and civilian officialdom.'

Presented with Embry's request, Hutton's fertile brain and drive did the rest. With only the RAF capable of taking the war to the Germans in Occupied Europe, he decided 'to divert all supplies of maps and compasses to units of the Royal Air Force'.

He was also being asked to provide a foodpack or, as he put it, 'an emergency ration box'. Its shape and size were suggested to him by the common 50-cigarette flat tin. The problem, however, was to obtain a sufficient quantity of the tins for his purposes. Never easily stumped,

---

* Official Secret *(Max Parrish, 1960)*.

Hutton went to see Wills of Bristol, the well-known cigarette manufacturers, and asked for 20,000 empties. One of the company directors implied that such an order was impossible as both tin and cardboard were in short supply. (There was, after all, a war on!) Hutton continues:

> 'A moment's reflection led me to the simplest way out of the impasse. "I'll take 20,000 full tins, then."'

That very day the first lorry-load of full 'flat fifty' tins was London-bound, and so the 'escape ration tin' was born. It took time, of course, to produce the right container and the right balance of foodstuffs and escape objects, but eventually the Mark IV plastic watertight container was produced. It was made by Halex, a company familiar today to thousands of table-tennis players. Hutton was justifiably proud of the kit which was little changed for the rest of the war and whose design was copied by the Americans. Many airmen would be grateful for it.

The escape kit, incidentally, to give an idea of its capacity, contained malted milk tablets, boiled sweets, plain chocolate, matches, benzedrine tablets for energy, halazone tablets for purifying water, a rubber bottle capable of holding almost a pint (of water), a magnetized razor blade, some soap, a needle and thread, and a fishing hook and line. The box was small enough to fit into the front pockets of battledress trousers.

The razor blade was usable as a compass but some airmen preferred to increase the odds by stowing other directional devices about their person, usually in a trouser fly-button (screwed on the wrong way to fool the Germans, which it frequently did) or sewn into a lapel of their battle-dress jacket.

Bibliography

Aders, Gebhard: *History of the German Night Fighter Force 1917–1945* (Jane's Publishing Company, 1979)

Anon: *Ceux du Maquis* (?)
La Résistance en Haute-Marne, Volumes II and III (Dominique Gueniot)

Baumbach, Werner: *Broken Swastika* (Robert Hale, 1960; George Mann, 1974)

Bennett, AVM D. C. T.: *Pathfinder* (Frederick Muller, 1958)

Brickhill, F/L Paul, & Norton, Conrad: *Escape To Danger* (Faber and Faber, 1956)

Cooper, Alan W.: *Free To Fight Again* (William Kimber, 1988)
In Action With The Enemy (William Kimber, 1986)

Cosgrove, Ed: *The Evaders* (Clarke, Irwin, 1970; Simon & Schuster 1976)

Craven & Cate: *Army Air Forces in World War II* (The University of Chicago Press, 1951)

Crawley, Aidan: *Escape From Germany* (The Popular Book Club, 1956)

Eisenhower, Dwight D.: *Report of the Supreme Allied Commander* (HMSO, 1946)

Embry, ACM Sir Basil: *Mission Completed* (Methuen & Company, 1957)

Encyclopaedia Britannica: *Encyclopaedia Britannica* (1947)

Farran, Roy: *Winged Dagger* (Collins, 1948)

Finn, Sid: *Black Swan* (Newton Publishers, 1989)

Foot, M. R. D.: *SOE In France* (HMSO, 1966)

Foot, M. R. D. & Langley, J. M.: *MI9 Escape and Evasion 1939–1945* (Book Club Associates, 1979)

Green, William: *War Planes of the Second World War*, Volume X (Macdonald, 1968)

Hammersley, Roland DFM: *Up The Creek* (Privately, 1989)

Harris, Sir Arthur MRAF: *Bomber Offensive* (Collins, 1947)

Harrison, Derrick: *These Men Are Dangerous* (Cassell, 1957; Blandford Press, 1988)

Hawken, Stanley A. OBE: *Missing Presumed Dead* (Hill of Content Publishing, 1989)

Hill, Robert: *The Great Coup* (Arlington Books (Publishers), 1977; Corgi, 1978)

Hutton, Clayton: *Official Secret* (Max Parrish, 1960)

Jones, R. V.: *Most Secret War* (Hamish Hamilton, 1978)

Jones, W. E.: *Bomber Intelligence* (Midland Counties Publications, 1983)

Lahanque, Pierre: *Les Grands Yeux Dans La Nuit* (?, 1974)

Laval, Pierre: *The Unpublished Diary of Pierre Laval* (The Falcon Press (London), 1948)

Margerison, Russell: *Boys At War* (Ross Anderson Publications, 1986)

Marlow, Roy MM: *Beyond The Wire* (Robert Hale, 1983)

McLuskey, J. Fraser: *Parachute Padré* (SCM Press, 1951)

Meynell, Laurence: *Airmen On The Run* (Odhams Press, 1963)

Neave, Airey: *Saturday At M.I.9* (Hodder & Stoughton, 1969)

Novick, Peter: *The Resistance Versus Vichy* (Chatto & Windus, 1968)

Patton, General George S. Jr: *War As I Knew It* (Houghton Mifflin, New York, 1947)

Price, Alfred: *Instruments Of Darkness* (Macdonald and Jane's, 1977; William Kimber, 1967)

Pritchard, David: *The Radar War* (Patrick Stephens, 1989)

Roche, Michel: *L'Aube Dans La Guerre 1939/1945* (Horvath, Troyes, 1985)

Sweets, John F.: *The Politics of Resistance in France, 1940–1944* (Northern Illinois University Press, 1976)

Teare, T. D. G.: *Evader* (Hodder & Stoughton, 1954)

Warner, Philip: *The SAS* (William Kimber, 1971; Sphere Books, 1983)

Webster, Sir Charles W. & Frankland, Noble F.: *The Strategic Air Offensive Against Germany 1939–1945* (HMSO, 1961)

Whitfield, Fred DFM: *We Sat Alone* (Privately)

Zuckerman, Lord OM FRS: *From Apes To Warlords* (Hamish Hamilton, 1978)

PRO Files

The following files were examined at the Public Record Office, Kew. Some are easy to read, others (particularly the squadron records held on microfilm) are not. There are, in addition, some files which I wished to examine but which are 'closed for 75 years'. These are files containing accounts from evaders and which presumably contain 'evidence' against persons who were not particularly pro-Allies. It was also impossible for me to obtain details of Lancaster crashes in France unless, that is, I was a close relative of the deceased airman (which I am not). I did, however, acquire a copy of the report of one of the crashes made soon after the 'liberation'. I obtained it from a Frenchman (living in France) who in turn got it from the Canadian authorities (some of the dead were Canadian)! I leave it to the reader to decide who is being protected by this unavailability, and why.

AIR 14:533; 727; 1017; 1146; 1864; 2073; 2081; 2145; 2202; 2318; 2411; 2421; 2476; 2495; 2679; 2688; 2766; 2799; 3015; 3066; 3120; 3121; 3224; 3456

AIR 22:157

AIR 24:284; 285; 286; 287

AIR 25:2; 13; 110

AIR 27:128; 129; 482; 488; 539; 579; 688; 797; 803; 816; 956; 1042; 1089; 1154; 1172; 1235; 1323; 1649; 1651; 1658; 1911; 1921; 1909; 1924; 1931; 2027; 2028; 2037; 2047; 2052; 2131; 2138; 2143; 2145; 2148; 2152; 2155

AIR 28:50; 65; 69; 114; 171; 215; 244; 255; 264; 283; 329; 352; 405; 416; 426; 479; 501; 536; 606; 682; 713; 722; 797; 869; 881; 945; 947; 952; 955

AIR 29:228; 341; 342; 343; 344; 850; 853; 854; 870; 873; 882

AIR 34:79; 81; 95

AIR 37:735; 1042; 1126; 1127

AIR 40:265; 317; 625; 1141; 1207; 1305; 1343; 1397; 1486; 1526; 1669; 1897; 2465

AIR 50:179; 288

WO 208:3319; 3320; 3321; 3322; 3323; 3324

WO 218:192; 197; 198; 199

WO 219:1462; 2401; 2413; 2414; 5092

Glossary

ABC *Airborne Cigar* – Airborne radar device for jamming German fighter transmissions

a/c aircraft

A/Cdre Air Commodore

ACM Air Chief Marshal

ACP Air Control Point; usually a caravan sited close to the runway in use

AEAF Allied Expeditionary Air Force

AFC Air Force Cross

AI Airborne interception apparatus

AM Air Marshal

AVM Air Vice-Marshal

BATF Beam Approach Training Flight

BDTF Bomber Defence Training Flight

BDTU Bomber Defence Training Unit

(B)GF (Bomber or Bombing) Gunnery Flight

B-17, B-24 US four-engined bombers

BS Bomber Support

CGM Conspicuous Gallantry Medal

CIU Central Interpretation Unit

CO Commanding Officer

corkscrew heavy bomber manoeuvre – up, down and sideways – to throw off enemy fighters

DFC Distinguished Flying Cross

DFM Distinguished Flying Medal

D/R dead-reckoning navigation; a term first used at sea and defined as the art of calculating where a ship should be at a given moment

Dr Doctor

DRAGOON Allied landings in the south of France on 15 August 1944

DSO Distinguished Service Order

DZ Dropping Zone

E/a enemy aircraft

ETA Estimated Time of Arrival

FFI *Forces Françaises de l'Intérieur* – 'official' French Resistance decreed in March 1944 by General de Gaulle

FIDO Fog Intensive Dispersal Operation; a system of pipes laid alongside a runway through which fuel was forced at high pressure and ignited; the heat from the flames would clear the fog

Fishpond A radar device used in conjunction with *H2S* to detect aircraft in vicinity

F/L Flight Lieutenant

F/O Flying Officer

F/S Flight Sergeant

FW190 Focke Wulf 190 – German single-seat fighter

G/C Group Captain

GP General purpose

GOODWOOD Operation in Normandy by British Second Army against the Germans launched on 18 July 1944

Gruppe Luftwaffe Group (plural – gruppen)

HCU Heavy Conversion Unit

H-Hour The time selected for the bombing to begin

H2S An airborne ground-scanner using a cathode-ray tube for display. For picking up *H2S* transmissions (used so profligately by most navigators) the Germans produced *FuG 350 Z Naxos Z* which, by July 1944, was capable of picking up the signal at a range of up to 50 kilometres

HQ Headquarters

ID Identification

IS9(WEA) Intelligence School 9 (Western European Area) – first set up to assist evaders, escapers and POWs in France after D-Day

'Jedburgh' 'Jed' for short. See page 134 for description

JG Jagdgeschwader – Luftwaffe Fighter Wing

Ju88 Junkers 88 – versatile German twin-engined night-fighter or bomber

Kriegie short for *Kriegsgefangener* (prisoner-of-war)

LFS Lancaster Finishing School

Lt Lieutenant (also 1/Lt or 2/Lt – First or Second Lieutenant)

Mandrel Powerful airborne transmitter

Maquis French resistance (named after the Corsican scrub)

MC Medium Capacity, or 'Master of Ceremonies'

Me109 Messerschmitt 109 – German single-seat fighter

Me110 Messerschmitt 110 – German twin-engined night-fighter

MI9 Military Intelligence 9

Monica An airborne transmitter and receiver to warn of the rearward approach of a night-fighter. A radio signal was emitted and reflected off any metal object within range. In 1943 the Germans developed the passive homing system *FuG 227 Flensburg* which enabled a fighter to close in to within 1,000 feet

MRAF Marshal of the Royal Air Force

NCO Non Commissioned Officer

NJG Nachtjagdgeschwader – Luftwaffe Night Fighter Wing

Op. operation

ORS Operational Research Section

OVERLORD Codename for the overall plan for the Allied landings in Normandy on 6 June 1944

Pct Parachutist

PFF Path Finder Force

P/O Pilot Officer

POW Prisoner-of-war (see Kriegie)

PRC Personnel Receiving Centre

PRU Photographic Reconnaissance Unit

RAAF Royal Australian Air Force

RAF Royal Air Force

RAMC Royal Army Medical Corps

RASC Royal Army Service Corps

RCAF Royal Canadian Air Force

R/G Rear Gunner

RNZAF Royal New Zealand Air Force

R/O Radio Operator

RSF Red Spot Fire (for marking targets)

R/T Radio telephone

SAS Special Air Service

Schräge musik Name for upward-firing guns carried in Luftwaffe night-fighters

SD Special Duties

SDF Special Duties Flight

Second dickie co-pilot, usually gaining operational experience before flying with own crew

s/e single-engined

Sgt Sergeant

Serrate Radar device carried in RAF night-fighters to combat the Luftwaffe's *Lichtenstein* device

SHAEF Supreme Headquarters Allied Expeditionary Force

S/L Squadron Leader or searchlight

SN2 Luftwaffe night-fighter radar device

SNCF Société Nationale des Chemin de Fer Français – the French national railway company

SOE Special Operations Executive

Sprog novice, beginner

SS Schutzstaffel (Protection Squad); German élite troops

Stalag short for Stammlager, German POW camp

TFU Telecommunications Flying Unit

TI Target Indicator

u/s unserviceable

USAAF United States Army Air Force

USStAF United States Strategic Air Forces

V-1 Vergeltungswaffe Ein – 'revenge weapon number one'; the infamous German 'doodlebug' flying bomb

VHF Very High Frequency (radio)

W/C Wing Commander

W/O Warrant Officer

W/Op Wireless operator

WOP/AG Wireless Operator/Air Gunner

W/T Wireless telephone or telegraphy

W/V Wind velocity

'Y' type Codename for RAF bomber equipped with H2S

Index